THE INTE

COURT

The International Court of Justice

HUGH THIRLWAY

UNIVERSITY PRESS

OXFORD
UNIVERSITY PRESS

Great Clarendon Street, Oxford, OX2 6DP,
United Kingdom

Oxford University Press is a department of the University of Oxford.
It furthers the University's objective of excellence in research, scholarship,
and education by publishing worldwide. Oxford is a registered trade mark of
Oxford University Press in the UK and in certain other countries

First Edition published in 2016
Impression: 1

Published in the United States of America by Oxford University Press
198 Madison Avenue, New York, NY 10016, United States of America

British Library Cataloguing in Publication Data
Data available

Library of Congress Control Number: 2016940854

ISBN 978–0–19–877908–7 (pbk)
ISBN 978–0–19–877907–0 (hbk)

Printed and bound by
CPI Group (UK) Ltd, Croydon, CR0 4YY

Preface

The purpose of this book is to give as full a picture of the International Court of Justice—its composition, how it works, and what it is achieving—as is possible within the compass of a single volume of moderate length. It is intended that it should be feasible for it to be read as a whole (though perhaps not in one sitting!), rather than being more suited to consultation, as are, for example, the mammoth works of Rosenne and Kolb, not to mention the vast Oxford Commentary on the Statute.[1] At the same time, the writer has endeavoured to include some mention, however brief, of most of the points that might occur to an interested enquirer. It is assumed that the reader already has a general knowledge of international law, and of the structure of international society, including the place of the International Court, and some acquaintance with its functioning and jurisprudence; but it is hoped that the exposition offered will be clear and informative in itself.

Notwithstanding the limitation declared by Article 59 of the Court's Statute, whereby the force of a judgment is restricted to the parties and to the particular case, it is common knowledge that the jurisprudence of the International Court forms a rich resource for the definition and elucidation of many areas of law. However, no attempt is made here to report on or discuss the actual content of the Court's decisions (except in so far as they relate to its own procedures and working); to try to do so would be to convert the book into an incomplete textbook on the whole field of international law. As for the separate and dissenting opinions of Members of the Court, these have become[2] an increasingly valuable source of material, including observations relating to the Court's procedures; but these are mentioned only when they add substantially to (or constructively contradict!) the Court's decisions. Any full and systematic treatment of judges' opinions would overbalance this book.

A further caveat: the book, and in particular the sections on procedure, evidence, etc., is not in any way intended as a manual for the conduct of proceedings, which would involve a much more detailed examination of precedents in this domain. It is hoped that those appointed as agents and counsel in cases before the Court may find the work of use, but for the general picture, not as a step-by-step guide.

It is evidently impossible to study the work of the Court without having the governing texts—primarily the Statute and the Rules of Court, but also the Practice Directions, Resolution Concerning the Internal Judicial Practice, etc.—to hand, and it is assumed that the reader will be making use of the Court's website for this

[1] A. Zimmermann, C. Tomuschat, K. Oellers-Frahm, and C. J. Tams (eds.), *The Statute of the International Court of Justice: A Commentary*, 2nd edn. (Oxford: Oxford University Press, 2012). Similarly, the present writer's study, *The Law and Procedure of the International Court of Justice: Fifty Years of Jurisprudence* (Oxford: Oxford University Press, 2013), has a different aim, concentrating more on the content of the Court's decisions.

[2] See Ch. 17 on developments in this domain.

purpose (or, of course, of those texts in printed form). The possibility of including the texts in the present volume was considered; but in the first place this would considerably increase its bulk (and price), and secondly, having to keep a finger in one page while reading another is probably much a less convenient method of study than looking from book to screen and back.

It is generally the policy of the Oxford University Press that gender-specific pronouns ('he', 'his', 'him', and so on) should be avoided in any reference that is relevant to both male and female persons. However, the present work is to a large extent a commentary on the ICJ Statute and Rules of Court, and uses frequent and extensive quotations from them. Those texts use the convention applicable at the time they were drafted or revised, that an unspecified member of a category comprising both males and females would be referred to by a masculine pronoun. To avoid a confusing alternation of style, it has therefore been thought preferable to use this earlier convention throughout the text, while recognizing that it is beginning to have an archaic character.

The word 'States', when referring to sovereign States, is spelled in the text with a capital S, as is the ICJ's own usage; where a passage quoted from another source employs a lower-case s, this has been left unchanged.

The bibliography appended makes no claim to be complete:[3] its scope is indicated in its prefatory Note. Contemplation of the number of published works about the Court calls to mind the admonition to the would-be author in Ecclesiastes.[4]

It is customary for the author of a work of this kind to accept full responsibility for any errors or omissions. This I do in the most literal sense, as no research assistants or secretaries have been involved in its preparation. Artur Brodowicz in the ICJ Library has been as courteous and helpful as ever; at the Press, my thanks go to John Louth and Merel Alstein for valuable discussions as to the form of the book, and encouragement during its writing. Sylvie Jaffrey, as copy editor, has meticulously picked up slips, omissions, and ambiguities and has borne my belated adjustments with great patience.

The decisions of the Court consulted, and other relevant developments noted, are those up to and including June 2016.

H.T.

The Hague
June 2016

[3] The Court's own *Handbook* gives merely a 'Short Bibliography' of thirty-five items.

[4] 'And further, my son, be admonished by these: of making many books there is no end; and much study is a weariness of the flesh', Eccles. 12: 12.

Table of Contents

V. THE DECISION

VI. INCIDENTAL PROCEEDINGS

List of Abbreviations

AJIL	*American Journal of International Law*
BIICL	British Institute of International and Comparative Law
BYBIL	*British Year Book of International Law*
ChJIL	*Chinese Journal of International Law*
CR	*Compte-rendu* (verbatim record of ICJ sitting)
ECtHR	European Court of Human Rights
EHRR	*European Human Rights Review*
EJIL	*European Journal of International Law*
ESIL	European Society of International Law
ICLQ	*International and Comparative Law Quarterly*
ITLOS	International Tribunal for the Law of the Sea
JIDS	*Journal of International Dispute Settlement*
LJIL	*Leiden Journal of International Law*
LPICT	*The Law and Procedure of International Courts and Tribunals*
NILR	*Netherlands International Law Review*
NYBIL	*Netherlands Yearbook of International Law*
PCIJ	Permanent Court of International Justice
RGDIP	*Revue générale de droit international public*
TLR	*Times Law Reports*
UNAT	United Nations Administrative Tribunal
UNRIIA	*United Nation Reports of International Arbitral Awards*
Kolb	Robert Kolb, *The International Court of Justice* (Oxford and Portland: Hart Publishing, 2013)

Rosenne	S. Rosenne, *The Law and Practice of the International Court, 1920–2005*
Thirlway, *Law and Procedure*	H. Thirlway, *The Law and Procedure of the International Court of Justice—Fifty Years of Jurisprudence*, 2 vols. (Oxford: Oxford University Press, 2013), assembling article published in *BYBIL*)
Zimmermann et al., *Commentary*	A. Zimmermann, C. Tomuschat, K. Oellers-Frahm, CJ Tams (eds.), *The Statute of the International Court of Justice: A Commentary*, 2nd edn. (Oxford: Oxford University Press, 2012)

I

THE COURT

1

The Court: Principal Judicial Organ of the United Nations

A. Introduction

The International Court of Justice was established by the United Nations Charter, and came into existence with the election of its first members (judges) in February 1946. It was created as the successor to the Permanent Court of International Justice (PCIJ), established pursuant to Article 14 of the Covenant of the League of Nations in 1921, and was modelled closely on that body.[1] Its constitution and operation are regulated, first by the Charter itself, Chapter IV (Arts. 92–6); secondly by its Statute, to which Article 92 refers, and which is there stated to be 'an integral part' of the Charter; thirdly by the Rules of Court, made by the Court itself under a power conferred by Article 30 of the Statute. The Rules may from time to time be amended by the Court; it is entitled also to propose amendments to the Statute, under Article 70 thereof. These, however, may only be effected by the same process as for amendment of the Charter itself (see Charter, Art. 108).[2]

It is not, however, the international equivalent of a national supreme court—a body of worldwide jurisdiction, empowered to pass judgment on the legal rights and duties of all States from a position of superiority and supervision. No such tribunal exists. The International Court can better be seen as a standing mechanism available for the peaceful settlement of disputes between States, to the extent that they wish to make use of it. No dispute can be the subject of a decision of the Court unless the States parties to it have consented to the Court's jurisdiction over that specific dispute, or over a class of disputes of which that dispute is one. Access to the Court is enjoyed by all members of the United Nations, but its 'compulsory jurisdiction' (a somewhat misleading term) is accepted by only a fairly small number of States, and for the most part with reservations that limit effective jurisdiction to certain classes of dispute, as will be explained in Chapter 5.

[1] Accordingly, reference to the jurisprudence of the PCIJ has frequently been useful to the Court in the past, but is becoming steadily less necessary. For the history of the two institutions, see O. Spiermann, 'Historical Introduction', in Zimmermann et al., *Commentary*.

[2] A proposal for amendment of the Statute has only been made on one occasion: see sect. B.

The Court is composed of fifteen judges, elected for a term of office of nine years, supplemented in some cases by judges ad hoc nominated by the parties; the system is examined in more detail in Chapter 2.

B. The Court and the United Nations

The Court is named in Article 7 of the Charter as one of the 'principal organs' of the United Nations, along with the Security Council, the General Assembly, the Economic and Social Council, the Trusteeship Council, and the Secretariat. It is therefore in principle not subject to any direction or control by any of the other principal organs; and there is no specific provision elsewhere in the Charter regulating the Court's relations with other organs. It would clearly be in conflict with the basic principle of the independence of the judiciary if any such control were to exist. There are, however, two ways in which pressure or influence could, at least in theory, be exercised by the General Assembly.

The election of judges is in the hands of the Security Council and the General Assembly, acting separately (Statute, Arts. 4–12), and arrangements are made so that information as to developments during the voting in one organ do not become known to, and thus influence, the other. It is an established convention that candidates (of their nationality) put forward by the five permanent Members of the Security Council will be elected, and the remaining seats are treated as appertaining to various geographical groupings of States. Even taking this arrangement into account, any sort of 'packing' of the Court seems to be excluded.

Under Article 16 of the Charter, it is the General Assembly that is empowered to 'consider and approve the budget of the organization', and the Court's budget forms part of this, and need not necessarily be approved as submitted by the Court, but this can hardly be regarded as a form of control or influence exercised on the judges.[3] To make assurance doubly sure, Article 32 of the Statute (an integral part of the Charter) provides that the judges' salaries and allowances 'may not be decreased during the term of office'; this has raised an interesting constitutional problem.[4]

By Resolution 61/262 (4 April 2007) the Assembly made certain adaptations of the remuneration of Members of the Court. One consequence of the resolution—not intended as such but recognized as unavoidable—was that there would be a significant difference between the remuneration of judges elected before 1 January 2007 and those elected after that date.[5] The President of the Court had expressed

[3] In the aftermath of the hugely unpopular 1966 decision in the *South West Africa* case, a few voices were heard in New York suggesting that the Court be 'punished' by some reduction in its budget, but this was never a serious proposal.

[4] See the brief but illuminating study by N. Blokker in *The Governance of International Courts and Tribunals: Organizing and Guaranteeing Independence and Accountability*, at http://papers.ssrn.com/sol3/papers.cfm?abstract_id=2709626 (accessed January 2016).

[5] There would consequently be a similar difference between judges ad hoc appointed before or after that date.

the Court's 'extremely serious and deep concern' that the proposed action 'would not be in conformity with the Statute of the Court'; it would infringe 'the equality of all judges', which was 'a fundamental principle underlying the Statute'.[6] After some further exchanges, the matter was considered by the UN Legal Counsel, who took the view that 'the concerns raised' by the Court 'are justified'.[7]

The proposal was replaced by a revised text which was regarded as not open to the objection of breach of equality.[8] If, however, the Legal Counsel had taken the opposite view, or if the Assembly had declined to be guided by him, and implemented the original proposal, what would be the situation? In a lengthy memorandum supplied by the Court to the Assembly, it stated that it 'considers that matters relating to the proper administration of justice require it alone to authoritatively interpret the Statute'.[9] In the context of its judicial work, this is undoubtedly true, 'authoritatively' then meaning 'in a manner binding on the parties before it' in a contentious case; in advisory proceedings probably also, in so far as the interpretation was what was requested, or necessarily entailed in replying to the request. The assertion that this is also the case when it is the lawfulness of the Assembly's exercise of the powers of governance conferred on it by the Statute does not seem to follow. Nor is there any way in which effect could be given to the Court's view so far as it differed from that of the Assembly. The Court would have had no alternative but to accept the new system; principal organ or no, it cannot evade the control of the purse-strings enjoyed by the General Assembly.

In what does the character of the Court *as a court* differentiate it from the other principal organs of the United Nations, or from other international bodies in general? Several points may be noted. First, its function is limited to deciding disputes; it is not in any way a legislative body, nor a forum for negotiations, nor does it have any political functions. Secondly, it shares with the Security Council, but not the General Assembly, the quality of having power to *decide*, to settle definitively any appropriate issue regularly brought before it; and such decision is binding on the parties to the dispute, and on them only. (The advisory opinions of the Court are non-binding advisory opinions, as their name implies; in giving these it may perhaps be considered as being to some extent—but only to some extent—transformed from a court into an advisory committee of jurists.) Thirdly, neither the Court nor any State other than the parties to a dispute has any power of initiative: it is only when it has been 'switched on', so to speak, by being seised of an issue that it can take action, and a contentious case can only be instituted by one of the parties to the dispute.[10] An international dispute may be festering, and the situation may be

[6] Letter of 3 April 2007, reproduced as UN Doc. A/1/8837, at. 1. The legal questions raised will be considered in Ch. 2 sect. B, in connection with the principle of equality among judges; here the issue is the limits (if any) of the powers of 'governance' (the useful term employed by Blokker (see n. 4) of the Assembly in relation to the Court.

[7] UN Doc. A/62/538 Ann. I.

[8] GA Decision 62/457, 3 April 2008.

[9] UN Doc. A/62/538 Ann. II para. 32.

[10] This is a general feature of international tribunals, the only exception having been the Central American Court of Justice (1907–14), which had power to 'call in' a case (*Oxford Handbook of the History of International Law*, ed. Bardo Fassbender (Oxford: Oxford University Press, 2012), 574).

crying out for the sort of unprejudiced and non-prejudicial holding operation that could result from a court Order for provisional measures; but it is only when a party initiates proceedings that the Court can make its contribution.[11]

The judicial work of the Court is generally quite distinct from the operations of the other principal organs; but there have been occasions when it has found itself involved in a matter of which the Security Council has also been seised.[12] There is nothing relating to the Court in the Charter parallel to the provision in Article 12 that '[w]hile the Security Council is exercising in respect of any dispute or situation the functions assigned to it in the present Charter, the General Assembly shall not make any recommendation with regard to that dispute or situation unless the Security Council so requests'.[13] When in 1979 the US Embassy in Tehran was seized by militants, the US brought the matter before the Security Council, and also instituted proceedings against Iran. The Court thought it appropriate 'to examine, *ex officio*, whether its competence to decide the present case, or the admissibility of the present proceedings, might possibly have been affected' by the parallel procedures involving the Security Council.[14] Its conclusion was that '[i]t is for the Court, the principal judicial organ of the United Nations, to resolve any legal questions that may be in issue between parties to a dispute; and the resolution of such legal questions by the Court may be an important, and sometimes, decisive, factor in promoting the peaceful settlement of the dispute'.[15] There may be a judicious hint here that the Council should stay on its own side of the fence, and not venture to determine a legal issue! Subsequent cases have confirmed the approach outlined in the US/Iran case, which has been called 'functional parallelism': in the Nicaragua/US case in 1984, the Court observed that '[t]he Council has functions of a political nature assigned to it, whereas the Court exercises purely judicial functions', these being thus 'separate but complementary'.[16]

C. Seat and languages

Article 22 of the Statute declares that '[t]he seat of the Court shall be established at The Hague'; like its predecessor, it occupies premises in the Peace Palace, under an agreement between the United Nations and the Carnegie Foundation, the owner of

[11] Once seised of a case, the Court 'may at any time decide to examine *proprio motu* whether the circumstances of the case require the indication of provisional measures . . .' See further Ch. 13.

[12] This most commonly occurs in the context of requests for provisional measures, as the time taken by ICJ proceedings normally signifies that the action in the Security Council has been completed well before the Court is called upon to take a decision.

[13] And cf. also Art. 36 para. 3, emphasizing the suitability of the Court for the settlement of inter-State disputes.

[14] *US Diplomatic and Consular Staff in Tehran* [1980] ICJ Rep 3, 20 para. 39. Iran was not appearing in the proceedings, and as the Court noted (21 para. 40), no query had been raised in the Council.

[15] [1980] ICJ Rep 22 para. 40.

[16] *Military and Paramilitary Activities in and against Nicaragua* [1984] ICJ Rep 392, 436 para. 95. See also *Genocide Convention (Bosnia* v *Yugoslavia)* [1993] ICJ Rep 3, 19 para. 33; *Armed Activities on the Territory of the Congo (DRC* v *Uganda)* [2000] ICJ Rep 111, 126 para. 36.

the building. Unlike the UN Headquarters District in New York, it is not extraterritorial, but Netherlands territory.[17] Any change in its seat would therefore require an amendment of the Statute; Article 70 of the Statute empowers the Court itself to propose changes in the Statute, and the Court did in 1969 present such a proposal, to insert the words 'or at such other place as shall at any time be approved by the General Assembly on the recommendation of the Court'. In support of the proposal, the Court suggested that a 'world court' should not be too closely linked with a particular locality.[18] There was no support in the Assembly for the proposal, and it was allowed to drop.[19] A new building for the Court in the grounds of the Peace Palace was then constructed at the expense of the Dutch Government, and inaugurated in 1978.[20]

Article 22 adds that the provision as to the seat 'shall not prevent the Court from sitting and exercising its functions whenever the Court considers it desirable'. It has never 'sat' in the sense of holding hearings or deliberations elsewhere, but it has (in the *Gabcíkovo/Nagymaros* case) exercised its power under Article 66 of the Rules to 'exercise its functions with regard to the obtaining of evidence at a place locality to which the case relates'.

The Statute provides (in Art. 39 para. 1) that '[t]he official languages of the Court shall be English and French'.[21] This appears in the section of the Statute headed 'Procedure', but it is perhaps more fundamental than might appear. In the first place, the Statute and the Rules themselves exist in the two languages; the Statute, as an annex to the Charter, also exists in the other official languages of the United Nations, and these texts are equally authoritative for purposes of interpretation,[22] even though only the French and English texts are 'official languages of the Court'. The Court, when interpreting the Statute (as is necessary from time to time) may, and possibly should, take into account all five language-texts. In practice it does not seem to have done so;[23] but the regular presence on the Bench of judges of Russian

[17] During the German occupation of the Netherlands, a notice on the Peace Palace gates declared it international territory, and the occupying authorities respected this de facto.

[18] It was rumoured at the time that relations with the Dutch Government were strained, and certainly it was around this date that a new system of precedence of judges vis-à-vis the diplomatic corps in The Hague was established, and plans were begun for a new building.

[19] It left a legacy in the form of GA Resolution 2520 (XXIV), providing for the participation in the procedure for amendment of the Statute of States parties to the Statute but no Members of the UN. For an account of the handling of the proposal, see Shaw, 'Article 22', in Zimmermann et al., *Commentary*, 429–30, paras. 11–14.

[20] The building was extended in 1997. In July 2014 it was discovered that asbestos was present in it, and it had to be temporarily closed for health reasons, reopening early in 2016.

[21] Being in the Statute, this provision can be modified only by amendment of the Statute. During one of the Court's internal sessions devoted to amendment of the Rules of Court, there was a move to confer a special status on Spanish, as a quasi-official language; but this did not find acceptance.

[22] Charter, Art. 111. Curiously, the Court in *LaGrand* cited this article, in conjunction with Art. 92, to establish that the English and French texts of the Statute, an 'integral part' of the Charter, are equally authentic, but did not consider what significance, if any, the other three language texts might have.

[23] See *Military and Paramilitary Activities in and against Nicaragua*, [1984] 392, 405–7, paras. 29–31 (Art. 36 para. 5); *LaGrand*, [2001] 466, 501–2, paras. 98–101 (Art. 41). This is also to some extent justifiable as the texts were originally drafted in English and French (see Judge Oda's analysis of Art. 36 para. 5 in the first of these cases, [1984] ICJ Rep 478–81).

and Chinese nationalities, and from Spanish-speaking countries, suggests that there is unofficial opportunity for verification. The two official texts, French and English, thus have equal status: if they differ, neither prevails over the other. Some examples exist of textual *cruces* resulting from discrepancies between the two texts; but generally the Court has been able to resolve any apparent inconsistency without doing violence to either text.[24]

Article 39 of the Statute provides that the parties may agree to conduct the case wholly in one of the two official languages[25] (and in that case the judgment will be given in that language); otherwise each party may use whichever language it chooses, and is free to employ both. The Court thus works in the two official languages, in the sense that all documents submitted to it are, in principle, to be in the one language or the other (or both); and in principle all documents are translated by the Registry (or the party submitting) into the other language.[26] Similarly, in principle all speeches in court have to be made in one or other of the official languages.[27] Consequently, while there is no provision in the Statute that candidates for election to the Court must be able to work in at least one of the official languages, this is effectively an essential requirement;[28] at the present time, there is never any difficulty in finding candidates with this qualification. Article 51 of the Rules deals in more detail with the use of languages: the underlying principle is that if a pleading, document, or speech in court is in one of the two official languages, the party concerned does not have to supply a translation (or interpretation) into the other, but if it is in any other language, the Court must be supplied with a translation, into one or other of the official languages.

[24] See, for example, the difficulty with the word 'dispute' in Articles 36, para. 2, and 60 of the Statute: below, Chapter 16, text and fn. 6.

[25] See e.g. Art. 5 of the Special Agreement between Burkina Faso and Niger for their *Frontier Dispute*, [2013] ICJ Rep 44, 51.

[26] This requirement used to be meticulously carried out; in the case of *Barcelona Traction*, for example, the time and the staff needed to translate the enormous mass of documents submitted on both sides placed great demands on the Registry. Nowadays it is possible to be more selective, while respecting the principle that a judge is entitled to call for any document to be translated into his working language.

[27] Art. 39 para. 3 of the Statute empowers the Court to authorize a party to use a language other than French or English; in practice this means at the hearings, as a pleading drafted in another language can of course be translated before it is filed. The provision does mean that counsel who do not speak either French or English sufficiently competently may argue in their own languages; but nowadays there are few international lawyers who are not fluent in at least one of the official languages.

[28] Rosenne, writing in 2006, was of the view that it would become 'imperative' that 'some modification of the language rules and practice of the Court' be made to temper this exigency (Rosenne, i, 362); if so, it would probably have to be informal, as amendment of the Statute is not lightly to be undertaken, and the additional expense for translation and interpretation would be considerable. The present writer's experience as a witness of judicial deliberations is that use of more than two languages for that purpose would not be desirable.

2

Composition of the Court and Role of the Registry

A. The Members of the Court

The Court consists of fifteen judges, elected by the Security Council and the General Assembly, in separate elections, for terms of nine years; in order to ensure continuity, the elections are staggered so that five judges complete their terms of office every three years.[1] The term of nine years was adopted from the pre-war Permanent Court system: it is clearly advisable for a judge to have considerable security of tenure, but appointment for life would be unacceptable, as conflicting with the equally desirable purpose of rotation among candidates of different nationalities and legal traditions. The Statute calls for 'the representation of the main forms of civilization and the principal legal systems of the world [to] be assured' (Art. 9), and such representation can hardly be the product of a static system of seat division. A judge may, however, be re-elected (and this has frequently occurred); it has at times been suggested that a non-renewable term would be preferable,[2] but Article 13 of the Statute expressly states that Members of the Court may be re-elected, so that any change would necessitate amendment of the Statute. One purpose of security of tenure is to ensure independence; it is not suggested that a judge nearing the end of his term, and seeking re-election, would be influenced in his judicial conduct, but the pressure for places among the 193 Members of the United Nations means that the judge's national State may have to 'push', and even bargain, for his re-election to an extent sometimes unfitting to the dignity of judicial office.

Even if not re-elected, a Member of the Court may sometimes be called upon to sit after the expiration of his nine-year term. Article 13 paragraph 3 of the Statute provides that 'The Members of the Court shall continue to discharge their duties until their places have been filled. Though replaced, they shall finish any cases which they may have begun.' The first sentence contemplates the possibility

[1] In order to establish this system, at the first elections, in 1946, lots were drawn to determine which five judges should hold office for five years only, which for ten, and which for the full fifteen-year term.

[2] This reform was introduced in the European Court of Human Rights in 2010 by Protocol No. 14 to the ECtHR Statute, replacing a renewable six-year term by a nine-year non-renewable term.

that a successful election of judges might not have been held before the expiry date of the terms of office of some of those sitting;[3] this has never yet occurred. The purpose of the second sentence is evident, but it raises three questions of interpretation.

The first—when has a judge 'begun' a case?—has been resolved by the Court itself: it normally proceeds on the basis that the judges who are sitting at the time of the opening of the oral proceedings in a case have 'begun' the case. For this reason, the Court is careful to arrange its judicial calendar so that oral proceedings held in an election year are timed to open after 5 February; if at the beginning of a calendar year a case is under deliberation, every effort is made to complete it and deliver judgment before 5 February. An exception to this is when the case is referred to a Chamber: as a result of an amendment to the Rules of Court in 1978, the Members of the Chamber, who (in that capacity) are chosen *intuiti personae* and are therefore not subject to 'replacement', continue to sit beyond a triennial renewal of the Court at which they have, for all other purposes, been 'replaced'.[4]

The second question concerns the meaning of 'finish a case'. The evident intention is that the judge should continue to sit until the Court gives judgment (or until the case terminates by a discontinuance, for example). But many cases fall into distinct stages, usually referred to as 'phases', e.g. proceedings on a request for provisional measures or on a preliminary objection.[5] If a judge is sitting when the oral proceedings open in such a preliminary phase, for example, on preliminary objections, and these are then rejected so that the case continues, has he 'finished the case' when judgment is given on the objections, or does he continue to sit until the case is disposed of on the merits? The practice of the Court is that the judge will cease to sit once the proceedings on the preliminary objection (or other intermediate stage) are completed. This is so even though the objection proceedings and the merits proceedings are all part of the same case, bearing a single number on the Court's General List; and the case bears throughout the same title, with the addition, where appropriate, of the words 'Preliminary Objections' in brackets after it.

The third question, while usually academic, is more difficult, since on a periodic election five judges are 'replaced' as a group, but strictly speaking it is not possible to say which new judge 'replaces' which new judge, even if on the retirement of, let us say, a judge of German nationality, another German lawyer is elected to the Court.[6] Judges are elected as individuals, not as representatives

[3] e.g. the General Assembly and the Security Council might have difficulty arriving at a consistent choice of candidates.

[4] See Art. 17 para. 4 of the Rules, and the Order of 28 February 1990 in the *Land, Island and Maritime Boundary Dispute* case (with a strong dissenting opinion by Judge Shahabuddeen), and Thirlway, 'Procedural Law and the International Court of Justice', in V. Lowe and M. Fitzmaurice (eds.), *Fifty Years of the International Court of Justice (Jennings Festschrift)* (Cambridge: Cambridge University Press, 1996), 389, 309–3. For Chambers generally see sect. C.

[5] Proceedings on a request for interpretation or revision of a judgment are not 'phases' of the case in which the judgment was given, but separate cases: see further in Ch. 7 sect. B(2).

[6] See further Thirlway, *Law and Procedure*, i. 902.

of their countries;[7] nevertheless, no two members of the Court may be of the same nationality.[8] The Statute (Article 9) directs that the election be such as to ensure the representation of 'the main forms of civilization and of the principal legal systems of the world'. There is no official allocation of seats on this (or any other) basis, but it is a long-standing convention that the candidate of each of the permanent members of the Security Council will always be elected (and the other seats are unofficially treated distributed between various regions of the world). Even in the case of these five judges it is, however, doubtful whether legally such a judge 'replaces' the retiring judge of the same nationality, since the convention is no more than that—a convention.

The qualifications required for election are laid down by the Statute (Art. 2): 'The Court shall be composed of a body of independent judges, elected regardless of their nationality from among persons of high moral character who possess the qualifications required in their respective countries for appointment to the highest judicial office, or are jurisconsults of recognized competence in international law.' Competence specifically in international law is thus not necessarily required;[9] nor is judicial experience.[10] The competition between States to see one of their nationals elected has become much more intense since the Court began to make its mark in international relations (say, since about 1990); whether this has resulted in improvement in the quality of candidates it would probably be impossible (and indiscreet) to say.

Members of the Court are required to make a solemn declaration in open court of impartiality in the exercise of their functions. A Member of the Court cannot be dismissed, according to Article 18 paragraph 1 of the Court's Statute, 'unless in the unanimous opinion of the other Members, he has ceased to fulfil the required conditions'. It is unclear whether the conditions referred to are solely those laid down in the Statute; there is no mention, for example, of sickness leading to physical or mental incapacity; does this mean that this could not be treated as a ground for removal, even with the unanimous vote?[11] More generally, solidarity among judges means that it would probably be very difficult to obtain the quasi-unanimity called for by the Statute for the removal of a judge, except perhaps in a case of such flagrant impropriety as the acceptance of bribes.

[7] Cf. the criticism, in the *Military and Paramilitary Activities* case, of the United States' suggestion that two of the Members of the Court were influenced by their national origins: see the dissenting opinion of Sir Robert Jennings [1986] ICJ Rep 528.

[8] But a judge ad hoc (see sect. B) may have the same nationality as an elected member of the Court.

[9] And there are examples of lawyers with other fields of specialization being elected, and proving themselves entirely equal to their colleagues in competence and insight.

[10] One criticism addressed to international investment arbitration tribunals is that their members are rarely, if ever, persons with judicial experience (except in the context of previous arbitrations of the same kind); see e.g. Mattias Kumm, 'An Empire of Capital? Transatlantic Investment Protection as the Institutionalization of Unjustified Privilege', *ESIL Reflections* 4:3 (May 2015).

[11] In the writer's experience, the state of health of one judge prevented him from attending in The Hague for more than a year preceding the end of his term of office; and another in similar circumstances attended but the influence of his health on his competence gave rise to great concern; in neither case did there appear to be any pressure to resign.

Members of the Court during their period of office may not 'exercise any political or administrative function, or engage in any other occupation of a professional nature'.[12] This is clearly an appropriate restriction, first to avert the risk of conflict of interest, and secondly to secure the full-time services of the judges. There has in this respect been a development of practice—one which is perhaps to be regretted. During the years when the Court had little or nothing to do (after the 1966 *South West Africa* judgment), Members of the Court sat as arbitrators in two major arbitrations.[13] There was at the time little on the Court's list to occupy the judges, so that there was no risk of interference with the orderly progress of cases at The Hague. While these were not the first cases of Members of the Court being appointed as arbitrators, both were conspicuous events, and appear to have set a trend. Judges have since been appointed as arbitrators with increasing frequency, to such an extent as to suggest doubts whether the work of the Court continued to be wholly unaffected.[14] Now, however, there are signs that this practice is becoming less frequent.

The Members of the Court receive an annual salary, and the President an annual allowance in addition (Statute, Art. 32) as part of the regular budget of the Organization; the amounts of these are determined by the General Assembly, and they may not be reduced during the term of office. The Members of the Court also receive travelling expenses during office, and pensions on retirement. Paragraph 8 of Article 32 provides that '[t]he above salaries, allowances and compensation shall be free of all taxation', and this of course results in a binding obligation on Parties to the Statute not to impose such taxation. This paragraph does not mention the judges' pensions; it is unclear whether this omission is deliberate, so that such pensions are taxable, or whether they are to be regarded as included in the general words of paragraph 8.[15]

Mention has been made (Ch. 1 sect. B) of the controversy that erupted in 2007 over the proposal in the General Assembly to modify the system of remuneration

[12] An interesting concession was made when Judge Ago was elected in 1979; he had been acting as the International Law Commission's Special Rapporteur on State Responsibility, and the work had reached a critical stage. On taking up his seat on the Court, he continued as Special Rapporteur until the work had reached a point when it could be conveniently handed over to his successor.

[13] Judges Waldock and Gros in the UK/France *Delimitation of the Continental Shelf* arbitration (18 *UNRIAA* 3–343), and Judges Dillard, Fitzmaurice, Gros, Onyeama, Petrén in the *Beagle Channel* arbitration (21 *UNRIAA* 53–264). The decision in the latter case was adopted by a unanimous vote of four members, Judge Petrén having died during the proceedings. The Award unfortunately prompted further disagreement between the Parties, eventually settled by agreement following papal mediation: see the Editorial Note to the text in *UNRIAA*.

[14] See the Report on the work of the Court prepared by the British Institute of International and Comparative Law, J. P. Gardner et al., *The International Court of Justice, Process, Practice and Procedure* (London: BIICL, 1997), 46 para. 27; Thirlway, 'The International Court of Justice 1989–2009: At the Heart of the Dispute Settlement System', 57 *NILR* (2010), 347 at 393. Where a person elected to the Court is already engaged in an arbitration he may of course be obliged, in fairness to the parties, not to withdraw at once.

[15] There is in existence, it is understood, a declaration by a President of the Permanent Court to the effect that the PCIJ Statute (identically worded on this point with the post-war Statute) does commit States to exempting judges' pensions from taxation, and this has been accepted, or at least tactfully left unchallenged, by a number of national taxation authorities.

of the judges (and the judges ad hoc), which involved a temporary difference in the amount of salary payable to judges according to whether they were elected before or after 1 January 2007. The objection made by the Court was that this infringed the 'fundamental principle' of equality of judges 'underlying the Statute'. The only specific reference to equality in the Statute is Article 31 paragraph 6 providing that judges ad hoc 'shall take part in the decision on terms of complete equality with their colleagues'. This is an aspect of the self-evident requirement of equality in the judicial sphere, to the extent that each judge has one vote on the decision, each judge has an equal opportunity of expressing his views to his colleagues, and hearing and commenting on theirs, etc.[16] Even in the financial sphere, as regards travel expenses, for instance, the judge from the Antipodes is entitled to full reimbursement just as much as his colleague from, say, Belgium. However, acceptance of the Court's contention signifies that the salaries of Members of the Court can never be decreased,[17] even if the UN were in the most dire financial straits, since a modification would either infringe Article 32 paragraph 5 of the Statute by decreasing remuneration after terms of office had begun, or (as the 2007 example showed) be seen as infringing equality. This would render meaningless the qualification in Article 32 paragraph 5 of the Statute that reduction must not be effected 'during the term of office'. All in all, it is suggested that the interpretation advanced by the Court, though accepted by the UN Legal Counsel, is not entirely convincing.[18]

A judge is not required to withdraw if a case is brought by or against the State of which he is a national; on the contrary, he is bound to sit in all cases before the full Court, and in any Chamber of which he is a member, unless there are special reasons, other than the mere fact of nationality, why it would be inappropriate for him to sit. The disqualification or withdrawal of a judge from a case is dealt with by Articles 17 and 24 of the Statute: the commonest reason for exclusion is that the judge has, prior to his election, already 'taken part in the case, as agent, counsel or advocate for one of the parties, or as a member of a national or international court, or of a commission of enquiry, or in any other capacity' (Art. 17 para. 2 of the Statute), but Article 24 of the Statute also provides for withdrawal or exclusion 'for some special reason'.[19]

[16] 'The members of the Court, in the exercise of their functions, are of equal status, irrespective of age, priority of election or length of service': Rules, Art. 3 para. 1: note the limitation to 'the exercise of their functions'. The Memorandum presented by the Court nevertheless asserts that this text (which was of course prepared by the Court itself) 'confirms that equality of status *and income* of members of the Court should be respected': UN Doc. A/62/538 Ann. II para. 36.

[17] As pointed out by N. Blokker, *The Governance of International Courts and Tribunals: Organizing and Guaranteeing Independence and Accountability*: ESIL Conference Paper No. 5/2015, Conference Paper Series, 5 (5).

[18] The Court's Memorandum also bases an argument on the fact that the parties before the Court are States, but this relates to the asserted need for equality between judges ad hoc and elected judges, and between judges ad hoc sitting in the same case (UN Doc. A/62/538 paras. 35 and 41–52), and its relevance to equality between elected judges is obscure.

[19] Little is known about the application of this text in practice. In the *Effect of Awards* case, Judge Basdevant did not sit, because the President of the Administrative Tribunal, the awards of which were to be discussed, was his daughter: see *ICJ Yearbook 1956–7*, 86.

B. Judges ad hoc

(1) Rationale

The possible presence on the Bench of a judge of the nationality of one of the parties was seen, when the Statute was drafted, as suggestive of inequality, despite the fact that members of the Court are required to act impartially. Rather than requiring withdrawal of the judge, in such circumstances the Statute ensures equality by enabling the other party to a case of this kind to nominate a person to sit as judge solely for that case, with the title of judge ad hoc.[20] There is, however, no requirement that the judge ad hoc be of the nationality of the party appointing him, and this is frequently not the case.[21] This system is defended on the ground that the presence of a 'national judge', even one bound to decide impartially, is still valuable to convince the State of which he is a national that justice will be achieved, since he can ensure that the case presented by the appointing State is fully understood; and this is held to be so even though the judge ad hoc does not have to have the nationality of the party appointing him. The Statute also provides, consistently with the idea of the benefit of a 'national judge', that in a case where neither party has a judge of its nationality on the Bench, and thus even though there is no inequality between the parties, each party may choose a judge ad hoc. In such cases, the parties sometimes agree on a mutual waiver of the right. Generally however practice suggests that the system meets a need felt by States.

There is no reason in theory why the Court should not sit with the inclusion of a judge ad hoc appointed by one party, the other party, equally entitled to appoint, having refrained from doing so; but for obvious reasons this is an unlikely scenario.[22]

Elected members of the Court not infrequently vote against the State of their nationality, but to date judges ad hoc have nearly always voted on most issues in favour of the State that appointed them;[23] and it is perhaps too much to expect that they should do otherwise.

[20] It has been suggested that the time has come, not merely to abolish the judge ad hoc, but to require the withdrawal of a Member of the Court having the nationality of a party to the case: A. Cassese, 'The International Court of Justice: It Is High Time to Restyle the Respected Old Lady', in Cassese (ed.), *Realizing Utopia: The Future of International Law* (Oxford: Oxford University Press, 2012), 239, 242.

[21] For an analysis of the function of a judge ad hoc, see the dissenting opinion of Judge ad hoc Franck in the case of *Sovereignty over Pulau Ligitan and Pulau Sipadan, ICJ Reports 2002*, 625 paras. 9–12, quoting the Separate Opinion of Judge ad hoc Elihu Lauterpacht in the *Application of the Convention on the Prevention and Punishment of the Crime of Genocide, Provisional Measures, Order of 13 September, ICJ Reports 1993*, 325 at 408–9 paras. 4–6.

[22] Except in the situation where the other party has refusing to participate in the proceedings at all: cf. *Fisheries Jurisdiction (Federal Republic of Germany* v *Iceland*), though in that case there was ultimately no judge ad hoc appointed by Germany (see sect. (2)).

[23] Exceptions include Judge ad hoc Bastid in *Application for Revision and Interpretation of Judgment, Continental Shelf (Tunisia/Libya)*, and Judge ad hoc Cot in *Territorial and Maritime Dispute (Nicaragua* v *Colombia)*.

(2) Case of parties 'in the same interest'

If two States bring proceedings jointly against another State, or proceedings are brought against two States jointly, each of the two remains a separate 'party'[24] to the proceedings. It would, however, obviously be unjust, and contrary to the purposes of Article 31 of the Statute, if each of the two States could appoint its own judge ad hoc. Paragraph 5 of that Article therefore provides that 'Should there be several parties in the same interest, they shall, for the purpose of the preceding provisions, be reckoned as one party only. Any doubt upon this point shall be settled by the decision of the Court.' It is rare that proceedings are instituted in a single case by, or against, more than one State, but the same situation results from the Court joining two cases (see Art. 47 of the Rules of Court and Ch. 7 sect. B(2)b). A joinder of this kind was ordered in the two *South West Africa* cases (*Liberia* v *South Africa*; *Ethiopia* v *South Africa*), and in the two *North Sea Continental Shelf* cases (brought by two special agreements: *Denmark/Federal Republic of Germany*; *Netherlands/Federal Republic of Germany*). As a result of the joinder, Ethiopia and Liberia were able to appoint only a single judge ad hoc; and similarly a single judge ad hoc was appointed jointly by Denmark and the Netherlands.

At the time of these decisions, the Rules of Court did not make any provision for joinder of cases. In 1961, when the Court joined the *South West Africa* cases, it stated that all States 'which, in proceedings before the Court, come to the same conclusion, must be held to be in the same interest'[25] for the purposes of Article 31 of the Statute. Since the pleadings of the two applicants were virtually identical, it was not difficult to conclude on that basis that they were 'in the same interest'. In the *North Sea Continental Shelf* cases, the three parties (Denmark, Netherlands, UK) had come to an agreement that the Court would be asked to join the cases, and that the two applicant States should be considered to be 'parties in the same interest'; the Court made an Order giving effect to this arrangement.[26]

It should not be overlooked that in these cases, had there been no joinder, the result would not have been a frustration of Article 31 of the Statute leading to possible injustice. The votes of the Ethiopian judge ad hoc and the Liberian judge ad hoc would not have been cumulative, since they would have been sitting in two different cases, decided by, in effect, two different courts; the same result would be seen in the *North Sea* cases. Article 47 of the Rules, introduced in 1972, does not indicate in what circumstances and on what grounds the Court may direct that two cases be joined,[27] but it seems that procedural economy in the administration of justice is the general basis, not specifically the implementation of the judge ad hoc system.

There followed, however, what is, it is suggested, an anomalous decision, in the *Fisheries Jurisdiction* cases, brought against Iceland by the United Kingdom and

[24] See also the discussion of the general significance of the term 'party' in Ch. 5 sect. C.

[25] Order of 20 May 1961, [1961] ICJ Rep 13, 14. The formula is taken from the PCIJ decision in the advisory case of *Customs Regime between Germany and Austria, PCIJ Series A/B, No. 41*, 89.

[26] Order of 26 April 1968, [1968] ICJ Rep 9.

[27] On this, see the discussion of the 2015 *Costa Rica/Nicaragua* cases in Ch. 7 sect. B(2)b.

by Germany. These cases were not joined, and Germany appointed a judge ad hoc. However, shortly before the hearings on the question of the Court's jurisdiction, the Court announced that, since there was a Member of the Court of British nationality sitting in the case, it was 'unable to find that the appointment of a judge ad hoc by the Federal Republic of Germany in this phase of the case would be admissible'.[28] In the subsequent judgment it stated that it had decided that 'there was in the present phase . . . a common interest in the sense of Article 31, paragraph 5, of the Statute which justified the refusal' of the German appointment.[29] The 'common interest' test of Article 41 was thus being read as satisfied if the two States of nationality of judges 'came to the same conclusion' in a case to which they were both parties *or in two separate cases*.[30]

Joinder had thus not been thought appropriate in the *Fisheries Jurisdiction* cases, nor was it in the two *Nuclear Tests* cases (*Australia* v *France*; *New Zealand* v *France*), in which each of the applicant States appointed a judge ad hoc (who was in fact the same person in each case). No suggestion seems to have been made that there was any relevant 'common interest', since the voting in the two cases would be separate, and neither applicant had a judge of its nationality among the elected judges.

The *Lockerbie* cases, brought by Libya against the UK and against the US on basically the same grounds, were not the subject of a joinder; and in the context of appointment of a judge ad hoc, three Members of the Court expressed doubts. The Court included a British judge (Higgins) and a US judge (Schwebel); but it happened that Judge Higgins had had to withdraw, in application of Article 17 of the Statute, and the UK therefore proposed to appoint a judge ad hoc. The Court decided that, 'in the two cases, the United Kingdom and the United States of America were not parties in the same interest within the meaning of Article 41, paragraph 5, of the Statute'.[31] This decision, taken by ten votes to three, was in effect a reversal of the *Fisheries Jurisdiction* decision, and in a joint declaration, Judges Bedjaoui, Guillaume, and Ranjeva explained their disagreement.[32]

A more complex picture emerges from the multiple cases of *Legality of the Use of Force* brought by Yugoslavia (Serbia). These were brought against the ten members of NATO, with a request in each case for the indication of provisional measures. Serbia appointed the same person to sit as judge ad hoc in each of the cases. At that initial stage of the proceedings the Court, unusually, removed two cases (those brought against Spain and the US) from the list on the basis that no title of jurisdiction had been shown. In the remaining cases, four of the respondent States had a judge of their nationality on the Bench: France, Germany, the Netherlands, and the UK; in principle, in each of the other cases the respondents (Belgium, Canada, Italy, Portugal) would have been entitled to appoint a judge ad hoc, and three of

[28] *ICJ Pleadings, Fisheries Jurisdiction*, ii. 421; quoted in [1971] ICJ Rep 37.

[29] [1973] ICJ Rep 49, 51 para. 7. The phrase 'a common interest' appears in the authoritative English text of the decision: the French has 'font cause commune', the phrase which in Art. 31 of the Statute corresponds to 'be . . . in the same interest'.

[30] The matter is further discussed in Thirlway, *Law and Procedure*, i. 882–6.

[31] [1998] ICJ Rep 9, 13 para. 9.

[32] [1998] ICJ Rep 32–45.

them (not Portugal) did so. The requirements of the Statute were thus met, in that in each case taken separately, the applicant and the respondent (except for Portugal) each had either a judge of their nationality or a judge ad hoc on the Bench. But in each of the cases involving a judge ad hoc, the Court also included the French, German, Dutch, and British judges; and, without any reflection on the judicial impartiality of these persons, the situation was hardly that of equality contemplated by the judge ad hoc system.

If all eight cases had been joined—and this in some ways would have been a logical step, since they all related to the same events, and asserted international responsibility on the same grounds[33]—then none of the respondent parties lacking a national judge would have been entitled to have a judge ad hoc on the bench, since they would all have been 'in the same interest' as France, Germany, the Netherlands, and the UK.

Until a few months before the opening of oral proceedings on the question of jurisdiction (all the respondents had raised preliminary objections), the judges ad hoc appointed by the respondent States were treated as sitting in the respective cases. Then a meeting was held between the President of the Court and the agents of the parties, with regard to questions of procedure, at which the agents were invited to discuss (*inter alia*) the 'presence on the Bench of judges ad hoc during the preliminary objection phase; possible joinder of the proceedings . . .'[34] Subsequently, each respondent party that had appointed a judge ad hoc was informed by the Registrar that 'the Court had decided, pursuant to Article 31, paragraph 5, of the Statute, that, taking into account the presence on the Bench of judges of British, Dutch and French nationality,[35] the judges ad hoc chosen by the respondent States should not sit during the current phase of the procedure in these cases . . .'[36] The Court was thus ruling, in effect, that for the purposes of entitlement to a judge ad hoc, a party to a case may be 'in the same interest' as a State not party to that case, but party to a 'parallel' case, and having a judge of its nationality on the bench for that case. This handling of the matter, it may be thought, ensured procedural justice in the context of the provisions of the Statute as to judges ad hoc (an institution that has always been somewhat anomalous); and there was clearly nothing that could be done about the fact that, opposite the Serbian judge ad hoc, there were four judges from NATO countries in a case directly involving action taken by NATO.

The Court might usefully have given rather more explanation of the reasoning behind its decision in each of these cases. The judge ad hoc appointed by Serbia devoted a substantial part of his separate opinion to 'The Issue of the Composition of the Court'; this included the suggestion that where the composition of the Court includes several elected judges of the nationalities of parties 'in the same interest', the other party should be entitled as many judges ad hoc as required to balance

[33] There was on the other hand considerable variation in the jurisdictional titles invoked.

[34] (e.g.) *Legality of the Use of Force (Serbia* v *Belgium)*, [2004-I] ICJ Rep 279, 286 para. 17.

[35] The German judge had retired in the meantime.

[36] *Legality of the Use of Force (Serbia* v *Belgium)*, [2004-I] ICJ Rep 279, 287 para. 18. It was also explained that the question whether judges ad hoc would sit in any later phases of the case was left open.

them,[37] which seems to go beyond what is compatible with the wording of the Statute.

The position of the judge ad hoc has always been anomalous, but the system is based on, or at least implies, the idea that his is a vote secured in advance. To permit appointment of a judge ad hoc to 'balance' an elected judge, as does paragraph 1 of Article 41, then comes near to implying that the latter's vote also may be treated (as least for this purpose) as secured in advance; and this is enshrined in the Statute. The innovation in the *Fisheries Jurisdiction* cases was to pursue this line of argument further: if the UK elected judge and the German judge ad hoc are both 'booked' on the same side, then it is appropriate to treat them as having been appointed by parties in the same interest for the purposes of Article 41 paragraph 5. In the case of parties to two different cases (e.g. *South West Africa*), the fact that they are so 'booked' is unimportant so long as that situation continues, as their votes are not cumulative: it is only when the cases are joined that the 'same interest' matters. As soon as one applies the 'same interest' test to an *elected* judge, however, the problem arises that that judge's vote will be counted in every case, and will necessarily be cumulative with that of a judge ad hoc voting the same way. In the *Lockerbie* case the Court was no longer willing to press the argument as far as in *Fisheries Jurisdiction*. In the *Use of Force* cases the Court swung from one solution to the other: individual judges ad hoc at the preliminary stage, and no judges ad hoc at the next stage.

So far, the test for 'same interest' involves the participation of the State having a national on the bench in a case before the Court, not necessarily the same case, and pursuing thereby the same ends. In the *Nauru* case, Nauru brought proceedings against Australia (alone) complaining of the actions taken under UN Trusteeship by Australia, New Zealand, and the United Kingdom. Neither party appointed a judge ad hoc; but if both Nauru and Australia had done so, could Nauru have objected that Australia and the United Kingdom were 'in the same interest' (since the harm complained of by Nauru was the act of the three States as trustees), so that the presence of a United Kingdom national on the bench debarred Australia from such appointment? Probably not; but the hypothesis demonstrates, it is suggested, that it was unwise of the Court in 1971 to apply the 'same interest' criterion in the case of an elected judge.

A case that involved something approaching manipulation of the system was that of *Whaling in the Antarctic*, brought by Australia against Japan; there was a Japanese Member of the Court (Judge Owada), but no Australian Member, and Australia appointed a judge ad hoc. New Zealand, which shared Australia's concerns about Japanese whaling activities, then applied to intervene under Article 63 of the Statute, and the intervention was admitted; this did not make New Zealand a party,[38] but enabled it to put its views before the Court. If the case had been brought by Australia and New Zealand jointly, they could not have appointed a judge ad hoc, as the Court also included Judge Keith, of New Zealand nationality.

[37] [2004-I] ICJ Rep 371, 416–26 paras. 67–75.

[38] See Ch. 15 sect. B.

Japan did not object, but expressed 'serious doubts'; and Judge Owada, in a declaration, expressed the view that a situation could have been created 'in which the principle of the fair administration of justice, including the equality of the Parties, would most likely be compromised'.[39] The Court emphasized the limited role of an intervenor, and considered that 'such an intervention cannot affect the equality of the Parties to the dispute'.[40]

C. The Chambers

The Court is authorized by the Statute to create standing chambers for particular categories of case, and a special chamber may be formed by the Court to deal with a specific case if the parties so request. There is also one standing chamber, which the Statute requires to be formed 'with a view to the speedy dispatch of business': the Chamber of Summary Procedure (Art. 29), which is regularly constituted but has, up to the present, never operated.[41] Article 26 authorizes the creation of chambers 'for dealing with particular categories of cases: for example, labour cases and cases relating to transit and communications'. These examples mirror the expectations of the drafters of the PCIJ Statute. There was for a while (1993–2006) a Chamber formed to deal with environmental matters, but States did not seem to be interested in using it, and after a while it was allowed to disappear.[42]

The number of judges to constitute a special chamber is determined by the parties, but the individual judges to be members of it are elected by the Court, and the composition of the chamber is thus, theoretically, outside the control of the parties. In practice, however, it has become accepted that if the parties indicate that certain names would be acceptable, the Court is virtually certain to elect them, if only because the creation of a chamber composed otherwise than as desired by the parties would be likely to result in the case being withdrawn and referred to some other method of settlement.[43]

[39] [2013] ICJ Rep 11, 13 para. 6.

[40] [2013] ICJ Rep 3, 9 para. 18. One wonders whether it was not more a matter of equality between parties *to the case*, which, it would seem, was affected.

[41] Two cases (or two stages of one case) were referred to the corresponding chamber of the Permanent Court, and decided by it: see *Paragraph 4 of the Annex following Article 179 of the Treaty of Neuilly, PCIJ Series A, No. 3*, and *Interpretation of Judgment No. 3, PCIJ Series A, No. 4*.

[42] See *ICJ Yearbook 1992–3*, 17; *2005–6*, 29. The most active specialized field in the work of the post-war Court has probably been the law of maritime delimitation, and the developing nature of this, it is suggested, called for the full Court to be involved; in a few cases, however, the Court has given effect to the desire of parties to cases in this field of law to have a special Chamber formed for the case. Experience with these suggests that a principal reason for the neglect of the standing chambers (Chamber of Summary Procedure and the Environmental Matters Chamber) is probably that their composition is determined in advance by the Court, and the parties have no say in it.

[43] The first request for a special chamber, by the United States and Canada in the *Gulf of Maine* case, was made pursuant to a treaty that provided explicitly that the case would be transferred to arbitration if the Chamber was not formed as the parties wished. Subsequent approaches to the Court have been more tactful.

The device of reference of a case to a special chamber formed for the purpose, a procedure long neglected, became more popular between 1984 and 2002, but may now be in decline.[44] To some extent the use of chambers makes for greater flexibility and thus tends towards speedier settlement of cases; the deliberation can also proceed faster, with fewer judges to present their views.[45] But simultaneous operation of two chambers is only practicable if no member of one chamber is also a member of the other; and the members of the Chamber also have to take part in any cases being heard and deliberated on by the full Court. In tribunals where the chambers are established by the tribunal itself, as sub-units (e.g. the International Criminal Tribunal for the Former Yugoslavia and the International Criminal Court), this can be arranged; but where the membership of chambers is in effect left to the parties to determine, experience suggests that overlapping membership may be a real problem. The use of chambers has thus not appreciably accelerated the procedure of the International Court.

A question that has been raised but not settled is whether a Chamber of the Court might give an advisory opinion;[46] the hypothesis of this being requested is somewhat unlikely.

D. The Presidency

The President and Vice-President of the Court are elected triennially by their colleagues. The President is to 'direct the work and supervise the administration of the Court' (Rules, Art. 12). The Statute provides that he is to 'reside at The Hague' (Art. 22 para. 2). Judicial hearings are 'under the control of the President, or, if he is unable to preside, of the Vice-President; if neither is able to preside, the senior judge shall preside' (Statute, Art. 45), and the same practice is adopted in administrative meetings. The President may be unable to preside because he is absent, either for practical reasons (e.g. illness),[47] or because he is excluded from participation in the case under Article 24 of the Statute. He may also be sitting in the case but not presiding, because he is a national of one of the parties to the case (see Rules, Art. 32 para. 1).

If the votes on a decision are equally divided, the judge presiding has a casting vote (Statute, Art. 55 para. 2). This has been applied for the adoption of a judicial

[44] The following cases have been decided by chambers: *Gulf of Maine* (1984); *Frontier Dispute (Burkina Faso/Mali)* (1986); *Elettronica Sicula* (1989); *Land, Island and Maritime Frontier Dispute* (1992); *Application for Revision of the Judgment of 11 September 1992 in the Land, Island and Maritime Frontier Dispute* (2003); *Frontier Dispute (Benin/Niger)* (2005).

[45] As already observed by Plato, who equates an over-large court with one of poor quality: *The Laws*, VI. 766.

[46] See discussion by P. Palchetti in Zimmermann et al., *Commentary, sub* Art. 26 para. 10.

[47] Article 23 of the Statute provides for Members of the Court to have periodic leave, that is, on an individual basis, apart from periods when the Court itself is on judicial vacation. With the present workload of the Court, this text has become virtually a dead letter.

decision on three occasions;[48] whether it is also regarded as applicable to administrative decisions when the Court is sitting privately is not known, but the published records of the Permanent Court's work on the revision of its Rules show that the casting vote was on occasion used in this context.

The President presides at the hearings (Statute, Art. 45), and has a number of powers to act in place of the Court, in particular for the regulation of the written proceedings, under Article 44 paragraph 4 of the Rules. That article provides that the President's exercise of such power is 'without prejudice to any subsequent decision of the Court'; but this apparently does not confer any power of appeal by an aggrieved party from the President's decision to the Court.[49] The President, as an individual, can generally act more rapidly than the Court, as a collegiate body that has to be convened and discuss what action to take. In the past, when the Court was less active than it is now, procedural Orders were quite frequently made by the President alone, but now the Court is assembled for much more of the year, it can usually act collectively.

If a party requests the indication of provisional measures under Article 41 of the Statute, the situation is, by definition, one for rapid action. Article 41 states that 'the Court shall have power' to indicate measures, and there is no indication that this power can be delegated. This seems to have been the consistent view of the Court in exercising its rule-making power: Article 74 paragraph 3 provides for a rapid hearing on the request, and paragraph 4 seems to go as far as possible for 'provisional' provisional measures by adding that '[p]ending the meeting of the Court, the President may call upon the parties to act in such a way as will enable any order the Court may make on the request for provisional measures to have its appropriate effects.'[50]

E. The Registrar and the Registry

Article 21 paragraph 2 of the Statute provides that '[t]he Court shall appoint its Registrar and may provide for the appointment of such other officers as may be necessary.' The duties of the Registrar are set out in Article 26 of the Rules of Court,[51] which also indicates that '[i]n the discharge of his functions the Registrar shall be responsible to the Court.' The Registrar and his staff are also

[48] *South West Africa (Second Phase)*, [1966] ICJ Rep 6, 51 para. 99; *Nuclear Tests* [1996] ICJ Rep 226, 266 para. 105 (2) E; *Legality of Nuclear Weapons* [1996] ICJ Rep 266, para. 105 (2) E; *Delimitation of the Continental Shelf between Nicaragua and Colombia beyond 200 miles*, [2016] ICJ Rep para. 126 (1) (*b*).

[49] Rosenne ('The President of the ICJ'), in Lowe and Fitzmaurice (eds.), *Fifty Years of the International Court of Justice*, refers in this connection to a ruling of the Permanent Court: *PCIJ Series E, No. 3* (1927), 230.

[50] See further Ch. 13.

[51] For a survey of the role of the Registrar by the present very experienced holder of the post, see Ph. Couvreur, 'Aperçu du statut et des fonctions du greffier de la Cour internationale de justice', in C. Apostolidis (ed.), *Les Arrêts de la Cour international de justice* (Dijon: Éditions Universitaires de Dijon), 2005), 65ff.

officials of the United Nations, but this provision makes clear that they are not under the direction of the Secretary-General. Similarly, the Staff Regulations for the Registry are quite distinct from those applicable generally in the Organization. What is now shared by Registry staff and general UN staff is the right of appeal to the UN Administrative Tribunal in case of disputes relating to their employment.[52]

In the relations with the Government of the Netherlands, the Registrar is assimilated to an Ambassador, and the Deputy-Registrar to a Counsellor; the other senior officials of the Registry are assimilated to the senior staff (First Secretaries and Secretaries) of embassies accredited to The Hague. Apart from general administration, their duties had for a considerable time a linguistic emphasis, in view of the Court's need for impeccable correspondence between its decisions in the two official languages. An increasing need was, however, found for legal support, and the Registry became more closely involved in the work of drafting legal texts for approval by the Court and its committees. In 2009, the Court asked the General Assembly, when approving its budget, to establish six posts of law clerks to work directly with individual judges, and the number of these was later increased; today each Member of the Court has the support of a secretary, a law clerk, and a University intern.

Article 26 of the Rules elaborates on the few mentions of the Registrar's duties in the Statute; the article adds that '[t]he Court may at any time entrust additional functions to the Registrar.' His responsibility as chief administrative officer is clear; less evident is the extent to which he is a judicial officer with the function of taking certain legal decisions. The Statute and Rules frequently indicate the action that the Registrar is to take in circumstances where a decision of this kind is needed: a simple example is the filing of an application instituting proceedings. First of all, is it a genuine application? The Registry receives enormous numbers of 'private applications for justice'; these call for no more than a polite acknowledgement, and indication of the effect of Article 34 of the Statute. But there are, very occasionally, approaches from entities whose international legal status is less clear.[53] In practice, in all these matters the Registrar works closely with, and under the direction of, the President. In one respect (the maintenance of the Court's General List of cases), Article 26 specifies that this is

[52] Following the example of the PCIJ, the Court for a considerable time preferred to keep settlement of disputes of this kind 'in house', even after the establishment of UNAT. In 1979 it set up a procedure before a 'Judge for Staff Appeals', a Member of the Court chosen for that role, with appeal from his decision to the Court itself; but this was never a system that was going to enjoy the confidence of the staff. Eventually, in 1997, provision was made for recourse to UNAT, subject to a prior conciliation procedure. See *ICJ Yearbook 1978–9*, 127–31; *1988–9*, 163–4; *1997–8*, 265–72. For a recent UNAT decision concerning a Registry staff member, which vividly illustrates the need for 'outside' intervention to 'defuse' the situation, see *Rangel* v *ICJ Registrar*, UNAT cases 2014–611, 2014–674, and 2014–689.

[53] There have been examples where the Registrar has thought it prudent to lay the matter before the Court: see *ICJ Yearbook 1966–7*, 88.

to be 'under the supervision of the President'. It would rash to deduce that none of the other tasks are to involve such supervision; but the conferral of various powers on him presumably signifies that it is his personal judgement that is to be exercised in their use.[54] The fact that he can presumably be overruled by the Court does not detract from this.[55]

[54] Rosenne, *Law and Practice*, i. 419, observes that 'in some legal systems, the registrar is given quasi-judicial powers to settle at least some procedural matters that arise during the process of litigation', and suggests that '[t]his tradition has been carried over into international litigation practice.'

[55] S. Yee comments that it 'may be somewhat difficult' for a party to appeal to the Court, and suggests that a party in that position might disregard the normal rule of communication through the Registrar, and address the President directly (Art. 50 in Zimmerman et al., *Commentary*, para. 36); though this has happened (personal recollection) the suggestion is still to be deprecated for its implied slur on the conscientiousness of the (hypothetical) Registrar.

II

THE JURISDICTION AND POWERS OF THE COURT

3

The Law Applied by the Court

A. International law in general

The present work is neither a general treatise on international law, nor a study of the application of that law, in all its variety, by the Court in its decisions.[1] It may, however, be useful to mention some general points concerning the application of international law by a tribunal, and specifically by the International Court.

It is axiomatic that the law applied by the Court as the basis of its decision is international law: Article 38 of the Statute states that its function is 'to decide in accordance with international law such disputes as are submitted to it'. The Court may nevertheless find itself obliged to resolve a point of municipal law (the national law of a particular country), but this will normally be because the point is one on which international law refers to national law,[2] the process known in private international law as *renvoi*. It is also possible for an issue that for international law is one of fact depends on the existence, or absence, of certain provisions of national law.

Where then is international law to be found? Article 38 paragraph 1 of the Statute contains the well-known list of what the Court is to apply:

a. international conventions, whether general or particular, establishing rules expressly recognized by the contesting states;
b. international custom, as evidence of a general practice accepted as law;
c. the general principles of law recognized by civilized nations;
d. subject to the provisions of Article 59,[3] judicial decisions and the teachings of the most highly qualified publicists of the various nations, as subsidiary means for the determination of rules of law.

For purposes of the work of the Court this is clearly a limitative enumeration, so that whether there are now other sources of international law is a question outside

[1] As was attempted by the present writer up to a fairly recent date in the *British Yearbook of International Law*, these contributions are collected in Thirlway, *Law and Procedure*.

[2] e.g. the application in matters of territorial title of the international law principle of *uti possidetis juris*, where, as was pointed out by a Chamber of the Court, 'the *jus* referred to is not international law but the constitutional or administrative law of the pre-independence sovereign': *Land, Island and Maritime Frontier Dispute*, [1992] ICJ Rep 351, 559 para. 333.

[3] Article 59: 'The decision of the Court has no binding force except between the parties and in respect of that particular case.'

our purview; nor is it the purpose of the present work to enquire into that wide-ranging subject of sources, even within the restraints of Article 38.[4]

A concept that has developed since the PCIJ era, and indeed since the current Statute was adopted, is that of 'soft law', that is, legal provisions, usually in treaty instruments, not intended to impose a binding obligation;[5] since the usual purpose of contentious proceedings before the Court is to press for compliance with an obligation, this area of law is one that does not usually concern it. There is, however, no reason why the Court should not find that such an obligation exists in principle: frequently a rule of soft law is created by a treaty, and the Court may apply the normal rules of treaty-interpretation to ascertain the existence of the rule. The soft nature of the rule may, however, then intervene to prevent the Court going on to say whether or not it has been complied with, or how it should be complied with. Many resolutions adopted by organs of international organizations amount to soft law, but have been taken into account, within these limits, by the Court.

B. Equity

Another question that is essentially one of the content of international law is that of the role of equity. The concept of equity is closely related to that of judicial settlement: it implies a balancing of competing considerations as distinct from the application of a more or less clear rule. Such balancing may be achieved by the parties to a dispute through negotiation; but achieving it is very much the speciality of the third party called in to judge or arbitrate.

The question whether something called 'equity' is part of international law is thus here viewed as the question: can the Court apply equity in reaching its decisions? Article 38 of the Statute, which directs the Court to decide 'in accordance with international law', itself contains a qualification in paragraph 2: 'This provision shall not prejudice the power of the Court to decide a case *ex aequo et bono*, if the parties agree thereto.' There has not yet been a case in which the parties have so agreed; but it is generally recognized that a decision on these lines means a decision on the basis of very general ideas of fairness or appropriateness, taking no account whatsoever of positive law.[6]

[4] The present writer has written on the subject elsewhere: Thirlway, *The Sources of International Law* (Oxford: Oxford University Press, 2014). For a more recent study of the matter, see Sienho Yee, 'Article 38 of the ICJ Statute and the Applicable Law: selected issues in recent cases', *ICJ 70th Anniversary Symposium* (2016), to appear shortly in *JIDS*.

[5] For a more detailed analysis of different categories of soft law, see D. Shelton (ed.), *Commitment and Compliance: the Role of Non-Binding Norms in the International Legal System* (Oxford: Oxford University Press, 2000), particularly the Introduction and Ch. 9 (E. Brown Weiss).

[6] That fairness has in any event some role to play is suggested by the incident concerning the appointment of the judge ad hoc in the *Whaling in the Antarctic* case: see Ch. 2 sect. A(2), and generally in the procedural context, Sarvarian et al. (eds.), *Procedural Fairness in International Courts and Tribunals* (London: BIICL, 2016).

The possible employment of equity in a stricter sense, as part of the 'international law' that the Court is directed to apply, was discussed in the *Frontier Dispute* case between Burkina Faso and Mali. The Chamber seised of the case had been invited by Mali to take account of 'that form of equity which is inseparable from the application of international law'.[7] The Chamber distinguished the application of equity *contra legem*, contrary to the law, which, it indicated, would be appropriate only if it were asked to adjust the respective interests of the parties; equity *praeter legem* (that is to say, equity alongside the law, a concept the Chamber did not explain); and equity *infra legem* (within the law), 'that is, the form of equity which constitutes a method of interpretation of the law in force and is one of its attributes [*qualités* in the French text]'.[8] In this connection it cited the *Fisheries Jurisdiction* cases: 'It is not a matter of finding simply an equitable solution, but an equitable solution derived from the applicable law.'[9] Specific application of this approach appears later in the judgment in the context of a pool lying close to the frontier; it proved impossible to determine which side of it the frontier passed. Accordingly,

> in the absence of any precise indication in the texts of the position of the frontier line, the line should divide the pool of Soum in two, in an equitable manner. Although 'Equity does not necessarily imply equality' (*North Sea Continental Shelf, I.C.J. Reports 1969*, p. 49, para. 91), where there are no special circumstances the latter is generally the best expression of the former.[10]

Under this head mention may also be made of the principle of good faith, which has been invoked before the Court as the basis for rights and obligations, or as affecting their exercise or discharge. The Court has recognized that 'the principle of good faith' is something it recognizes and should take account of (with the implication that it forms part of the law that the Court is to apply), nevertheless it has made clear that while it is a principle 'governing the creation and performance of legal obligations', yet 'it is not in itself a source of obligation where none would otherwise exist'.[11]

C. Humanitarian considerations

A number of cases involving the application of the death penalty in the United States have raised the delicate question of the relevance of strictly non-legal considerations, specifically considerations of humanity.[12] When the first of these cases, the

[7] [1986] ICJ Rep 554, 567 para. 27. [8] [1986] ICJ Rep 554, 567–8 para. 27.

[9] [1974] ICJ Rep 3, 33 para. 78; 175, 202 para. 69.

[10] *Frontier Dispute* [1986] ICJ Rep 554, 633 para. 150. There is perhaps here some disproportion between the ponderous legal substructure and the simple solution!

[11] *Boundary and Transboundary Armed Actions (Nicaragua* v *Honduras)*, [1988] ICJ Rep 69, 105 para. 94; followed in *Land and Maritime Boundary between Cameroon and Nigeria*, [1998] ICJ Rep 275, 297 para. 39.

[12] See also V. Chetail, 'The Contribution of the International Court of Justice to International Humanitarian Law', *International Review of the Red Cross* 85:850 (2003), 235–69.

Breard case, came before the Court in the form of a request for provisional measures, Judge Oda made it very clear in a Declaration that he 'voted in favour of the Order' indicating measures intended to postpone Breard's execution 'for humanitarian reasons', and that as matter of law the request 'should have been dismissed'.[13] He made the same point still more emphatically in a Declaration appended to the Order indicating measures in the *LaGrand* case;[14] and in a dissenting opinion attached to the eventual judgment on the merits, he expressed regret at having voted in favour of the Order, 'since I did so against my juridical conscience'.[15] The reason why Judge Oda considered that the Order indicating measures should not have been made was that such measures may be indicated only to preserve rights of States asserted in the application instituting proceedings, not any other rights, and this requirement was not satisfied.

The question of interest here is not whether he was right on this point, but whether, on the supposition (adopted purely for the sake of argument) that a majority of the Court had substantial doubts on the point, it would have been judicially correct to issue the Order. It was very understandable for the Court to take such action as it could to preserve human life, and to let the chips fall subsequently as they might; and its Members were left very little time for consideration: an Order had to be made instantly if it was to serve any purpose at all.[16] But Judge Oda raises a good point: to what extent, if any, may humanitarian considerations of this kind impede the strict application of the law? So long as capital punishment is in itself not contrary to international law,[17] it is difficult to justify impeding a State's right to carry it out. It is for that reason that the applications in the death penalty cases have contrived (if the term may be permitted) to rely on claims of non-compliance with treaty obligations concerning access to consular assistance.[18] In another death penalty case, the request by Mexico for interpretation of the *Avena* judgment, a strong minority held that '[h]umanitarian considerations which clearly underlie the decision cannot override the legal requirements of the Statute of the Court.'[19]

In the case of *Jurisdictional Immunities of the State*, the Court was invited to find that the general rule of international law of State immunity, on the basis of *par in parem non habet imperium*, should yield when it was sought to enforce responsibility

[13] [1998] ICJ Rep 260, 262 paras. 1, 8. He also drew attention to humanitarian considerations in relation to Breard's victims.

[14] [1999-I] ICJ Rep 18, 20 paras. 1, 7.

[15] [2001] ICJ Rep 525, 531.

[16] See the details of the timing of the request given by Judge Oda, [2001] ICJ Rep 525, 531–2, and by Judge Buergenthal, ibid. 548–9. The Order was made *proprio motu* without hearing the parties; this was objected to by the US, but does not seem to be improper in principle.

[17] On the limitations on its use, see International Covenant on Civil and Procedural Rights, art. 6, which probably represents customary law.

[18] A parallel may be seen in the case of *Construction of a Road in Costa Rica along the San Juan River*, where Nicaragua sought to prevent alleged damage to wetlands threatening many animal species with extinction, but relied for this purpose on 'transboundary harm' and thus infringement of sovereignty, rather than any public interest in preserving the environment: see Order of 13 December 2013, [2013] ICJ Rep 398, 406, 407 paras. 28 and 34 *in fine*.

[19] Dissenting opinion of Judges Owada, Tomka, and Keith, *Request for Interpretation (Avena)*, Order of 16 July 2008, [2008] ICJ Rep 311, 341.

for violation of humanitarian law, but declined to do so.[20] Similarly, it had already held that the nature of genocide, and its recognition of its prohibition as a matter of *jus cogens* (see next section) did not invalidate a reservation made by a State when acceding to the Genocide Convention, excluding the jurisdiction of the Court.[21]

D. Peremptory norms

The concept of peremptory norms, or *jus cogens*, is comparatively new to international law, at least as known by that name.[22] The essence of a peremptory norm is that it is universally applicable, in the sense that it cannot be excluded, varied, or modified by agreement between two or more States for the purposes of their mutual relations.

The Court has since 1970 made numerous allusions to the existence of norms of this character. However, while it has indicated, on a number of occasions, recognition of the defining feature of the concept: the legal impossibility of contracting out of such a norm, it has never yet had occasion actually to strike down an agreement between two States on this ground. The concept therefore, while widely recognized, still lacks, to this extent, judicial confirmation; nor is there complete unanimity among scholars or among States that the concept has a real existence, in the form generally asserted, in general customary law.[23]

Cases in which a peremptory norm made an appearance were the *Armed Activities* case just referred to, and the case of *Jurisdictional Immunities of the State*,[24] where the concept was more directly related to the Court's activity. The Court there declined to set aside, or make an exception to, the recognized rules of State immunity on the grounds that the obligation sought to be enforced derived from what were recognized to have been breaches of peremptory norms.

A difficult question that has attracted comment in this connection[25] is how the concept applies to the principle of *ne ultra petita*, the principle that a court may only decide what it has been asked to decide. This will be examined in Chapter 7 section C. A similar issue has been raised in connection with the effect of reservations to declarations of acceptance of jurisdiction under the 'optional clause' (Art. 36 para. 2 of the Statute), but only as a hypothesis in argument: see further Chapter 4 section A.[26]

20 [2012] ICJ Rep 99, 139 para. 91.

21 *Armed Activities on the Territory of the Congo (DRC* v *Rwanda)*, [2006] ICJ Rep 6, 32 para. 67, and para. 68 citing previous decision in the same sense.

22 On the historical development of the concept, and generally, see the First ILC Report on the subject, A/CN.4/693, 8 March 2016, sect. IV.

23 For A. Mark Weisburd, for example, 'the concept of *jus cogens* makes no sense': *Failings of the International Court of Justice* (Oxford: Oxford University Press, 2016), 78; and see R. Kolb, *Peremptory International Law:* Jus Cogens, *A General Inventory* (Oxford: Hart, 2015), particularly ch. 2.

24 [2012] ICJ Rep 99.

25 In particular by A. Orakhelashvili in *Peremptory Norms in International Law* (Oxford: Oxford University Press), 492 ff.

26 See the case there referred to of *Application of the Genocide Convention (Croatia* v *Serbia)* [2015] ICJ Rep para. 87.

E. The principle *jura novit curia*

A general principle concerning courts of justice that is regarded as applicable to the ICJ is that defined in the Latin phrase *jura novit curia*, 'the court knows the law'. This signifies that whatever arguments of law are addressed to it by the parties, it is the Court that determines for itself what the law is;[27] it may uphold the legal arguments of the one side or the other, or may dismiss them all as incorrect or incomplete. While a litigant may lose his case if he fails to prove the facts upon which his claim is based, he will in principle not fail merely because he has not produced a convincing argument that the claim is sound in law. The court cannot be expected to make its own enquiry into the facts of the dispute, but will decide upon such evidence of those facts as is placed before it; but it is the whole function of a court to know the law and apply it to those facts.[28]

Theoretically at least, therefore, an applicant State might merely expound the facts and leave the law to the Court; but this is of course impracticable, since it is the legal nature of the claim that defines what facts are relevant; and no counsel would take the risk of leaving the Court unguided as to the law. What if a party does not submit argument at all? Article 53 of the Statute, dealing with the case of non-appearance of a party (and discussed in Ch. 7 sect. B(3)(c), empowers the Court to decide in favour of the claim of the other party provided it is satisfied 'that the claim is well founded in fact and law'. The Court will therefore accept the facts as established by the appearing party (unless the evidence of them is patently unconvincing); but, in application of the *jura novit curia* principle, may reject the claim on the grounds that the law is not as contended for by that party.

The parties may conclude a treaty in a particular field, and expect the Court, if it becomes the subject of litigation, to apply the rules adopted in the treaty in preference to such rules of general international law;[29] what then if they agree that the legal rules, of a general or customary nature, applicable to the transaction being litigated, are such and such? A question of this kind was touched on in the *Military and Paramilitary Activities* case. The Court there stated the *jura novit curia* principle, but added, '[n]evertheless the views of the parties to a case as to the law applicable are very material, particularly . . . when those views are concordant.'[30] The application of this observation later in the judgment came when the Court was considering what are the rules of customary law on the use of force; it found that there was evidence 'of a considerable degree of agreement between the Parties as to the content of the customary international law relating to the non-use of force and

[27] 'It used to be said that the common law of England resided in the breasts of His Majesty's Judges': Darling J in *Gray* v *Gee* (1923) 39 *TLR* 429, 430.

[28] A question of interest, but unlikely to arise in practice, is whether the Court could reject the ground of jurisdiction alleged by the Applicant, but (in the application of *jura novit curia*) invoke a different ground. Jurisdiction is, however, usually a question of mixed law and fact.

[29] Always subject of course to such principles as may constitute *jus cogens* (peremptory norms).

[30] *Military and Paramilitary Activities in and against Nicaragua* [1986] ICJ Rep 14, 29 para. 29.

non-intervention'. But it then continued, '[t]he mere fact that States declare their recognition of certain rules is not sufficient for the Court to consider these as being part of customary international law. . .'[31] The weight attached to the 'views of the parties', *as parties*, and not merely as members of the international community whose *opinio juris* is needed for custom formation, remains obscure.[32]

The principle does not mean that the Court must always be able, and be required, to find an applicable rule of law and apply it; the extent to which it can develop the law is controversial, but if it finds that there is no rule that, for example, either forbids or specifically authorizes some conduct alleged, then it must say so, and leave the dispute unresolved. This is shown by the case of *Legality of the Threat or Use of Nuclear Weapons,* in which the Court found that it '[could] not reach a definitive conclusion as to the legality or illegality of nuclear weapons' in certain defined circumstances.[33]

This dictum appears in the context of a request for advisory opinion, where the role of the Court is to state the law, not to resolve a dispute. The outcome must, however, be the same in a contentious context: the Court has no more power to fill gaps in the law in a contentious case than it has in advisory proceedings. But the procedural context may still affect the way in which the decision is conveyed. If the applicant alleges the breach by the respondent of a specific rule of law, and the Court finds that no such rule exists, that is sufficient as basis for a rejection of the claim. It does not need to go on and consider whether the action of the respondent was legally justified, or was legally neutral, in the sense that there is no relevant rule of law on the point. This may explain why the only example so far in the Court's jurisprudence of a finding of this kind was in an advisory opinion. For the development of the law, there is not much to choose between these situations; but the first might be read to suggest an insufficiency on the part of the Court, of the law, rather than on that of the applicant or the evidence that it adduces.

[31] Ibid. 97 para. 184.

[32] The Court was perhaps making a rhetorical point by saying, in effect, to the United States, 'You apply these rules when it suits you, so they apply here too.'

[33] [1996-I] ICJ Rep 226, 263 para. 97.

4

Jurisdiction in Contentious Cases (I)

A. The concept of jurisdiction

The 'jurisdiction' of a court or tribunal is essentially the power to decide according to law (*jus dicere*) a dispute of a particular nature between specific parties.

One distinction that should be made at the outset is that between jurisdiction in relation to a party, or potential or alleged party, to a dispute, and jurisdiction over the dispute itself: jurisdiction *in personam* and jurisdiction *in rem*. The national courts within a State have jurisdiction in principle to decide disputes between any persons (natural or legal) present within the national territory (and in some circumstances also where a party is outside that territory); this is jurisdiction *in personam*. Also in domestic law, in the judicial system of a State, there will in principle be some court empowered to decide any specified dispute, though some courts may be confined to disputes of a particular nature (e.g. commercial courts, or courts dealing solely with landlord/tenant relations), or may for example only be empowered to disputes involving claims not exceeding a particular amount or value. Sometimes it is possible for such limitations to be waived by the parties. A question of jurisdiction of this kind, jurisdiction *in rem*, will therefore often be of importance, but not finally determinative as to the enforceability of a claim, since the question is, in the domestic sphere, a relative rather than an absolute one, in the sense that all legal disputes are, in that context, also justiciable disputes.

At the international level, the picture is markedly different. There is in fact no court, not even the International Court of Justice, that has universal jurisdiction in this sense, either in relation to all States, or in respect of all possible subjects of legal dispute. For many international disputes, if not the majority, no tribunal exists which has *ab initio* jurisdiction to resolve them, in the sense that proceedings for the purpose can be set in motion unilaterally. International jurisdiction *in rem* raises issues of a more general nature than jurisdiction *in personam*, and will be examined first.

It is with regard to jurisdiction *in rem* that the basic principle of international judicial jurisdiction operates most directly, the principle that jurisdiction is the product of the consent of the parties, and exists only to the extent that that consent has conferred it.[1] That consent may be very immediate, as when two States

[1] For a recent very fully worked-out theory on a totally different basis, see A. von Bogdandy and I. Venzke, *In Whose Name? A Public Law Theory of International Adjudication* (Oxford: Oxford University Press, 2014).

conclude an agreement to establish a one-off arbitral tribunal to decide a particular dispute; or it may be wider in scope, and more long-lasting in operation, as when two States conclude a general treaty for the settlement of future disputes; or a multilateral convention (on whatever subject) includes a clause providing for the judicial settlement of any dispute between parties to it concerning (for example) the interpretation or application of the convention.

Since jurisdiction is created by consent, it may also be said that all judicial jurisdiction derives from treaty-law. There is no such thing as jurisdiction deriving from custom or customary international law. A rule of customary international law may be binding on a State that did not *expressly* give its consent, provided that State has not qualified for the status of 'persistent objector' by its timely and consistent opposition to the rule;[2] but no such 'deemed' consent or tacit acceptance can commit a State to acceptance of the jurisdiction of the Court, or any other international tribunal.[3] The moment at which jurisdiction must exist is the time of seisin of the Court, that is to say the filing of an application instituting proceedings;[4] and the lapse or withdrawal, subsequent to that date, of the instrument embodying the respondent's consent to jurisdiction, does not deprive the Court of jurisdiction.[5] In one exceptional case, the applicant State returned to the Court nearly twenty years after a judgment had been given in its favour, containing (most unusually) a provision for the matter to be re-examined if the other party were to take certain action. The basis of jurisdiction originally invoked had long since ceased to exist, but the Court impliedly accepted that it could act in the matter, presumably on the basis that it was sufficient that it had been in force at the time that the Court was seised of the original case.[6]

This is not to say, however, that the existence and extent of the Court's competence[7] is definitively limited to what had been accepted by the parties at the moment that a case is brought before the Court—the moment at which it becomes 'seised' of the case. Where what is claimed at that moment goes beyond the limits

[2] See the Norwegian *Fisheries* case [1951] ICJ Rep 116; M. Fitzmaurice, 'The Problem of the Single Recalcitrant State', 92 *Recueil des cours* [1957-II] 131; M. Byers, *Custom, Power and the Power of Rules* (Cambridge: Cambridge University Press, 1999), 102–5; Hugh Thirlway, *The Sources of International Law* (Oxford: Oxford University Press, 2014), ch. III 2(c).

[3] But note the possibility of *forum prorogatum*, discussed at Ch. 5 A(3).

[4] And it is also at that date that the *dispute* must exist: see *Alleged Violations of Sovereign Rights and Maritime Spaces in the Caribbean Sea*, [2016] ICJ Rep paras. 50, 52.

[5] See *Right of Passage over Indian Territory*, [1957] ICJ Rep 125, 142, where it was held that a right, reserved in a declaration accepting jurisdiction, to modify or limit its scope, could not be interpreted as asserting a right effectively to exclude a case already instituted against the State author of the declaration.

[6] *Request for an Examination of the Situation in accordance with paragraph 63 of the Court's Judgment of 20 December 1974 in the* Nuclear Tests (New Zealand *v* France) *case*, [1995] ICJ Rep 288. This is not the only possible interpretation of the Court's Order; it was hotly debated at the time whether the Court could take any action at all. The case is examined further in Ch. 8 sect. A.

[7] The usual term for 'jurisdiction' in French is *compétence*, and the English word 'competence' is not infrequently used in the same sense, particularly in the context of advisory proceedings: cf. Rosenne, ii. 522 ff.

of existing jurisdiction, but the respondent State does not wish to insist on those limits (or fails to notice the discrepancy), it may omit (deliberately or by oversight) to raise the matter when pleading its side of the case. In such circumstances, the Court acquires jurisdiction by *forum prorogatum*, prorogated jurisdiction, that is to say jurisdiction deriving from the shared agreement (possibly to some extent tacit) of the parties that the Court should decide. A case may even be brought by a State that openly recognizes at the moment of bringing it that the Court has, at that moment, no jurisdiction to deal with it, but couples its application to the Court with an invitation to the respondent State to accept jurisdiction ad hoc by allowing the case to proceed without objection. Such cases involve certain procedural complication (see Ch. 5 sect. A(3)), but exemplify rather than contradict the principle that consent equals jurisdiction.

The corollary of this is that a respondent State that *does* wish to raise and rely on a defect in the jurisdiction of the Court to deal with the case brought should—indeed, must—make that clear at an early stage if it is not to be treated as having waived any objection, and filled any jurisdictional lacuna by giving the consent that is thus implied.[8] The definitive stage in the procedure is the filing by the respondent State of its first written pleading, usually the Counter-Memorial; any jurisdictional objection not formally raised before or at that stage is liable to be treated as waived or abandoned. In practice, a State will generally show the most extreme caution in communications with the Court in the early stages of a case which has been brought without its advance specific consent, making it clear at every moment that it is reserving its position on jurisdiction, if not flatly denying its existence. Formally it will state its position, at the moment when its Counter-Memorial is due, by filing, in place of that pleading, a 'preliminary objection' to jurisdiction. The preliminary objection procedure is however not limited to jurisdictional issues: Article 79 of the Rules of Court, under the heading 'Preliminary Objections', refers to '[a]ny objection by the respondent to the jurisdiction of the Court or to the admissibility of the application, or other objection the decision upon which is requested before any further proceedings on the merits . . .' This procedure will be examined in more detail in Chapter 14.

The Court endeavours to show itself scrupulous in respecting the limits on its jurisdiction imposed by the consent principle; but it has come increasingly to succumb to the temptation to declare its position on grave matters that are recognized to be beyond its jurisdiction in the specific case before it. In the recent case of *Application of the Genocide Convention (Croatia* v *Serbia)*, its jurisdiction was based on the compromissory clause (Art. IX) of that Convention. The events complained of involved, according to Croatia, not merely acts to be characterized as genocidal, but also breaches of obligations protecting human rights in armed conflict, existing under peremptory norms, or owed *erga omnes*. The Court

[8] For an example of extreme caution in this respect, see the *Seizure and Detention of Certain Documents* case; at the provisional measures stage Australia reserved its right to raise jurisdictional objections at the merits stage: Order of 3 March 2014 [2014] ICJ Rep 147, 151–2 para. 20.

emphasized that, since Article IX confined it to disputes regarding genocide, it had no power to rule on alleged breaches of these other obligations; but did not leave matters there.[9] It also observed that its jurisdiction under the Genocide Convention did not extend to allegations of violation of the customary law of genocide, but indulged in admittedly irrelevant flourishes as to the Convention containing obligations *erga omnes*, and the prohibition of genocide having the character of a peremptory norm.[10] Whether this kind of proclamation on a basis of moral rather than legal authority nevertheless has a certain value may be debatable.[11]

B. Consent and the principle of *la compétence de la compétence*

It is a generally recognized principle of international judicial settlement that a tribunal has the power to decide on the existence and extent of its own jurisdiction in respect of any dispute brought before it, and such a decision is binding on the parties to that dispute.[12] Such power does not therefore need to be conferred specifically in the text (treaty, statute, etc.) that brings the tribunal into existence; it is inherent in the status of a judicial or arbitral body; it may in fact not be limited to jurisdictional organs, but apply also to political organs (though the term 'jurisdiction' then has a different significance).[13] The alternative would be a situation in which the mere denial by a party of the court's jurisdiction would be determinative, and bring the proceedings to an end, which would defeat the whole object of a dispute-settlement process.[14]

[9] [2007-I] ICJ Rep 104 para. 147, repeated in [2015] ICJ Rep para. 85. Thus in the latter decision the Court also recalled 'that the absence of a court or tribunal with jurisdiction to resolve disputes about compliance with a particular obligation does not affect the existence and binding force of that obligation. States are required to fulfil their obligations under international law, including international humanitarian law and international human rights law, and they remain responsible for acts contrary to international law which are attributable to them', [2015] ICJ Rep para. 86. This statement of the obvious is perhaps regrettable, as it suggests that the Court was inclined to accept the validity of allegations with which it had admittedly no right to concern itself.

[10] [2015] ICJ Rep para. 87. For earlier examples of *obiter dicta* of this kind, see *Armed Activities on the Territory of the Congo (DRC* v *Rwanda)* [2006] ICJ Rep 31–2 para. 64; 52–3 para. 127; *Application of the Genocide Convention (Bosnia* v *Serbia)* [2007-I] ICJ Rep 104 para. 148; 110–11 para. 161.

[11] A distinction has been suggested that such extraneous matter is harmless provided it is not included in the operative clause: *Avena (Interpretation), Declaration of Judge Abraham,* [2009] ICJ Rep 27, 28. On the tendency of the Court to throw in pronouncements outside its jurisdiction, see also Ch. 10, text and nn. 30 and 31, and Ch. 16, text and n. 28.

[12] It is 'generally recognized . . . that, in the absence of any agreement to the contrary, an international tribunal has the right to decide as to its own jurisdiction and has the power to interpret for this purpose the instruments which govern that jurisdiction': *Nottebohm*, [1953] ICJ Rep 111, 119.

[13] See e.g. *Certain Expenses of the United Nations* [1962] ICJ Rep 151, 168: 'each organ [of the UN] must, in the first place at least, determine its own jurisdiction'; but the jurisdiction of a political organ may not be to make binding decisions.

[14] The situation becomes more complex when one tribunal (*in casu* the Court) is seised of an appeal from another: see the *Appeal Relating to the Jurisdiction of the ICAO Council* [1972] ICJ Rep 46, and Thirlway, *Law and Procedure*, i. 714.

In the case of the ICJ, the principle is given expression in Article 36 paragraph 6 of the Statute: 'In the event of a dispute as to whether the Court has jurisdiction, the matter shall be settled by the decision of the Court.'[15]

It has however been argued in one case that the Court there lacked even the *compétence de la compétence*: the proceedings had been instituted by a State that was at the time (it was contended) not a party to the Statute, so that the act of seising the Court was, it was said by the respondent, a nullity.[16] The Court did not accept this argument: '[n]ot being "properly seised" does not mean that the Court lacks the competence necessary to decide on its own jurisdiction, in other words to decide whether it has been properly seised and whether the conditions necessary to allow it to hear the case on the merits have been satisfied.'[17] Clearly a line has, however, to be drawn somewhere: the numerous applications addressed to the Court by individuals, unaware that only States may be parties, receive a summary rejection from the Registrar. It may perhaps be said that in such cases it is not a question whether the Court has been 'properly seised', but whether it has been seised at all.

The *compétence de la compétence* thus exists in every judicial proceeding: it is not for either party to prove its existence. However, there can be no presumption in any case that jurisdiction exists, or that it does not exist, so that it would be for the party asserting it (or, as the case may be, denying it) to prove the contrary.[18] The Court must be satisfied that it has jurisdiction before acting, but that is not the same as saying that there is a presumption that it has none.

C. The Court as a standing tribunal

The application of the consent principle is further complicated as a result of the fact that the Court is a permanent institution. In the first place, the Court is a treaty-based institution: as already indicated, it is created and regulated by the United Nations Charter and the Statute of the Court as an 'integral part' of the Charter); this means that the general scope of its jurisdiction, and the conditions of its exercise, are defined *ne varietur* by those instruments. Jurisdiction in this sense, relating to access to the Court, and to the general nature of the powers it possesses, is thus a

[15] It is thus here argued that Art. 36 para. 6, is declaratory of a general principle; but an alternative view might be that the *compétence de la compétence* rests on the intention of the parties to the Statute (or other text constituting a tribunal). For the first view, cf. *Arbitral Award of 31 July 1989* [1991] ICJ Rep 53, 69 para. 46; for the opposite view, the opinion of Judge Shahabuddeen in the same case, p. 109.

[16] *Application of the Genocide Convention (Croatia* v *Serbia)* [2008] ICJ Rep 412, 440–1, para. 84. On the requirement of the status of party to the Statute, see sect. C below.

[17] *Application of the Genocide Convention (Croatia* v *Serbia)* [2008] ICJ Rep 412, 441, para. 86. See further Thirlway, *Law and Procedure*, ii. 1629–30.

[18] Note the devastating observation of President Tomka in his separate opinion in the *Genocide (Croatia* v *Serbia)* case: 'The challenge for the Court remains to strengthen the confidence of States not only by its display of objectivity, impartiality and independence, but also by strictly interpreting the provisions which confer jurisdiction on it. It can do that by focusing its inquiries on whether jurisdiction has been conferred on it, rather than by endeavouring to find ways how to assume it.' [2015] ICJ Rep.

function of the will of the body of States parties to the Charter and Statute, not of the will of the specific parties to a given dispute. The consent of the parties to the dispute cannot therefore abrogate or modify statutory provisions of this kind;[19] it is in fact those provisions that determine how, for example, the necessary consent may be given for the creation of jurisdiction in specific cases.

The Statute regulates in particular the question of jurisdiction *in personam*, that is to say who or what entities may be parties to proceedings before the Court. Article 34 paragraph 1 of the Statute provides that '[o]nly States may be parties in cases before the Court.' As to what bodies are or are not States, reference may still be made to the definition in the 1933 Montevideo Convention on the Rights and Duties of States, Article 1.[20] This is the most basic limitation on the Court's jurisdiction. The reference is of course to sovereign States in the sense of the principal category of subjects of international law, and excludes the component States of federations, for example. A case could not be brought by or against a non-State entity, such as an individual, a non-governmental organization, or a multinational, even if the other party were a State and consented to the case being brought.[21] Nor can an intergovernmental international organization (not even the United Nations itself) be a party to a contentious case, though the Court may request information from public international organizations, under Article 34 of the Statute;[22] and the major bodies are empowered to ask the Court for advisory opinions.

To be a party to a case, a State must also be one of those to which the Court is 'open', or having 'access' to the Court, under Article 35 of the Statute. The principal category of States with such access is that of parties to the Statute of the Court; Article 35 paragraph 1 provides that '[t]he Court shall be open to the parties to the present Statute';[23] this category automatically includes the members of the United

[19] Discussing Art. 35 para 2 of the Statute, the Court has observed that 'it would have been inconsistent with the main thrust of the text to make it possible in the future for States to obtain access to the Court simply by the conclusion between themselves of a special treaty', *Legality of the Use of Force (Serbia and Montenegro* v *Belgium)*, [2004-I] ICJ Rep 279, 319 para. 102.

[20] 'The state as a person of international law should possess the following qualifications: a) a permanent population; b) a defined territory; c) government; and d) capacity to enter into relations with the other states.' The Convention itself in fact never came into force, but this is regarded as defining the criteria for effective Statehood.

[21] The position is apparently different in advisory proceedings, in which there are strictly speaking no 'parties': cf. the participation by Palestine in the case concerning *Legal Consequences of the Construction of a Wall in the Occupied Palestinian Territory,* [2004-I] ICJ Rep 136, 142 para. 4; *Accordance with International Law of the Unilateral Declaration of Independence by the Provisional Institutions of Self-Government of Kosovo* [2008] ICJ Rep 409. The Court has also indicated in Practice Direction XII that where an international non-governmental organization submits a statement in advisory proceedings, while 'it is not to be considered part of the case-file', the Court may refer to it as 'a publication readily available', and it may thus be referred to by, and before, the Court. See further Ch. 9 sect. A(3).

[22] See Ch. 7 sect. B(3). Note that this text only provides for information to be requested by the Court; the provision of information unasked, which is essentially the role of an *amicus curiae*, is not contemplated by the Statute or Rules (but see Practice Direction XII, applicable in advisory proceedings).

[23] Paragraph 2 of that Article continues: 'The conditions under which the Court shall be open to other States shall, subject to the special provisions contained in treaties in force, be laid down by the Security Council, but in no case shall such conditions place the parties in a position of inequality before the Court.' Security Council resolution 9 of 1946 lays down these conditions, and provides for the deposit with the Secretary-General of a declaration accepting the jurisdiction of the Court and undertaking to comply with its decisions. The resolution used to be printed with the Statute and Rules

Nations.[24] The application of these requirements is normally simple, inasmuch as it is generally evident at the outset of a case whether the parties are States, and States having access to the Court;[25] and if one of them is not, then the case cannot proceed, even with the consent of the other party. If, for example, an individual attempts to bring a case before the Court (as frequently happens), the Registrar draws his attention to the provisions of Article 3r, and no further action is necessary. This also has the effect of excluding what may be called 'would-be States'; entities whose statehood has been self-declared but not recognized by other States; since, whether or not a particular entity in this class is a 'State', it will not be a party to the Statute.

A second limitation is that, according to Article 35 paragraph 1 of the Statute, the Court is open only to States that are parties to the Statute. Since Members of the United Nations are *ipso facto* parties to the Statute,[26] and membership in the Organization is now practically universal, this limitation—for it is a limitation—of the Court's jurisdiction is easily overlooked. To become a party to the Statute—or at least to seek to become a party—is an act of choice on the part of a State, and a matter of consent of that State; but admission as a party to the Statute requires a decision of the General Assembly upon the recommendation of the Security Council.[27] Article 35 paragraph 2 of of the Statute, however, contemplates States

in the Court's *Acts and Documents Series*, but has been omitted since it lost relevance as participation in the UN became quasi-universal. For the significance of the reference to 'treaties in force' see n. 24.

[24] UN Charter, Art. 93 para 1. Paragraph 2 of Art. 35 of the Statute contains an obscure reference to 'the special provisions contained in treaties in force'. At the provisional measures stage of the *Bosnia* v *Yugoslavia* case, the Court took the view that this might authorize proceedings against a State which was not a party to the Statute and had not complied with the conditions laid down by the Security Council: *Application of the Convention on the Prevention and Punishment of the Crime of Genocide, Provisional Measures*, [1993] ICJ Rep 3 paras. 18–19, but at the preliminary objections stage this view was abandoned: [1996] ICJ Rep 595. The Court also took the opposite position in the NATO cases: see e.g. *Legality of the Use of Force (Serbia and Montenegro* v *Belgium)*, [2004-I] ICJ Rep 279, 323–4 paras. 113–14, and it is submitted that this is the better view.

[25] An exception is the case of the *Application of the Convention on the Prevention and Punishment of the Crime of Genocide*. Following the break-up of the former Socialist Federal Republic of Yugoslavia, for a time the new Federal Republic of Yugoslavia (Serbia and Montenegro) was treated by the United Nations as the successor of the former Yugoslavia, and on that basis it was made respondent to the proceedings before the Court. On 1 November 2002, however, after the Court had indicated certain provisional measures in the case, and had given judgment dismissing certain preliminary objections, the Federal Republic of Yugoslavia was admitted to the United Nations as a new member. Yugoslavia filed an Application for Revision of the Court's judgment on the preliminary objections on the basis that this admission showed that it had not previously been a party to the Statute. The Court however dismissed the Application on the ground that this event was not a 'new fact' within the meaning of Art. 61 of the Statute (see Ch. 16 sect. B). The question then arose again in the cases brought by Yugoslavia against ten member States of NATO: at a late stage in the proceedings, Yugoslavia withdrew its claim to have been a party to the Statute (and to the Genocide Convention) and invited the Court 'to decide on its jurisdiction'. The Court ruled that Yugoslavia had not been a party to the Statute when its Application was filed: *Legality of the Use of Force (Serbia and Montenegro* v *Belgium)* [2004-I] ICJ Rep 279, 311 para. 79, and seven similar judgments dated 15 December 2004.

[26] See Article 93(2) of the Charter provides that a State may become a party to the Statute without becoming a Member of the Organization: the conditions for this are to be laid down by the General Assembly, on the recommendation of the Security Council.

[27] Cf. the history of the problem of the membership of the Federal Republic of Yugoslavia in the United Nations, examined in the *Legality of the Use of Force* cases mentioned in n. 24.

non-parties to the Statute having access to the Court under conditions to be laid down by the Security Council; and the Council has implemented this text in resolution 9 (1946).[28] A declaration has to be deposited with the Registrar of the Court, but the text does not provide for any control of the validity or regularity of the declaration at that stage.[29]

A further consequence of the fact that the Court is a permanent, standing, tribunal is that the consent creative of jurisdiction is not always simple and direct, but may have been given (or may be alleged to have been given) in general terms, perhaps many years ago. An ad hoc arbitration is established by the consent of the parties given directly in respect of a dispute that is already defined. The jurisdiction of the Court, however, may be, and frequently is, asserted on the basis of treaty instruments of a general nature that conferred what was then future jurisdiction over a range or category of disputes. When the instrument was concluded, no such disputes may yet have been in existence, but the possibility that such might arise will have been foreseen, and consent given in advance to the binding determination of them by the Court. When a dispute is subsequently brought before the Court on the basis of a clause of this kind, that advance consent creative of jurisdiction is still operative (assuming that the treaty has not been denounced), but it may well not be accompanied, at the time that the matter is brought to the Court, by actual contemporary consent or willingness to have that particular dispute settled by decision of the Court. The respondent State may therefore seek to deny that the general consent given in the past applies to the specific dispute, because, for example, it does not really fall within the category of disputes contemplated, or because any conditions attached to it have not been met in the specific case. The Court, in order to be satisfied that consent to its dealing with the dispute has actually been given, will have to analyse, in sometimes painstaking detail, the provisions of the relevant instruments in order to trace a link between the consent given, often in wide general terms, by the respondent and the facts of the particular case. The principle remains simple: has the respondent State given consent to jurisdiction? Its application may, however, involve much subtle and complex argument, frequently in the context of the procedure to resolve preliminary objections to jurisdiction, the decision on which may be as lengthy and complex as that on the merits of a case.

[28] Text in *ICJ Yearbook 2012–13*, 20–21.

[29] There have been cases in the past of a 'would-be State' depositing a purported declaration under the Council resolution, the presumed object being either to become prima facie entitled to bring a case to the Court, or at the least to bolster politically a claim to Statehood.

5

Jurisdiction in Contentious Cases (II)

A. Methods of creating jurisdiction

(1) Special agreements, treaties, and compromissory clauses

As explained in Chapter 4, the simplest means of putting into effect, in relation to a specific dispute, the principle that jurisdiction is conferred on the Court by the consent of the parties is for the two States that wish such dispute to be settled by the Court to enter into an agreement to that effect.[1] This is the classic *compromis* or 'special agreement', used for many years prior to the establishment of the Permanent Court for the submission of a dispute to arbitration, and now also one of the two methods of bringing a case before the Court as defined in Article 40 paragraph 1 of the Statute (supplemented by Art. 39 of the Rules). Such an agreement will define the dispute, and usually will record the agreement of the parties to accept the decision on it as binding, though while this last provision is appropriate in the case of an agreement to go to arbitration, it is at least theoretically unnecessary in view of the provisions of the Charter and Statute.[2] The agreement may also contain provisions as to the procedure to be followed (number and order of written pleadings, possibly mention (or waiver) of the right to appoint judges ad hoc, etc.).

Normally no jurisdictional problems arise in a case brought before the Court by special agreement, since the consent of the parties is real and contemporaneous, rather than given in advance and in general terms.[3] This does not, of course, exclude disagreements over what exactly it was agreed to submit to the Court, so that a case brought by special agreement may still lead to a finding of lack of jurisdiction over certain aspects of it, on the basis of the Court's interpretation of the meaning of the special agreement.[4]

[1] A valuable guide to methods of creating jurisdiction is the *Handbook on Accepting the Jurisdiction of the International Court of Justice*, produced in 2014 by a group of seven UN Member States and circulated as a UN document: A/68/963 of 19 August 2014.

[2] The Statute does not state directly that a judgment is binding, but does so indirectly: '[t]he decision of the Court has no binding force except between the parties and in respect of that particular case.' The PCIJ rejected an attempt by the parties to a case to obtain a non-binding decision, a sort of 'advisory' judgment (*Free Zones of Upper Savoy and the District of Gex, PCIJ Series A, No. 22*), but something of this nature was the outcome of the *North Sea Continental Shelf* cases; see further Ch. 10 sect. B.

[3] There may, however, be limitations on the exercise of jurisdiction resulting from issues not under the control of the parties: see the *Monetary Gold Removed from Rome in 1943*, [1954] ICJ Rep 19, and sect. C below.

[4] '[I]n cases where the special agreement forms the only basis of jurisdiction, it goes without saying that any request made by a party in its final submissions can fall within the jurisdiction of the Court

When a special agreement has been concluded, the procedural step by which a case is brought before the Court—in technical language the 'seising' of the Court—is the notification of the agreement to the Court (Statute, Art. 40; Rules, Art. 39). Whether this is done by one party or by both parties jointly (or indeed separately, as has sometimes been done), the essence of a case of this kind is that it is a joint approach to the Court, not an action commenced by one party against the other.

A treaty may of course be concluded between two States with a view to the *future* submission of disputes to the Court: either all disputes, or more commonly disputes falling into specified categories; or a bilateral treaty may contain a 'compromissory clause', a clause whereby any dispute concerning, for example, 'the interpretation or application' of the treaty may be so submitted.[5] Treaties and conventions of this kind have been relied on as jurisdictional basis in a number of cases before the Court. Similarly, multilateral conventions may follow either pattern: general dispute settlement conventions (e.g. the General Act for the Pacific Settlement of International Disputes, or the Pact of Bogotá), or a convention concluded for another purpose, particularly one intended to be of a general lawmaking character, will frequently contain a clause conferring jurisdiction on the Court for any disputes arising out of the treaty. This has become common practice for major lawmaking treaties (e.g. the Genocide Convention, or the Racial Discrimination Convention, invoked in recent major cases before the Court).[6]

Where jurisdiction is asserted on the basis of some instrument other than a special agreement, the Court will be seised unilaterally, by an application, indicating the subject of the dispute and the parties (Statute, Art. 40 para. 1; Rules, Art. 38). Normally (but not necessarily—see Ch. 5 sect. A(3)) it will also be indicated which pre-existing instrument is relied on as basis of jurisdiction. The applicant State in such circumstances will claim that the other party to the dispute has in the past consented to settlement of disputes of a particular category being referred unilaterally to the Court for settlement, and that the current dispute falls into that category. The treaty or convention relied on must of course be in force for the State named as respondent at the moment when the proceedings are instituted.[7]

only if it remains within the limits defined by the provisions of the special agreement, a matter which is for the Court to ascertain': *Frontier Dispute (Burkina Faso/Mali)* [2013] ICJ Rep 44, 68–9 para. 42. This does not, of course, exclude the widening of claims accepted (tacitly or otherwise) by the other party: see sect. A(3), '*Forum prorogatum*'.

[5] It is even possible for such a treaty to be 'asyllagmatic' (the term is that of Rosenne) in that only one of the parties is entitled to institute ICJ proceedings, but the other party is committed in advance to the decision (and is of course entitled to appear and defend its case): see the agreements entered into by Iceland with the UK and the FRG and invoked in the *Fisheries Jurisdiction* cases, [1974] ICJ Rep 3 and 175.

[6] *Application of the Convention on the Prevention and Punishment of the Crime of Genocide (Bosnia and Herzegovina* v *Serbia and Montenegro*) [2007-I] ICJ Rep 43; *(Croatia* v *Serbia*) [2015] ICJ Rep; *Application of the International Convention on the Elimination of All Forms of Racial Discrimination (Georgia* v *Russian Federation)* [2011-I] ICJ Rep 70 (Preliminary Objections). The number of clauses of this kind included in treaties in recent years has declined: see D. Akande, 'Selection of the ICJ as a Forum for Contentious and Advisory Proceedings', *ICJ 70th Anniversary Seminar* (2016), to be published shortly in *JIDS*.

[7] See the *Certain Violations* case, where the Respondent (Colombia) had denounced the treaty, but the provisions in the treaty for denunciation posed something of a conundrum as to identification of the moment when Colombia ceased to be bound: [2016] ICJ Rep paras. 36 ff.

(2) The 'optional clause' system

a. The clause and its operation

At an early stage of the preparation of the Statute of the Permanent Court of International Justice, it was envisaged that the new Court would have universal compulsory jurisdiction, in the sense that any State party to the Statute could bring before the Court, by unilateral application, 'any dispute of an international character' with any other State party to the Statute. The necessary consent conferring jurisdiction would thus be given simply by accession to the Statute. However, a proposal on these lines encountered objections from States Members of the League, and it was contended that the idea went beyond the scope of Article 14 of the Covenant; it was soon realized that the majority of States were not ready for so radical an innovation, and the optional clause system, now to be explained, was devised as being the furthest that it was then possible to go in the direction of compulsory jurisdiction.[8] The system was then carried over, without change of substance, into the Statute of the post-war Court,[9] and it is in that context that it will be examined here. Continuity was also ensured so far as possible by Article 36 paragraph 5 of the post-war Statute, which preserves, as between parties to that Statute, any declarations of acceptance of jurisdiction made under the PCIJ Statute.[10]

Under Article 36 paragraph 2 of the Statute, a State may deposit with the UN Secretary-General a declaration that it accepts the jurisdiction of the Court, 'in relation to any other State accepting the same obligation', for disputes in respect of all or some of the matters enumerated in Article 36. These are:

a. the interpretation of a treaty;
b. any question of international law;
c. the existence of any fact which, if established, would constitute a breach of an international obligation;
d. the nature and extent of the reparation to be made for the breach of an international obligation.

The keywords in this text are 'in relation to any other State accepting the same obligation'. The intended effect of this was that those States that were ready to accept compulsory jurisdiction could do so among themselves, while other States would

[8] For a brief account of the controversy, see O. Spiermann, paras. 11–16 of 'Historical Introduction', in Zimmermann et al., *Commentary*, 54–6.

[9] The acceptability of a system designed on these lines, enabling 'tailor-made' acceptances of jurisdiction within an overall conventional system, had in the meantime been confirmed by its adoption also for the 1928 General Act for the Pacific Settlement of International Disputes, relied on in e.g. the *Nuclear Tests* cases [1974] ICJ Rep 253 and 457, and the *Aegean Sea Continental Shelf case* [1978] ICJ 3.

[10] Cf. *Military and Paramilitary Activities in and against Nicaragua Jurisdiction and Admissibility*, [1984] ICJ Rep 392, 398–9 para 14. This provision of the Statute did not specifically regulate the position of States parties to the Statute of the Permanent Court who did not become members of the United Nations, and thus parties to the Statute of the new Court, until many years after the Permanent Court had ceased to exist. For the handling of lacunas of this kind, see *Temple of Preah Vihear, Preliminary Objections*, [1961] ICJ Rep 17; *Barcelona Traction, Light and Power Company, Preliminary Objections*, [1964] ICJ Rep 6.

have to rely on obtaining the consent ad hoc of any State with which they might have a dispute, if that dispute were to be brought before the Court—assuming, that is, that there was no pre-existing disputes settlement treaty or other basis of jurisdiction accepted in advance. There would be two classes of 'clients' of the Court, those within the 'optional clause' system and those outside it.

Declarations of this kind may be regarded as unilateral acts, since whether such a declaration is made at all, and if so upon what terms, is a matter solely of the will of the declarant State. That does not prevent them creating binding obligations; the Court found in the *Nuclear Tests* cases that a unilateral statement could create such obligations;[11] and in the *Military and Paramilitary Activities* case it applied this reasoning to declarations under the optional clause.[12] In their operation, however, the declarations necessarily become bilateral, as is contemplated by the phrase 'in relation to any other State accepting the same obligation' in Article 36.

The expression 'the same obligation' refers simply to the essential obligation under Article 36, and does not mean that States may not choose to subject their declarations to differing limitations and conditions; the effect of these is considered in subsection b. Article 36 is also imprecise as to date: the States that have filed declarations under this provision have naturally done so at various different dates. There must, in relation to any case brought on the basis of the clause, be at least one moment when the declaration of the applicant State and that of the respondent are both in force. It was decided in the *Nottebohm* case that the key date in this respect is, logically enough, the date on which the proceedings are instituted, so that a withdrawal by the respondent of its declaration after proceedings have begun is without effect on the Court's jurisdiction.[13] However, in the present age of instant communication, it may be appropriate to recall that for much of the earlier period, the filing of a State's declaration with the Secretary-General might not become known to other Member States, and in particular to those that had also filed declarations, until some time had elapsed; so that the notification from the Registrar that an application had been filed might be the first time that the respondent became aware that the applicant had become one of those States entitled to invoke the optional clause against it. Could this be reconciled with considerations of procedural justice?

Two attempts have been made to convince the Court that it should reject proceedings brought in these circumstances: the first was in the *Right of Passage* case, in which the Court held that it was on the day of making of the second (in time) declaration that 'the consensual bond, which is the basis of the Optional Clause, comes into being between the States concerned'.[14] In the case of the *Land and Maritime Boundary between Cameroon and Nigeria*, Nigeria put forward a similar argument, and endeavoured first to convince the Court that it was not bound to follow the *Right of Passage* precedent, and should not do so; the reasons for this part of the decision are discussed elsewhere.[15] On the issue of the effect of an optional clause

[11] [1974] ICJ Rep 267 para. 43 and 472 para. 46.
[12] [1984] ICJ Rep 418 paras. 59–60.
[13] [1953] ICJ Rep 111, 122.
[14] [1957] ICJ Rep 146.
[15] See Ch. 11, text and nn. 18, 19.

of which the other party to a case was not aware, the Court maintained its position. Nigeria cited the provisions of the Vienna Convention on the Law of Treaties as to notifications, but the Court regarded the provisions of that text applying to instruments expressing an intention to be bound as more relevant.[16] Similar reasoning led to the Court's dismissal of the view that, just as 'the right of immediate termination of declarations with indefinite duration is far from established', so also was the alleged immediate effect of the deposit of a declaration.[17]

The possibility of withdrawal of a declaration depends in the first instance on its terms; if it is expressed to be in force for a fixed time, then it can only be denounced with effect from the date at which that time runs out; if it is terminable on notice of a specified length of time, then this too must be respected.[18] If no specific time is fixed, as the Court noted in the judgment in the Cameroon/Nigeria case quoted in the previous paragraph, it is unsettled whether the declaration can be withdrawn with immediate effect.

b. Reservations

At the time of writing, seventy-two States have deposited declarations under this provision.[19] However, the simple vision here outlined became complicated as a result of the recognition by Article 36 paragraph 3 of the possibility of making an optional-clause declaration either 'unconditionally', or with reservations attached: specifically, the reservations foreseen were 'a condition of reciprocity on the part of several or certain States' and acceptance 'for a certain time'. Reciprocity was generally insisted on expressly, usually in the terms of Article 36 paragraph 2, 'in relation to any other State accepting the same obligation'. The meaning of the term was that if State A brought proceedings against State B, it would have to show (at least if challenged by State B) that in similar circumstances, the roles being reversed, State B could have brought proceedings against State A.

On one occasion a declaration was made under the optional clause that purported expressly to *exclude* the requirement of reciprocity. This was the special declaration deposited by Malta in 1981 which was limited to disputes concerning the delimitation of the continental shelf, and was expressed to be made 'without the condition of reciprocity and without reservations'.[20] There was of course a special reason for this exceptional form: Malta was anxious to intervene in the proceedings currently before the Court between Tunisia and Libya for the delimitation of their

[16] [1998] ICJ Rep 293–4 paras. 29–31.

[17] [1998] ICJ Rep 295–6 paras. 33–5, quoting *Military and Paramilitary Activities in and Against Nicaragua*, [1984] ICJ Rep 392, 420, para. 63.

[18] *Military and Paramilitary Activities in and against Nicaragua*, [1984] ICJ Rep 419 para. 61.

[19] This figure has remained more or less stable rather than increasing in proportion to the increased number of current States Members of the United Nations; cf. Thirlway, 'The International Court of Justice 1989–2009: At the heart of the dispute settlement system', 57 *NILR* (2010) 347, 357; Akande, 'Selection of the International Court of Justice', to be published shortly in *JIDS*.

[20] See text in *ICJ Yearbook 1981–2*, 78; the declaration was withdrawn in 1983.

continental shelves, and argued that it was thereby creating a jurisdictional link with those two States.[21]

The other explicitly recognized possibility, of acceptance 'for a certain time', permitted a State to dip a cautious toe in the water of obligatory judicial settlement; it also implied that an acceptance once given would, unless a time-limit was specified, generally be irrevocable until the time allotted expired.[22] In the *Military and Paramilitary Activities* case brought by Nicaragua against the United States, Nicaragua relied on a US optional-clause declaration of 1946, which was stated to be in force, after an initial fixed period, 'until the expiration of six months after notice may be given to terminate the declaration'. The US endeavoured to frustrate Nicaragua's proceedings by depositing, three days before Nicaragua filed its application, a declaration purporting to modify the 1946 declaration so as to exclude the matters that Nicaragua was about to raise.[23] The Court said:

> Declarations of acceptance of the compulsory jurisdiction of the Court are facultative, unilateral engagements, that States are absolutely free to make or not to make. In making the declaration a State is equally free either to do so unconditionally and without limit of time for its duration, or to qualify it with conditions or reservations. . . . However, the unilateral nature of declarations does not signify that the State making the declaration is free to amend the scope and the contents of its solemn commitments as it pleases.[24]

In other words, while a State need not commit itself to jurisdiction in advance further than it pleases, and may impose whatever restrictions or limitations on its acceptance as it wishes, once it has committed itself for a specified period (or subject to a specified period of notice) it is not free during that period to impose fresh restrictions or limitations, let alone withdraw the acceptance. Once proceedings have been instituted in reliance on an acceptance of jurisdiction by the respondent State, they can validly continue to judgment even if the acceptance expires, or is terminated, during the proceedings.[25] The Court has emphasized in this respect the important role of good faith in the optional-clause system.[26] Nevertheless, a State may still reserve to itself in its declaration the power to terminate its acceptance with immediate effect, so that on becoming aware of the intention of another State to commence proceedings it can frustrate this, provided it acts before the Court is seised.[27]

21 See Thirlway, *Law and Procedure*, i. 783–5.

22 Or of course until terminated by notice in the exercise of a power reserved in the declaration.

23 Texts of both the 1946 and 1984 declarations at [1984] ICJ Rep 398 para. 13.

24 [1984] ICJ Rep 392, 418 para. 59. The US endeavoured to rely on a distinction between terminating a declaration and merely modifying it, but the Court thought the distinction 'without consequence' (417 para. 58).

25 'It is a rule of law generally accepted . . . that once the Court has been validly seised of a dispute, unilateral action by the respondent State in terminating its Declaration, in whole or in part, cannot deprive the Court of jurisdiction': *Right of Passage over Indian Territory* [1957] ICJ Rep 125, 142, citing *Nottebohm* [1953] ICJ Rep 111.

26 *Military and Paramilitary Activities in and against Nicaragua*, [1984] ICJ Rep 392, 418 para. 60.

27 *Right of Passage over Indian Territory* [1957] ICJ Rep 125, 141–2. In that case the respondent, India, would have wished to exercise the right it had reserved to terminate its declaration with

The simplicity of the system was thus already compromised by the facility of making reservations of the two kinds specified; but the question soon arose whether any *other* reservations were permitted and effective (e.g. the exclusion of disputes of a specified type, or of disputes arising before or after a specified date). Under the Statute of the Permanent Court the inclusion of reservations became standard practice. The prevailing view became that, since a State was free to decide to accept or not to accept the optional clause jurisdiction in its entirety, it was also free to accept it subject to whatever reservations it saw fit to make, on the basis that the greater (freedom not to accept jurisdiction) included the less (freedom to accept subject to conditions).[28]

Furthermore, as already noted, Article 36 paragraph 2 of the Statute employed the term 'reciprocity', and provided for acceptances of jurisdiction 'in relation to any other State accepting *the same obligation*'. If a State which had made a reservation to its acceptance brought proceedings against a State which had made none, was the jurisdiction of the Court affected by the reservation? The Permanent Court held that it was; that the respondent State could invoke the applicant State's reservation, or to put it another way, that the Court's jurisdiction was defined by the narrower of the two acceptances.[29] As the Court put it in the *Interhandel* case, 'Reciprocity enables the State which has made the wider acceptance of the jurisdiction of the Court to rely upon the reservations to the acceptance made by the other party'.[30] Similarly, the Court has held that the an applicant having made a declaration which contained no provision limiting its right of termination (and therefore presumably able to terminate without notice) had still 'accepted the same obligation' as the respondent whose declaration was expressed to be only terminable on six months' notice.[31]

Some of the cases concern reservations that must necessarily operate bilaterally, for example the reservation limiting jurisdiction to disputes arising after a certain date: if a dispute arises after such date for one party to it, then it must equally do so for the other.[32] A more striking example of the application of this principle is afforded by the *Certain Norwegian Loans* case, in which the reservation made by

immediate effect, but it did not become aware that Portugal, by depositing a declaration, had become entitled to bring proceedings, until after Portugal had already done so.

[28] See the statement in the report of Subcommittee IV/1/D of the San Francisco Conference that drafted the Statute of the post-war Court: UNCIO, xiii. 391, 559. The League Assembly had taken the view as early as 1928 that reservations were not limited to those specifically contemplated in the Statute: see the resolution of the Assembly quoted in *Aerial Incident of 10 August 1999 (Pakistan* v *India)*, [2000] ICJ Rep 12, 29 para. 37.

[29] *Electricity Company of Sofia and Bulgaria, Judgment, 1939, PCIJ Series A/B, No. 77*, 64 at 81; see also *Certain Norwegian Loans* [1957] ICJ Rep 9, 24. For a fuller examination of the problem, see Thirlway, 'Reciprocity in the Jurisdiction of the International Court', 15 *NYBIL* 1984.

[30] [1959] ICJ Rep 6, 23.

[31] *Military and Paramilitary Activities in and against Nicaragua* [1984] ICJ Rep 392, 419 para. 62.

[32] See e.g. the Orders on provisional measures in the cases concerning the *Legality of Use of Force*, brought by Yugoslavia against the member States of NATO, and the question of events before the key date continuing afterwards: e.g. *Yugoslavia* v *Belgium, Provisional Measures*, [1999-I] ICJ Rep 134–5 paras. 28–30.

France, the applicant, excluding disputes within the domestic jurisdiction of France could be turned against it by Norway, the respondent, so as to exclude a dispute on the ground that it was within the domestic jurisdiction of Norway.[33]

The consequence of the recognition of freedom to make whatever reservation might seem useful was that, instead of the simple system of universal compulsory jurisdiction within a limited group of States, foreseen by the draftsmen of the Statute, the jurisdiction of the Court under Article 36 paragraph 2 became a complex network of bilateral relationships. The fact that two States have each made a declaration of acceptance does not signify that any dispute between them can be brought by either of them unilaterally before the Court, unless both acceptances are entirely without reservations. If that is not so, it is necessary to find the lowest common denominator of the jurisdiction *not* excluded by reservations on each side, and consider whether the particular dispute falls within it.

Another disruptive development, though one that has now more or less passed out of use, was the invention of the 'self-judging' reservation, designed to retain control of the extent of the jurisdictional obligation in the hands of the State making the declaration. In the form pioneered by the United States, and known as the 'Connally reservation',[34] this was a reservation excluding matters within the domestic jurisdiction of the reserving State *as determined by the reserving State*. This reservation was intended to enable the reserving State to declare, even after the Court had been seised of a dispute on the basis of the optional clause declaration, that the dispute was a matter of domestic jurisdiction, and that the Court had therefore no jurisdiction. A reservation of this kind may be felt to be incompatible with the system of Article 36, and in particular with the principle of the *compétence de la compétence*, or with the requirements of good faith, but when a declaration on these lines was first relied on, the Court nevertheless gave effect to the reservation; it did so in a case where the reservation was invoked by reciprocity, and was thus used against the State that had included it in its declaration.[35] This may have reduced the popularity of the device;[36] and the Court had declined to examine the question of its compatibility with the Statute simply on the grounds that that issue had not been raised by the other party. It has in fact been convincingly argued that to rule that the reservation was invalid would lead to the consequence that the whole declaration of acceptance was invalid, so that the reserving State would still be able to escape the jurisdiction of the Court.[37]

[33] *Certain Norwegian Loans*, [1957] ICJ Rep 9: the reservation was in fact of the 'Connally' type (see next para.). Cf. also the *Aegean Sea Continental Shelf*, [1978] ICJ Rep 3, where a reservation made by Greece (applicant) excluding matters of the 'territorial integrity' of Greece applied to exclude a matter concerning the territorial integrity of Turkey (respondent). This case, however, related, not to Art. 36 para. 2 of the Statute, but to the parallel provision in the 1928 General Act for the Pacific Settlement of International Disputes.

[34] After the US Senator who proposed its inclusion in the declaration.

[35] *Certain Norwegian Loans*, [1957] ICJ Rep 9, 26–7.

[36] Though it still figures in a number of current declarations.

[37] See *Certain Norwegian Loans*, [1957] ICJ Rep 9, Separate Opinion of Judge Sir Hersch Lauterpacht, 34, 56ff. This was on the basis that it would not be proper to 'sever' the reservation from the acceptance, since to do so would be to impose on the State concerned an obligation that it had clearly not consented to accept. The European Court of Human Rights, on the basis of a virtually

It has thus never been judicially determined whether a statement by the reserving State that the subject of a dispute brought before the Court is a matter of domestic jurisdiction is final and determinative, however remote that subject may be from what is generally regarded as within domestic jurisdiction; or whether the Court could disallow reliance on the reservation in such circumstances. In the last case in which a declaration containing the reservation (that of the United States) was relied on as basis of jurisdiction, in *Military and Paramilitary Activities in and against Nicaragua*, the US did not invoke the reservation, either because it was confident of obtaining a finding of lack of jurisdiction on other grounds, or conceivably because the alleged activities were so evidently not matters of domestic jurisdiction.

There is, however, nothing illicit about attaching even extensive reservations to an acceptance of jurisdiction. The fact that a reservation to an optional-clause declaration excludes jurisdiction over acts of which the legality may, in the view of other States, be doubtful does not render the reservation invalid; the reservation may have been made specifically because there is doubt about the matter, and this does not mean that the reserving State is claiming a licence to commit wrongful acts with impunity. It was in a case of this kind that the Court took the opportunity to emphasize the 'fundamental distinction between the acceptance by a State of the Court's jurisdiction and the compatibility of particular acts with international law'.[38] This is another application of the principle that, since a State is free not to accept the jurisdiction of the Court at all, it must also be free to decide for itself what limitations it will impose on such acceptance as it does consent to make.

(3) *Forum prorogatum*

If a case is thus brought before the Court by unilateral application, there exists normally a pre-existing title of jurisdiction in the form of a treaty between the parties of this kind, or in the form of acceptances of jurisdiction under the 'optional clause'; and this will be specified. This does not mean, however, that an application that fails to specify such a pre-existing title is invalid; the Statute of the Court (Art. 40) only requires an application to specify 'the subject of the dispute and the parties', and the Rules of Court (Art. 38 para. 2) only require that it indicate 'as far as possible' the basis of jurisdiction relied on. This permits of an application being made that in effect invites the State named as respondent to consent to jurisdiction simply for the

identical provision in its constituent instrument, has, however, taken a different view on this point: see *Belilos* v *Switzerland*, Judgment of 29 April 1988, Ser. A no. 132; 10 *EHRR* 418, and *Loizidou* v *Turkey (Preliminary Objections)*, Judgment of 23 March 1995, Ser. A no. 310, 20 *EHRR* 99. In *Fisheries Jurisdiction (Spain* v *Canada)*, Judge Bedjaoui enumerated some conceivable reservations to acceptances of jurisdiction that in his view were clearly improper and would be void; he was presumably reasoning, on the basis of the *Belilos/Loizidou* case-law, that they would be struck out, leaving the acceptance standing: [1998] ICJ Rep 516, 533–4. Judge Weeramantry drew attention to a similar argument by Spain, that a reservation concerning 'commercial issues' could not be invoked to cover the commercial exploitation of children: ibid. 496, 502 para. 26.

38 *Fisheries Jurisdiction (Spain* v *Canada), Jurisdiction of the Court*, [1998] ICJ Rep 432, 456 para. 55.

purposes of that particular case, a process known as *forum prorogatum*. Whatever the intention of the omission, it is established that an existing basis of jurisdiction may be indicated in a later pleading or communication.[39]

At one time the possibility of filing claims unsupported by any existing title of jurisdiction, with an invitation to accept jurisdiction by *forum prorogatum,* was being employed against States whose known attitude to judicial settlement made it certain that no such acceptance would be forthcoming, the object being to publicize the claim and to demonstrate the applicant State's readiness to accept judicial settlement.[40] A new paragraph 5 was included in Article 38 of the Rules of Court in 1978, whereby an application of this kind would be treated for procedural purposes as ineffective until the consent of the named respondent was forthcoming.[41] This means, in particular, that until then the application would not be circulated to Members of the United Nations under Article 40 paragraph 3 of the Statute, nor would the case be entered on the General List maintained under Article 36 para. 1 *(b)* of the Rules.[42] While this may be regarded as a somewhat bold exercise of the Court's rule-making power, it rendered such an approach much less attractive.[43]

Where, on the other hand, there is a shared will to achieve a settlement of a legal dispute, the possibility of beginning proceedings with an invitation to accept jurisdiction may be valuable. More recently there have been cases brought in good faith where there was (presumably, in the mind of the applicant Government) a real possibility that the State named as respondent would agree to defend the case; and this does indeed happen. For example, in two recent cases, both brought against France, following applications on this basis, France later gave its consent to ad hoc jurisdiction.[44]

Forum prorogatum can thus result from the simple participation in the proceedings of a respondent State which has not previously accepted jurisdiction, without any formal statement of acceptance of jurisdiction, but only if such participation amounts to 'an unequivocal indication' of acceptance of jurisdiction in a 'voluntary

[39] See Ch. 6 sect. A. There are, however, limits: *see Use of Force (Yugoslavia v Belgium)* [1999-I] ICJ Rep 124, 139 para. 44.

[40] See e.g. the *Aerial Incident* cases ([1956] ICJ Rep 6, 9) and the *Antarctica* cases ([1956] ICJ Rep 13, 15).

[41] See the Court's explanation of the motivation for the amendment in *Certain Questions of Mutual Assistance in Criminal Matters (Djibouti* v *France)* [2008] ICJ Rep 177, 204–5 para. 63.

[42] The General List being provided for only in the Rules, the Court presumably has discretion as to what is entered on it: but the provision for non-circulation seems to fly in the face of the statutory text. The result is, as intended, that the application gets no publicity; this has been deprecated, and a suggestion made that a suitable corner be found on the Court's website for this sort of application: A. Miron. 'Les Méthodes de travail de la Cour', *ICJ 70th Anniversary Seminar*, to be published in *JIDS* 2016. This would, however, defeat the original purpose of the modification of Art. 38.

[43] Though such applications have not disappeared completely: see the case brought by Argentina against the US in 2014 (ICJ Press Release 2014/25), concerning US arbitration decisions relating to restructuring of Argentina's sovereign debt.

[44] See *Certain Criminal Proceedings in France (Republic of the Congo* v *France)* (2003: case later withdrawn) and *Certain Questions of Mutual Assistance in Criminal Matters (Djibouti* v *France)*, [2008] ICJ Rep 177; see paras. 39–43 and 63–95 of that decision for the complications involved in ascertaining the precise extent of such jurisdiction.

and indisputable' manner.[45] The doctrine is relevant to a greater extent in determining, not whether a State named as respondent has consented to jurisdiction at all, but the extent to which it may tacitly have accepted jurisdiction over matters not covered by the original title relied on. Thus for example if a State waives, or simply does not invoke, a reservation to its optional-clause declaration that might otherwise have applied,[46] the jurisdiction to deal with the matter that might have been excluded is, in effect, a form of *forum prorogatum*.

B. The existence of a dispute as a condition of jurisdiction

Article 36 paragraph 2 of the Statute refers to the acceptance of jurisdiction by a State 'in all legal disputes' concerning the matters referred to in that paragraph. In a number of cases, jurisdiction in this respect has been challenged on the grounds that there is no dispute between the parties as alleged (thus a dispute whether there is a dispute, a 'dispute-dispute'[47]); or that if there is, it is not a *legal* dispute. The first objection may seem somewhat surprising at first sight; if the parties are really not in dispute, why, one might ask, has the applicant come to the Court at all? Matters are however not so simple. One possibility is that there is a dispute but, in the contention of the respondent, it is a dispute between the applicant and some State other than the respondent.[48] The moment at which a dispute must have existed is the date of the institution of proceedings.[49]

The English word 'dispute' appears in three articles of the Statute, but the French version uses two different words to translate it. In Articles 36 and 38, the French term is *différend*, while in Article 60, concerning requests for revision of a judgment, it is *contestation*. The Court has indicated that

> although in their ordinary meaning, both terms in a general sense denote opposing views, the term 'contestation' is wider in scope than the term 'différend' and does not require the same degree of opposition; whereas, compared to the term 'différend', the concept underlying the term 'contestation' is more flexible in its application to a particular situation.[50]

This explanation was clearly intended to justify an interpretation of Article 60 that was less strict than would have been appropriate for Articles 36 and 38, but does not throw much light on the treatment of these two articles.

45 *Armed Activities on the Territory of the Congo (DRC* v *Rwanda)*, [2006] ICJ Rep 18–19.

46 e.g. the United States' 'Connally Reservation' in the case of *Armed Activities in and against Nicaragua*.

47 By analogy with *Kompetenz-Kompetenz*!

48 As e.g. in *Application of the International Convention on the Elimination of All Forms of Racial Discrimination (Georgia* v *Russia)*, [2011-I] ICJ Rep 70, where the Court had to examine a lengthy and complex history of relations between the parties in order to reach the conclusion that there *was* a dispute between them, but only at a comparatively late stage (p. 120 para. 133).

49 *Alleged Violations of Sovereign Rights and Maritime Spaces in the Caribbean Sea* [2016] ICJ Rep paras. 50, 52.

50 *Request for Interpretation of the Judgment of 31 March 2004*, Order of 16 July 2008, [2008] ICJ Rep 311, 325 para. 53.

However, the Court had already defined the key requirements, and has subsequently re-enumerated them in its decision on preliminary objections in *Application of the Convention on the Elimination of All Forms of Racial Discrimination*.[51] The principal elements are that 'it must be shown [by the applicant] that the claim of one party is positively opposed by the other',[52] and 'the matter is one of substance, not of form';[53] in the *Georgia/Russia* case, it also observed that

> the existence of a dispute may be inferred from the failure of a State to respond to a claim in circumstances where a response is called for. While the existence of a dispute and the undertaking of negotiations are distinct as a matter of principle, the negotiations may help demonstrate the existence of the dispute and delineate its subject-matter.[54]

The other side of the medal is however that, as has been pointed out, if the Court is too ready to see negotiations over a contentious issue as evidence that there is already a dispute between the States concerned, so as to trigger a jurisdictional clause in a treaty, this could 'have negative effects on the readiness of States to engage in attempts at peaceful settlement of disputes'.[55]

When what is being complained of is simply an act that has been committed, allegedly contrary to international law, which has caused injury to the applicant, and the applicant has indicated its dissatisfaction or indignation, no problem arises as to the existence of a dispute. Less clear is the situation where what is asserted is non-compliance with some obligation (under a convention, for example), and the respondent asserts that there has been no breach yet because instant compliance is not required, but that a *locus penitentiae* (a period of time in which to put things right) is allowed, or an alternative course of action is available and legally permissible. Does that mean that there is as yet no jurisdiction? A good example is the case of *Obligation to Prosecute or Extradite* between Belgium and Senegal, in which Belgium sought the prosecution or extradition of a Senegalese national, M. Habré, who had allegedly been responsible for acts of torture. It was recognized that the obligation in question (under the Torture Convention[56]) was subject to the principle *aut judicare aut dedere*, that is to say that Senegal was obliged either to prosecute the offender or extradite him, but was free to choose between these courses of action. Thus so long as it was not clear that Senegal was refusing to do either, it could not yet be said to be in breach of the Torture Convention. Senegal's position was interpreted by the Court as a contention that the relevant texts 'grant a party some latitude with regard to the time within it may take the actions required'.[57] The

[51] [2011-I] ICJ Rep 70, 84 para. 30.

[52] *South West Africa (Preliminary Objections)* [1962] ICJ Rep 328.

[53] *Application of the International Convention on the Elimination of All Forms of Racial Discrimination, Georgia* v *Russian Federation* [2011-I] ICJ Rep 84 para. 30.

[54] [2011] ICJ Rep 70, 84 para. 30.

[55] Judge Fleischhauer, opinion in *Certain Property* [2005] ICJ Rep 69; quoted with approval by Vice-President Tomka in his Declaration in the *Racial Discrimination Convention* case, [2011] ICJ Rep 181, 182.

[56] United Nations Convention against Torture and other Cruel, Inhuman or Degrading Treatment or Punishment, 10 December 1984.

[57] [2012-II] ICJ Rep 444 para. 51.

Court appears to have accepted this in principle, but found that there was nevertheless a dispute over the interpretation and application of the Convention.[58] At a later stage of the decision, the Court held that, while the Convention did not lay down any 'time-frame for performance of the obligation ... it is necessarily implicit in the text that it must be implemented within a reasonable time'.[59] This, however, was at the stage of deciding, not on jurisdiction, but on whether Senegal had or had not complied with its obligation. At the jurisdictional stage, what mattered was that there was a dispute over, in effect, what was a reasonable time, and the claim by Senegal that (in effect) that time had not yet elapsed did not demonstrate the absence of a dispute, but rather the opposite.

This exemplifies that settlement of a jurisdictional issue does not have to await determination of an issue of the merits; so stated this point is obvious, since merits cannot be determined by a court which has not established jurisdiction, but it tends to be obscured by such circumstances as those of the *Belgium* v *Senegal* case.

If a respondent State accepts the view advanced by the applicant as to the legal position, and as to the obligations of the respondent, may there nevertheless exist a 'dispute' if the respondent State has not yet complied with those obligations, because it has not been able to ensure compliance by its internal subdivisions? This was the problem in the case of *Request for Interpretation of the Judgment of 31 March 2004 (Avena)*; but the key text in that case was Article 60 of the Statute, which refers to a 'dispute concerning the meaning or scope of the judgment', and the French text uses, for 'dispute', the word *contestation* rather than *différend* as in Article 36. The Court was able to leave the question undecided; but it appears that much may depend on the nature of the obligation; the obligation in question was an obligation under a previous judgment, which had left to the respondent 'a choice of means ... in the implementation of its obligation'.[60] As the *Belgium* v *Senegal* case illustrates, there can be a 'dispute' over whether or not delay in performance of the obligation (as to the existence of which there is no longer any dispute) may be equivalent to non-performance.

C. Jurisdiction and its exercise

In principle, if the Court finds that it has jurisdiction to entertain a particular case, it is under a duty to exercise that jurisdiction, to the extent that it has been conferred and to the extent of the claims of the parties before it (and no further—this principle is known as the rule *ne ultra petita*).[61] In a few cases, the Court has, however, found that, even before inquiring into the existence of jurisdiction, it sees reasons for not exercising it. One example of a category of cases of this kind is where to decide the case would involve determining the legal situation of a State not a party

[58] [2012-II] ICJ Rep 444 para. 52. [59] [2012-II] ICJ Rep 444 para. 114.

[60] *Request for Interpretation of the Judgment of 31 March 2004 (Avena)*, [2009] ICJ Rep 3, 18 para. 47.

[61] See e.g. *Continental Shelf (Libya/Malta)* [1985] ICJ Rep 13, 23 para. 19.

to the case; it is for this sort of situation that the system of intervention (examined further in Ch. 15) is designed. Where, however, a State whose position would be affected by the decision has not chosen to intervene, the principle laid down in the *Monetary Gold* case may come into play.[62]

In that case, what was in issue was entitlement to a quantity of monetary gold removed from Rome by the Germans in 1943 which 'might be held' to belong (and, according to an arbitral award, did belong) to Albania. The United Kingdom had, in the *Corfu Channel* case, obtained judgment against Albania for monetary compensation, and was anxious to intercept the gold in order to meet its claim. Italy also asserted that it had a legal claim against Albania, and also sought to intercept the gold. France, the UK, and the USA were jointly in actual possession of the gold in 1954, and an Agreement made in Washington in 1951 between those States provided that the gold should be handed over to the UK unless, within a 90-day period, the Court was seised either by Albania or by Italy to press their respective claims. Albania took no action, but Italy brought proceedings against the three parties to the Washington Agreement (who had in that text accepted in advance the jurisdiction of the Court for the purpose) asserting that Italy's claim 'must have priority over the claim of the United Kingdom'.[63] The problem the Court saw was that if it were to uphold Italy's claim to the gold[64] it would have to satisfy itself that that State's claim against Albania was valid; and Albania was not before the Court. The Court said:

> It is also contended that any decision of the Court on the questions submitted by Italy in her Application will be binding only upon Italy and the three respondent States, and not upon Albania. It is true that, under Article 59 of the Statute, the decision of the Court in a given case only binds the parties to it and in respect of that particular case. This rule, however, rests on the assumption that the Court is at least able to render a binding decision. Where, as in the present case, the vital issue to be settled concerns the international responsibility of a third State, the Court cannot, without the consent of that third State, give a decision on that issue binding upon any State, either the third State, or any of the parties before it.[65]

It was argued that it was open to Albania to intervene and become a party to the proceedings; but it had chosen not to do so. Here, however, the Court drew a distinction: if the interests of an absent State would merely *be affected* by the decision, then if that State chose not to exercise its right to request intervention, the proceedings could continue to judgment; but if the legal interests of the absent State 'would form the very subject matter of the decision', then the Court could not exercise its jurisdiction in the absence of that State.[66]

This would seem to raise problems when the Court is asked to delimit an international territorial boundary in an area where the end-point of the boundary, hitherto

[62] *Monetary Gold Removed from Rome in 1943, Preliminary Question* [1954] ICJ Rep 19.

[63] [1954] ICJ Rep 22.

[64] Italy in fact raised an objection to the proceedings it had itself instituted before the Court (for reasons that are not here material), and it was therefore argued that it had abandoned its claim; but the Court did not accept this: [1954] ICJ Rep 30.

[65] [1954] ICJ Rep 19, 33.

[66] [1954] ICJ Rep19, 32.

undefined, lies on the boundary of a third State, not party to the proceedings. This question arose in the *Frontier Dispute* between Burkina Faso and Mali, and the Chamber of the Court seised of the case dealt with it as follows:

The rights of the neighbouring State, Niger, are in any event safeguarded by the operation of Article 59 of the Statute of the Court, which provides that 'The decision of the Court has no binding force except between the parties and in respect of that particular case'. The Parties could at any time have concluded an agreement for the delimitation of their frontier, according to whatever perception they might have had of it, and an agreement of this kind, although legally binding upon them by virtue of the principle *pacta sunt servanda*, would not be opposable to Niger. A judicial decision, which 'is simply an alternative to the direct and friendly settlement' of the dispute between the Parties (*P.C.I.J., Series A, No. 22,* p. 13), merely substitutes for the solution stemming directly from their shared intention, the solution arrived at by a court under the mandate which they have given it. In both instances, the solution only has legal and binding effect as between the States which have accepted it, either directly or as a consequence of having accepted the court's jurisdiction to decide the case.[67]

The distinction offered between the two cases is narrow, but convincing. In *Monetary Gold* it was equally true that the parties before the Court could have 'concluded an agreement' to gain their end—in fact they had done so; but there is no doubt that a judgment in the *Monetary Gold* case would have had an impact on Albania going beyond any theoretical and unenforceable infringement of the rights of Niger in the later case.

Another reason for declining to exercise jurisdiction and give a decision is where any judgment given would be ineffective, because the legal situation is such that the decision would have no 'forward reach',[68] or because the claims of the applicant have in effect been satisfied, so that the case has become 'without object' or 'moot'.[69] Since a refusal to exercise jurisdiction would normally be a renunciation of the very function of the Court, these cases are, however, highly exceptional.[70] The first involved a claim for breach of a Trusteeship Agreement that had been validly terminated; the second, a situation in which the respondent State, while declining to appear in the proceedings,[71] had indicated that, of its own choice, it would not continue the conduct complained of, and which it was the object of the proceedings to condemn as unlawful. The decision has been much criticized on the procedural level, as having, in effect imposed on the applicant parties a discontinuance that they did not desire.[72] However, it enabled the Court to avoid

[67] [1986] ICJ Rep 554, 577 para. 46. Niger does not appear to have raised any difficulty as to the position of the tripoint: the later boundary dispute between Niger and Burkina Faso, dealt with by the Court in 2013, related to a quite different section of the boundary: see [2013] ICJ Rep 44.

[68] *Northern Cameroons*, [1963] ICJ Rep 15, 37.

[69] *Nuclear Tests (Australia* v *France)* [1974] ICJ Rep 253, 270–2 paras. 55–9; *Nuclear Tests (New Zealand* v *France)* [1974] ICJ Rep 457, 476–7 paras. 58–62.

[70] When a point of this kind was raised in the cases concerning the *Aerial Incident at Lockerbie*, the Court declined to deal with it as a preliminary issue (and the cases were subsequently discontinued). See *Questions of Interpretation and Application of the 1971 Montreal Convention arising from the Aerial Incident at Lockerbie (Libyan Arab Jamahiriya* v *United Kingdom)* [1998] ICJ Rep 9, 26–9 paras. 46–50.

[71] On non-appearance, see Ch. 7 sect. B(3)c.

[72] Relying on a debatable 'inherent jurisdiction': see sect. D.

having to give a decision on the legality or otherwise of atmospheric nuclear tests, a question that was controversial and probably not, as a legal matter, ripe for judicial decision.[73]

D. Inherent jurisdiction and the powers of the Court

A question that arises from time to time is that of the precise nature and extent of the powers vested in the Court, particularly those that are not specifically stated in the governing texts.

Clearly its most essential power—and duty—is, in the context of contentious proceedings, that of deciding the issues before it with binding force; and in advisory proceedings, that of supplying the requesting organization with an opinion on the question submitted. In the latter context, it has also the power of declining to give an opinion—an option examined in Chapter 6 section E. In contentious proceedings this option, that of refusal, is not in terms made available to it by its Statute, and the Court cannot simply give no judgment at all; but, as already noted, it has on occasion found it appropriate, for good and sufficient reason, to issue a 'judgment' that does not judge, that does not determine the issues laid before it.

A subsidiary but vital power is that of determining the extent of its own jurisdiction, the *compétence de la compétence*. This is expressly conferred by Article 36 paragraph 6 of the Statute; but it is a power generally recognized as necessarily appertaining to a judicial body—an inherent power. Its scope and conditions have been examined in Chapter 4 section B.

Yet another important power is that of 'indicating provisional measures', that is to say, issuing interim orders during the course of the proceedings with the purpose, broadly speaking, of requiring the parties not to do anything that would frustrate the eventual decision; and comparatively recently it has become recognized that, in the case of the ICJ, this is a power to bind the party or parties addressed, not merely, as the use, in Article 41 of the Statute, of the term 'indicate' might suggest, to propose measures to this end that the party concerned is free not to follow. Whether this power, conferred by the Statute, is inherent in the judicial office is less certain.[74]

[73] Cf the 'dusty answer' given by the Court to the request for an opinion on the question of the legality of the use of nuclear weapons: *Legality of the Threat or Use of Nuclear Weapons* [1996-I] ICJ Rep 226, 263 para. 97.

[74] Such a power seems to have been assumed, in the absence of textual warrant, by the European Commission and Court of Human Rights, and then codified in Rule 39 of the ECtHR Rules. On the other hand, it was thought necessary to provide specifically in UNCLOS for such a power to be exercised by any court or tribunal agreed between the parties for a maritime dispute (Art. 290 para. 1), and the measures so indicated are binding (para. 6). The PCIJ recognized a duty of parties to a dispute to 'abstain from any measure capable of exercising a prejudicial effect in regard to the execution of the decision to be given' (*PCIJ Series A/B, No. 9*, 194, 199). C. Brown, *A Common Law of International Adjudication* (Oxford: Oxford University Press, 2007), 126–7, argues from this for the existence of a general principle of law authorizing a tribunal to grant provisional measures; but the existence of a legal duty does not automatically confer jurisdiction on a tribunal to direct compliance.

Another power stated in the Statute is that of sitting *in camera*, that is to say hearings closed to the public: this is indicated as an exception to the principle of public hearings in Article 46 of the Statute: see further Chapter 8 section F.

These are the powers, or jurisdictions, conferred expressly on the Court. Are there examples to be found of other powers, not so mentioned, that are to be regarded as inherent in the Court's role, or perhaps in the operation of any court of justice, as such? In the *Nuclear Tests* cases, the Court made this statement:

> [T]he Court possesses an inherent jurisdiction enabling it to take such action as may be necessary, on the one hand to ensure that the exercise of its jurisdiction over the merits, if and when established, shall not be frustrated, and on the other, to provide for the orderly settlement of all matters in dispute, to ensure the observance of the 'inherent limitations on the exercise of the judicial function' of the Court, and to 'maintain its judicial character' (*Northern Cameroons, Judgment, I.C.J. Reports 1963*, at p. 29). Such inherent jurisdiction, on the basis of which the Court is fully empowered to make whatever findings may be necessary for the purposes just indicated, derives from the mere existence of the Court as a judicial organ established by the consent of States, and is conferred upon it in order that its basic judicial function may be safeguarded.[75]

The first of these powers appears to be no more than the power to indicate provisional measures,[76] which as already noted is, in the case of the ICJ, a power expressly conferred. A power 'to ensure that [the Court's] jurisdiction over the merits, if and when established, shall not be frustrated' might also include preventing evasion of an acceptance of jurisdiction.[77]

The second 'inherent jurisdiction' is stated in very wide terms. Certainly the Court can and does 'provide for the orderly settlement of all matters in dispute', in the most routine manner by making orders for the conduct of the proceedings. The actual exercise of the power in the case in point (*Nuclear Tests*) was directed to the Court's 'tak[ing] cognizance of a situation in which the dispute has disappeared because the final objective which the Applicant has maintained throughout has been achieved by other means', and acting *sua sponte* to bring the case to an end—certainly not a routine act of direction of the procedure.[78] Another example may be afforded by the assertion of a Chamber of the Court that the admission of an application by a third State to intervene in a case, without seeking or obtaining the status of party thereto, does not require the consent of the existing parties because the Court's competence

[75] *Nuclear Tests (Australia* v *France)* [1974] ICJ Rep 259–60 para. 23; similar text in the *New Zealand* v *France* case, [1974] ICJ Rep 463 para. 23.

[76] At the time of this decision it was by no means certain that provisional measures indicated by the ICJ were binding, this only being judicially pronounced in the *LaGrand* case a quarter of a century later (*LaGrand* [2001] ICJ Rep 466, 506 para. 109).

[77] e.g. in *Nottebohm* [1953] ICJ Rep 111, 119–20 (the expiration, after it had been seised of a claim, of the basis of jurisdiction relied on did not deprive the Court of jurisdiction); *Right of Passage over Indian Territory* [1957] ICJ Rep 142–4 (no retrospective withdrawal of jurisdictional acceptance); A similar effect of the so-called 'self-judging' or 'Connally reservation' is apparently also to be excluded for the same reason: see sect. A(2)b above.

[78] *Nuclear Tests (Australia* v *France)* [1974] ICJ Rep 271 para. 55; similar text in the *New Zealand* v *France* case, [1974] ICJ Rep 476 para. 58.

to admit such an intervention derives 'not from the consent of the parties to the case, but from the consent given by them, in becoming parties to the Court's Statute, to the Court's exercise of its powers conferred by the Statute'.[79]

The underlying reason stated for these powers—the safeguarding of the 'basic judicial function'—can well be understood in connection with the first power, since lack of provisional measures might make the judgment unenforceable or pointless. The second power, at least in the cases quoted, to put a stop to a case on the grounds that no decision is needed otherwise than at the request or the suggestion of the applicant,[80] is less easy to attribute to a need to 'safeguard the judicial function'. Is there an 'inherent limitation on the exercise of the judicial function' such that the Court may not give, as it were, a confirmatory judgment on a point on which the parties have come to agreement?[81]

The passage is, however, authority for recognizing that the powers of the Court are not limited to those specifically indicated in the Statute or the Rules. The Rules, being in effect delegated legislation, cannot add to the statutory powers, though they might declare a recognized inherent power not mentioned in the Statute. An example of this might be the power to direct that two or more cases be joined, and heard as one case, which is not mentioned in the Statute, but provided for in Article 47 of the Rules.[82] But in addition, the course of the proceedings in a case may well raise many minor procedural issues which it must be possible for the Court to determine authoritatively without any specific basis in the Statute.

To say that this is so that 'the basic judicial function may be safeguarded' is somewhat high-flown and imprecise language. Similarly, the Court has sometimes indicated that its action or inaction (particularly in procedural matters) is dictated by considerations of 'the good administration of justice',[83] which, it has been suggested, acts as a sort of 'compass' in procedural questions.[84] The danger of these expressions, particularly the second, is their lack of precision; if their use amounts to saying, 'This seems the right course to follow, but it is difficult to explain exactly why', this is hardly satisfactory, either for the instant dispute or for the future. It is in procedural matters also that 'Freedom slowly broadens down | From precedent to precedent'.[85]

[79] *Land, Island and Maritime Frontier Dispute (El Salvador/Honduras), Application to Intervene*, [1990] ICJ Rep 92, 133 para. 96; see further in Ch. 15.

[80] The applicant Governments were at the time reported to be by no means pleased with the Court's initiative.

[81] See the powerful remarks of Judges Onyeama, Dillard, Jiménez de Aréchaga, and Waldock in their joint dissenting opinion in *Nuclear Tests* [1974] ICJ Rep 321–2 paras. 22–3; [1974] ICJ Rep 504–5 paras. 21–2.

[82] 'The Court may at any time direct that the proceedings in two or more cases be joined. It may also direct that the written or oral proceedings, including the calling of witnesses, be in common; or the Court may, without effecting any formal joinder, direct common action in any of these respects.'

[83] The first appearance of the phrase is probably in *Frontier Dispute (Burkina Faso* v *Mali) (Provisional Measures)* [1986] ICJ Rep 3, 9 para. 19. It has been used e.g. for a joinder of cases: Order of 17 April 2013 in the two *Costa Rica/Nicaragua* cases, [2013] ICJ Rep 166, 170 para. 18 ('sound administration of justice').

[84] Miron, 'Les Méthodes de travail de la Cour', *ICJ 70th Anniversary Seminar* (2016) JPICT.

[85] Alfred, Lord Tennyson, 'You Ask Me, Why, Though Ill at Ease'.

6

Jurisdiction in Advisory Proceedings

A. Historical background

The idea of a standing international tribunal for the settlement of inter-State disputes developed from the long-established practice of international arbitration of inter-State disputes. It was generally agreed at the time of setting up an arbitration that the decision of the arbitrators in such cases was to be accepted as binding; generally the whole purpose was to achieve a settlement in circumstances in which negotiation had shown that any foreseeable solution would fail to satisfy at least one of the parties, and thus had to be definitive and accepted in advance.

So long as international legal questions arose in the form of inter-State disputes, submission of them to an international body would only be advantageous if the outcome was a settlement one way or the other. However, the establishment of the League of Nations meant that legal questions might be among those debated by its organs, and in some circumstances an independent and impartial legal opinion might be sufficient to advance the settlement of a problem.[1] The Covenant of the League of Nations therefore provided, in Article 14, that the Court that was being established should have power to give advisory opinions. This provision was not, however, carried over into the PCIJ Statute as originally adopted, as a result of some procedural complications.[2] Article 14 in itself sufficed for the new Court to be asked for, and give, its first two advisory opinions: in the 1922 Rules, however, provision was made for advisory opinions; and when the PCIJ Statute was revised in 1929, a chapter was added effectively incorporating these texts into the Statute. The usefulness of the advisory function was demonstrated by the fact that the PCIJ was asked for, and gave, five advisory opinions in all.

The Statute of the post-war Court contains a Chapter IV (Arts. 65–8) on Advisory Opinions, essentially re-enacting the relevant terms of the PCIJ Statute. One unobtrusive change was made that had considerable significance. It was generally understood that if the PCIJ was asked to give an advisory opinion, it was under a duty to give it;[3] but Article 65 of the ICJ Statute reads, 'The Court *may* give [*peut*

[1] e.g. even before the new Permanent Court was established, the Council of the League had obtained an opinion in 1920 from a specially established Commission of Jurists on the *Aaland Islands question*.

[2] See Zimmermann et al., *Commentary*, 1608–10 *sub* 65(1).

[3] The French and English texts of Art. 14 of the Covenant did not agree. The French text used an apparently prescriptive form 'donnera des avis consultatifs', while the English text read 'The Court

donner] an advisory opinion on any legal question at the request' (italics added) of any of the bodies specified; and, as explained in sect. E, this has regularly been interpreted as signifying that the Court has a discretion to refuse to give an opinion. The provisions of the Statute are completed by Part IV (Arts. 102–9) of the ICJ Rules; these in 1946 effectively took over the PCIJ Rules on the subject, and subsequent revisions (in 1972 and 1978) made no material change.

B. Jurisdictional issues in the advisory context

The Court has stated as a general rule that '[w]hen seised of a request for an advisory opinion, the Court must first consider whether it has jurisdiction to give the opinion requested and whether, should the answer be in the affirmative, there is any reason why it should decline to exercise any such jurisdiction'.[4] These are two distinct questions, but it may well happen that a reason put forward why the Court lacks jurisdiction is, as such, rejected, but is also advanced as a reason for a refusal to exercise the jurisdiction, and be accepted as such.

Jurisdictional issues in the context of requests for advisory opinion differ from those arising in contentious cases. Consent remains the basis of jurisdiction, but in relation to advisory opinions, it is solely the collective consent of States, expressed in the Charter and Statute, and any other international agreements underlying the proceedings,[5] that governs the matter. This is also relevant to contentious jurisdiction (to take an obvious example, the Court has no jurisdiction if an entity other than a State endeavours to bring proceedings, because the Statute permits this only to States), but in that context most issues in this sphere concern the existence *vel non*, or the extent, of the consent of the parties. The willingness, or lack of it, on the part of States involved in a dispute to see the Court deliver an advisory opinion on a question relating to that dispute is irrelevant to the Court's jurisdiction to give such an opinion (though it may, as will be seen, be relevant to the exercise of the Court's discretion to decline); and there is no room for the operation of *forum prorogatum*.[6] The questions that do arise may also be regarded as constitutional questions, or as matters of interpretation of the Charter, the Statute or whatever other agreement is relied on.

Similarly, there are in advisory proceedings no States or other entities that will be bound by the decision to be given, and whose consent would therefore, as a matter of legal principle, be required to create jurisdiction over them. Even the

may also give' (cf. Judge Keith in *Accordance with International Law of the Unilateral Declaration of Independence of Kosovo*, separate opinion, [2010-II] ICJ Rep 482).

[4] *Legal Consequences of the Construction of a Wall in the Occupied Palestinian Territory* [2004] ICJ Rep 136, 144 para. 13, citing *Legality of the Threat or Use of Nuclear Weapons* [1996-I] ICJ Rep 226, 232 para. 10.

[5] e.g. the Convention on Privileges and Immunities of the United Nations; the UN Headquarters Agreement; the Statute of the ILO Administrative Tribunal; etc.

[6] Discussed in Ch. 5 sect. A(3).

international organization requesting the opinion is, in principle, not bound by the Court's conclusions; still less is there any binding or authoritative effect as regards the States that may have participated in the proceedings, or to whose action the opinion may be relevant. The exception is where there has been advance agreement that an advisory opinion given in a particular case or cases shall be regarded as binding.[7]

One aspect, or corollary, of the principle of consent as the basis of jurisdiction that probably does apply in advisory cases is the application of the rule *ne ultra petita*: just as the Court in a contentious case may not decide matters not submitted to it by the parties, similarly when asked for an advisory opinion its duty is to answer the question put, and no other, and no more.[8]

C. The right to request an opinion and its limits

The power to request advisory opinions from the Court has from the outset been reserved for international bodies: in relation to the Permanent Court, for the Council of the League and the Assembly, and in the post-war era primarily for the United Nations Security Council and General Assembly. As already noted, in contentious cases States have usually sought judicial assistance and decision for the settlement of legal disputes, not mere legal advice; though such cases as *North Sea Continental Shelf*, in which the Court was asked to decide, not a 'dispute' but a 'question',[9] show that more recent developments in international law may lead States to find such advice useful. It remains the case, however, that there is no mechanism for individual States to obtain advisory opinions; and such machinery does not seem to be needed.[10]

Under Article 96 paragraph 1 of the Charter, the General Assembly and the Security Council are entitled to request the Court 'to give an advisory opinion on any legal question'; and paragraph 2 provides that '[o]ther organs of the United Nations and specialized agencies, which may at any time be so authorized by the General Assembly, may also request advisory opinions of the Court

[7] e.g. the various cases reviewing decisions of the UN Administrative Tribunal; also *Applicability of the Obligation to Arbitrate under Section 21 of the UN Headquarters Agreement*, [1988] ICJ Rep 12; and *Applicability of Section VI, Article 22, of the Convention on the Privileges and Immunities of the United Nations*, [1989] ICJ Rep 177.

[8] It may, however, have to re-interpret the request for opinion, in order to 'ascertain what are the legal questions really in issue in questions formulated in a request' (*Interpretation of the Agreement of 25 March 1951 between the WHO and Egypt*, [1980] ICJ Rep 73, 88 para. 35) so as to arrive at the 'true legal question' (ibid.), which may look rather different from the question formulated in the request.

[9] See the Special Agreement, Art. 1(1), quoted at [1969] ICJ Rep 6.

[10] In this sense, Schwebel, discussing whether States might be able to seek advisory opinions 'through' the General Assembly or the Security Council (or a specially authorized standing committee), suggested that since the *North Sea* case had shown that much the same result could be achieved through the contentious route, there would no longer be much demand by States for access to the advisory process: 'Was the Capacity to Request an Advisory Opinion Wider in the Permanent Court of International Justice than it Is in the International Court of Justice?', 1991 *BYBIL* 77–118, 116–17.

on legal questions arising within the scope of their activities.'[11] This is purely a faculty: nowhere in the Charter is there any obligation laid on any organ to seek the advice of the Court, and the Court has no power to offer it unasked.[12]

Authorizations under paragraph 2 of Article 96 have in fact been given to the Economic and Social Council and to practically all the specialized agencies. Unlike the two principal organs, however, these bodies are only authorized by that text to seek opinions on 'legal questions arising within the scope of their activities'. This restriction was held to debar the World Health Organization, which had received a general authorization from the General Assembly to request opinions, from asking for an opinion on the question whether the use of nuclear weapons by a State would be a breach of its obligations under international law 'including the WHO Constitution'. The Court held that, under the 'principle of speciality', the WHO could not deal with matters beyond what was authorized by its Constitution; that the question of the legality of nuclear weapons was outside that Constitution; and accordingly the question was not one 'arising within the scope' of the activities of the Organization.[13] In another case, the question was raised whether a subsidiary organ of the General Assembly, whose sole function was in fact to ask for advisory opinions (on the validity of judgments of the United Nations Administrative Tribunal), had any 'activities' of its own for the purposes of this text; the Court ruled in the affirmative.[14]

One notable omission—or apparent omission—from the category of bodies that may be authorized to request advisory opinions of the Court is the Secretary-General, who is neither an 'organ'—it is the Secretariat that is the organ—nor a specialized agency.[15] Whether the Secretariat could therefore be authorized to request an advisory opinion on 'questions arising within the scope of its activities' is doubtful. If the General Assembly may be reluctant to give the Secretary-General such authorization, the reasons may be less legal than political, as the authorization

[11] The wording of paras. 1 and 2 of Art. 96 suggests that a request from the Security Council or General Assembly can relate to a question not 'within the scope of their activities', but there are dicta of the Court suggesting that this approach may be too wide: see *Legal Consequences of the Construction of a Wall in the Occupied Palestinian Territory, Advisory Opinion,* [2004-I] ICJ Rep 136 para 16, and references there cited.

[12] Interpretation of the Charter by the Court is, however, 'an interpretative function which falls within the normal exercise of its jurisdictional powers': *Conditions of Admission of a State to Membership in the United Nations* [1947–8] ICJ Rep 57, 61.

[13] *Legality of the Use by a State of Nuclear Weapons in Armed Conflict, Advisory Opinion,* [1996-I] ICJ Rep 6, 66.

[14] *Application for Review of Judgement No. 158 of the United Nations Administrative Tribunal, Advisory Opinion,* [1973] ICJ Rep 166, 173–5 paras. 19–23. This body, the Committee on Applications for Review of Administrative Tribunal Judgments, no longer exists, having been abolished in 1995 (GA Res. 50/54, 11 December 1995), with no immediate substitute (see Ch. 9 sect. A(4)).

[15] It was also noted by Kelsen in 1950 that Art. 65 of the Statute refers to 'whatever *body* may be authorised' by the General Assembly, and the Secretary-General is not a 'body' in that sense: *The Law of the United Nations* (1950), 547. This interpretation is disputed by K. J. Keith, *The Extent of the Advisory Jurisdiction of the International Court of Justice* (Leiden: Sijthoff, 1971), 38, on the basis of the principle of internal consistency of interpretation of treaties.

once given (unless limited to a particular question) would enable him to obtain an opinion on a matter that the Assembly itself might prefer not to be the subject of legal advice.[16]

The decision of a particular organ or agency to request an advisory opinion is of course to be taken in accordance with its regular rules of procedure, and by a normal majority (thus in the Security Council, with the affirmative vote of the Permanent Members). If the question concerns an issue in dispute between two or more States, or between the State and the organization, the consent of that State or States is not required (though lack of it may, as will be explained, have significance for the Court's discretion to give or refuse an opinion).[17]

The consent of the States parties to a dispute is the basis of the Court's jurisdiction in contentious cases; but since the Court's reply to a request for an advisory opinion has no binding force, 'it follows that no State . . . can prevent the giving of an Advisory Opinion which the United Nations considers to be desirable in order to obtain enlightenment as to the course of action it should undertake'.[18] Similarly, the motives of any State or States putting forward or sponsoring the resolution making the request are irrelevant;[19] the Court 'will not have regard to the origins or to the political history of the request, or to the distribution of votes in respect of the adopted resolution'.[20]

It has been argued that, in respect of the General Assembly, a further important limitation on its power to request an opinion lies in in Article 12 paragraph 1 of the Charter. This is the provision that when the Security Council is exercising its functions in respect of any 'dispute or situation', the General Assembly is debarred from making any 'recommendation' with regard to that dispute or situation. In two cases[21] it was contended that the Security Council was so acting at the time that the General Assembly adopted its request for an advisory opinion, and that the request was thus *ultra vires*. In neither case did the Court uphold the objection, declining to see the request as a 'recommendation'; but it did note that Article 12 might limit

[16] In 1984 it was strongly urged by Schwebel that the Secretary-General be given authorization: 'Authorizing the Secretary-General to Request Advisory Opinions of the International Court of Justice', in J. Makarczyk (ed.), *Essays in International Law in Honour of Judge Manfred Lachs* (Dordrecht: Nijhoff, 1984), 519.

[17] There is also some suggestion, in the advisory opinion on *Applicability of the Convention on the Privileges and Immunities of the United Nations*, that if an opinion were requested to give effect to a disputes-settlement provision in such a convention, the opposition of a State party to the dispute that had made a reservation to that provision might 'act as a bar to the operation of the procedure of request for advisory opinion': [1989] ICJ Rep 177, 190 para. 34; but the observation is *obiter*.

[18] *Interpretation of Peace Treaties with Bulgaria, Hungary and Romania, First Phase*, [1950] ICJ Rep 65, 71.

[19] *Accordance with International Law of the Unilateral Declaration of Independence of Kosovo*, [2010-II] ICJ Rep 403, 417 para. 33.

[20] *Legality of the Threat or Use of Nuclear Weapons*, [1996-I] ICJ Rep 226, 237 para. 16.

[21] *Legal Consequences of the Construction of a Wall in the Occupied Palestinian Territory* [2004-I] ICJ Rep 3, 148 para. 3; *Accordance with International Law of the Unilateral Declaration of Independence of Kosovo* [2010-II] ICJ Rep 403, 414 para. 24.

what use the Assembly might make of the opinion given. It also returned to the question of the possible relevance of Article 12 paragraph 1 in the context of its discretionary power to decline to give an opinion even in response to a valid request (sect. (E)).[22]

D. Nature of the question: a 'legal' question?

Since Article 96 of the Charter and Article 65 of the Statute both refer to advisory opinions being given on 'any legal question',[23] it has on occasion been argued that a particular question submitted for opinion was not truly a 'legal' question, and therefore inappropriate for the application of the advisory procedure. It does not appear that any proposal to request an opinion has been successfully blocked on this ground; but once the request has been made, the Court has of course to satisfy itself that the question submitted to it is a legal one: 'If a question [submitted for opinion] is not a legal one, the Court has no discretion in the matter: it must decline to give the opinion requested.'[24]

The basis for the suggestion that the question is not a legal one has usually been either that the question is one of fact, or is political rather than legal, or that, while there is or may be a legal question, it cannot be answered without first establishing a complex body of facts, which the Court in advisory proceedings is not equipped to do.[25] In a number of cases in which the political nature of the question was asserted, this was more in order to urge the Court to decline (as a matter of discretion) to reply to the request than to assert that it would be exceeding its jurisdiction if it replied.[26] In the case of *Legality of the Threat or Use of Nuclear Weapons*, however, the issue was raised squarely; and the Court found that the question was 'indeed a legal one, since the Court is asked to rule on the compatibility of the threat or use of nuclear weapons with the relevant principles and rules of international law'.[27]

[22] *Accordance with International Law of the Unilateral Declaration of Independence of Kosovo* [2010-II] ICJ Rep 403, 419–22 paras. 39–42.

[23] Note the absence of the qualifying adjective 'international'; may the Court give an advisory opinion on a question of pure municipal law? It has certainly done so on questions of the internal law of an organization, that governing relations with its staff: see the cases mentioned in Ch. 9 sect. A(4).

[24] *Certain Expenses of the United Nations* [1962] ICJ Rep 155.

[25] See e.g. *Eastern Carelia, PCIJ Series B, No. 5*, 29. The reasoning of the decision seems to blend two ideas: that the real question was one of fact, and that the Court had no means of ascertaining what were the true facts; and that the Court would not be acting as a court if it were to try to decide a factual rather than a legal question. The exact significance of the decision as a precedent is therefore somewhat obscure.

[26] See e.g. *Certain Expenses of the United Nations* [1962] ICJ Rep 155; *Interpretation of the Agreement of 15 March 1951 between the WHO and Egypt* [1980] ICJ Rep 87 para. 33.

[27] *Legality of the Threat or Use of Nuclear Weapons* [1996] ICJ Rep 234 para. 13, where it added that 'The fact that this question also has political aspects . . . does not suffice to deprive the Court of a competence conferred on it by its Statute'.

E. The Court's discretion to refuse an opinion

An essential difference between the Court's rule in the settlement of contentious cases and its role in giving advisory opinions is that the Court is in principle obliged to give judgment on any legal dispute submitted to it,[28] but it has a discretion to decline to give an advisory opinion. The textual warrant for this is that Article 65 paragraph 1 of the Statute provides that '[t]he Court *may* give an advisory opinion on any legal question at the request of' the authorized bodies (italics added); this is contrasted with Article 38, whereby the Court's 'function is to decide in accordance with international law such disputes as are submitted to it'. The text of Article 65 gives no indication of the circumstances contemplated as possibly pointing to a refusal by the Court to give an opinion; and since the post-war Court has never yet refused to give one when requested (and its predecessor only did so on one occasion in rather special circumstances, and for reasons that are not entirely clear[29]), there is no clearly directing precedent. It seems doubtful, for example, that the Court would ever consider itself authorized in its discretion to substitute itself for the requesting organ so as to act on a different view of the political desirability or appropriateness of an opinion.

An important distinction is visible in the statement of the principle made in the *Western Sahara* case, that it would be 'incompatible with the Court's judicial character' if 'to give a reply would have the effect of circumventing the principle that a State is not obliged to allow its disputes to be submitted to judicial settlement without its consent'.[30] The word 'circumvent' carries an implication of *intention*, that the outcome would not merely chance to involve settlement notwithstanding opposition of the State concerned, but that there was the intention to achieve this. An intention on whose part? The Court has made it clear that 'the motives of individual States which sponsor, or vote in favour of, a resolution requesting an advisory opinion are not relevant to the Court's exercise of its discretion'.[31] But if it was the requesting organ, or the organization that sought to circumvent the

[28] There are exceptions: see the case of *Monetary Gold removed from Rome in 1943*, discussed in Ch. 10 sect. B.

[29] See n. 25. In 1950, the Court gave a different interpretation: it stated that the Permanent Court had 'declined to give an Opinion because it found that the question put to it was directly related to the main point of a dispute actually pending between two States, so that answering the question would be substantially equivalent to deciding the dispute between the parties, and at the same time it raised a question that could not be elucidated without hearing both parties': *Interpretation of Peace Treaties*, [1950] ICJ Rep 65, 72. The case was connected with a dispute between Russia and Finland, and Russia was refusing all participation in the case. It seems that it was not this refusal as such that determined the PCIJ to decline to act, but that refusal coupled with the practical difficulty of determining questions of fact (as to the intentions of the two parties when concluding a treaty) in the absence of one party: see pp. 28–9 of the advisory opinion.

[30] [1975] ICJ Rep 12, 25 para. 33.

[31] *Accordance with International Law of the Unilateral Declaration of Independence of Kosovo* [2010-II] ICJ Rep 403, 417 para. 33. See also *Legality of the Threat or Use of Nuclear Weapons* [1996-I] ICJ Rep 226, 237 para. 16: the Court 'will not have regard to the origins or to the political history of the request'.

consent principle, this reading would fit uncomfortably well with the background to the requests for opinion in *Namibia* and in the *Wall* case, which were accepted. The Court has indicated that it will not second-guess the requesting organ and consider whether the opinion will actually serve the purpose intended, or indeed any useful purpose: 'it is for the organ which requests the opinion, and not for the Court, to determine whether it needs the opinion for the proper performance of its functions'.[32]

In fact the principle, repeatedly stated by the Court, that its complying with a request for advisory opinion represents 'its participation in the activities of the Organization, and, in principle, should not be refused',[33] seems (despite *Eastern Carelia*) to be overriding. The Court, however, regularly raises, at the beginning of each advisory opinion, the question whether there is any reason to decline to give the opinion asked for, and has thus built up some case-law on what are *not* compelling reasons for doing so. It has on several occasions expressed marked hesitation, principally in a number of cases involving appeals by staff-members of international organizations, and these serve to delineate at least some of the areas of doubt. They include some aspects already mentioned that, having been advanced as reasons why a request for opinion was one that *could not* be dealt with, were rejected by the Court in that respect, and that were then found also not to be grounds for exercising the discretion to refuse.

Mention has been made of the possible relevance of Article 12 paragraph 1 of the Charter, and the relationship between the General Assembly and the Security Council. A similar but wider issue that the Court found it necessary to examine, in the context of its discretion, in the *Kosovo* case was

> whether, in view of the respective roles of the Security Council and the General Assembly in relation to the situation in Kosovo, the Court, as the principal judicial organ of the United Nations, should decline to answer the question which has been put to it on the ground that the request for the Court's opinion has been made by the General Assembly rather than the Security Council.[34]

This was a much more complex question, the ramifications of which are matters of the constitutional law of the United Nations, not of the powers and discretion of the Court, and thus need not be gone into here. It should be emphasized that the Court dealt with the point as one of discretion, not as one of legal prohibition of action on its part.[35]

[32] *Kosovo* case (see n. 31) [2010-II] ICJ Rep 403, 417 para. 34.

[33] *Kosovo* case (see n. 31) [2010-II] ICJ Rep 403, 416 para. 30, citing *Interpretation of Peace Treaties with Bulgaria, Hungary and Romania*, [1950] ICJ Rep 65, 71; *Difference Relating to Immunity from Legal Process of a Special Rapporteur of the Commission on Human Rights*, [1999-I] ICJ Rep 62, 78–9 para. 29; *Legal Consequences of the Construction of a Wall in the Occupied Palestinian Territory* [2004-I] ICJ Rep 136, 156 para. 44.

[34] [2010-II] ICJ Rep 403, 418 para. 36.

[35] Thus the Court drew the distinction with the *Wall* case, in which the argument had been 'whether or not the Court possessed the jurisdiction to give an advisory opinion, rather than whether it should exercise its discretion not to give an opinion': *Kosovo* case (see n. 31) [2010-II] ICJ Rep 403, 420 para. 42.

Where the question submitted relates to a dispute between two States, or between a State and an international organization, the attitude of the States concerned, irrelevant to the question of the Court's jurisdiction to give the opinion, needs to be examined in relation to a possible discretionary refusal of an opinion. As the Court declared in the *Western Sahara* case, 'lack of consent [of an interested State] might constitute a ground for declining to give the opinion requested', in the exercise of the Court's discretion, 'if, in the circumstances of a given case, considerations of judicial propriety should oblige the Court to refuse an opinion'.[36] The Court offered as an instance of this (and probably the most compelling instance), 'when the circumstances disclose that to give a reply would have the effect of circumventing the principle that a State is not obliged to allow its disputes to be submitted to judicial settlement without its consent'.[37] This might be so, it continued, if the object of the requesting organ (*in casu* the General Assembly) were 'to bring before the Court, by way of a request for advisory opinion, a dispute or legal controversy, in order that it may later, on the basis of the Court's opinion, exercise its power and functions for the peaceful settlement of that dispute or controversy'.[38] This criterion appears however to have been tacitly abandoned in the *Wall* case;[39] and the Court may be becoming generally more favourable to requests for an opinion where there is in the background a dispute with one or more States. It did not even refuse in the case of a dispute between the General Assembly and a State, in which the Assembly, unable to obtain a binding advisory opinion under the provisions of the Convention on the Privileges and Immunities of the United Nations, because of a reservation to that Convention made by the State concerned, sought and obtained a non-binding opinion of the Court on the point in dispute,[40] which looks very like a circumventing of the principle stated.

As to the staff appeal cases mentioned above, the most recent such case, in which much of the earlier jurisprudence was reviewed, was *Judgment No. 2867 of the Administrative Tribunal of the International Labour Organization upon a Complaint filed against the International Fund for Agricultural Development.*[41] On the general point, the Court noted that the discretion to give or refuse an opinion 'exists for good reason';[42] unfortunately it did not indicate what that reason was, but previous jurisprudence shows that it is 'to protect the integrity of the Court's judicial function and its nature as the principal judicial organ of the United Nations'.[43] This

[36] *Western Sahara*, [1975] ICJ Rep 12 para 32.

[37] [1975] ICJ Rep 12 para 33. This passage was later criticized, by Judge Kooijmans in the *Wall* case, as containing 'purely circular reasoning': *Wall* case (n. 33) [2004-I] ICJ Rep 227, para 27.

[38] *Western Sahara*, [1975] ICJ Rep 12, para 29.

[39] See the Separate Opinion of Judge Higgins, *Wall* case (n. 33) [2004-I] ICJ Rep 136, p. 210, paras. 12–13.

[40] *Applicability of Article VI, Section 22, of the Convention on the Privileges and Immunities of the United Nations*, [1989] ICJ Rep 177, 191 para. 38, on the basis of a fine distinction between a dispute between the United Nations and a State 'as to the *applicability* of the Convention' to a particular individual, and a dispute between the same parties 'with respect to the *application* of the [same] Convention in the case of' that individual.

[41] [2012-I] ICJ Rep 10.

[42] [2012-I] ICJ Rep 10, 24–5 para. 30.

[43] *Accordance with International Law of the Unilateral Declaration of Independence of Kosovo* [2010-II] ICJ Rep 403, 416 para. 33, citing *Eastern Carelia, PCIJ Series B, No. 5*; *Application for Review of*

formula is impressive, but not singularly helpful; and it was backed by rehearsal of the well-established principle that a request for opinion should not be refused. It appears however that what the Court had in mind was the need for 'the Court and its predecessor . . . to maintain their integrity as judicial bodies', and in this respect to have in mind 'a central aspect of the good administration of justice: the principle of equality before the Court', specifically such equality between 'the organization on the one hand and the official [author of the appeal] on the other'.[44] However, when the Article was drafted, incorporating the possibility of refusing an opinion, it is hardly likely that this is the sort of case that was contemplated as one that would justify a refusal, since at that time there was no possibility of the Court's being involved in staff matters. While the possibility of advisory opinions as a staff appeal mechanism goes back to the Statute of the League's Administrative Tribunal, this was adopted in 1927,[45] long after Article 14 of the Covenant was adopted.

Judgement No. 158 of the United Nations Administrative Tribunal [1973] ICJ Rep 166, 175 para. 24; *Application for Review of Judgement No. 158 of the United Nations Administrative Tribunal* [1982] ICJ Rep 325, 334 para. 22; Legal Consequences of the Construction of a Wall in the Occupied Palestinian Territory [2004-I] ICJ Rep 136, 156–7 paras. 44–5.

[44] [2012-I] ICJ Rep 10, 25, paras. 33, 34, 35.

[45] Text in *Clunet* 77 (1950) 346.

III

CONTENTIOUS PROCEEDINGS

7

Overview of Contentious Proceedings

A. The governing texts

The procedure of the Court is regulated primarily by its Statute, specifically, as regards contentious proceedings, by Chapter III (Arts. 39–64). These texts provide both for the procedure before the Court, that is to say the procedure to be followed by States bringing and conducting cases, and for the procedure to be followed by the Court itself, in conducting hearings, directing the proceedings, and deliberating. The Statute also provides, in Article 30, that the Court has power to make rules 'for carrying out its functions', including rules of procedure, and in practice the provisions of these are at least equally important. Both the Statute and the Rules of Court adopted in 1946 were modelled closely on those of the Permanent Court.

The Rules of Court, being drawn up by the Court itself, may freely be amended by it;[1] they were revised in part in 1972, and more radically in 1978; further revisions of detail have been effected in more recent years. While the Permanent Court published the minutes of the debates leading to the adoption and the amendment of its Rules, no comparable documents have ever been made public by the post-war Court.[2]

The Court has found it useful to regulate detailed matters of procedure in a more informal way, by issuing 'Practice Directions' interpreting and implementing the Statute and Rules. The hierarchy of norms is of course that Rules cannot be inconsistent with the Statute,[3] but since the Rules and the Practice Directions are both made by the Court, if there were any inconsistency the Direction might be taken to express the more recent will of the Court. The Practice Directions are of course published, with the Statute and Rules, and are amended and extended from time to time.

[1] But remain imperative for the parties: cf. Kolb, 99–101.

[2] Some years after leaving the service of the Court, the writer was involved in discussions with it over arrangements for such a publication, but ultimately it did not prove possible for agreement to be reached on this.

[3] For an example of a challenge to a provision in the Rules on the ground that it was inconsistent with the Statute, see the dissenting opinion of Judge Shahabuddeen in the *Land, Island and Maritime Frontier Dispute, (El Salvador/Honduras), Application to Intervene, Order of 28 February 1990, ICJ Reports 1990*, 3 at 18ff., and Thirlway, 'Procedural Law and the International Court of Justice', in V. Lowe and M. Fitzmaurice (eds.), *Fifty Years of the International Court of Justice (Jennings Festschrift)* (Cambridge: Cambridge University Press, 1996), 389, 391–4.

Generally, the extent to which the broad lines of the procedure laid down in the Statute of the Permanent Court, and in the Rules adopted by that body, have been maintained is a tribute to the work of the jurists of the inter-war period; and the complete revision of the Rules effected in 1978 has also stood the test of time.

A question that has arisen in the application of the Statute and Rules is that of a possible residual discretion in their application, or at least in the application of the Rules, since the Statute, being, as it were, imposed on the Court, must presumably be applied meticulously. Specifically, the point was the admission of a counterclaim: if the counterclaim fulfilled the conditions laid down by Article 80 of the Rules,[4] was the Court bound to admit it; or did the Court enjoy a degree of discretion, to refuse to admit it on grounds not contemplated by the Rule? Two judges were of the opinion that such discretion existed.[5] One of them drew a distinction between cases where the Rule being applied was one made to give effect to a provision of the Statute, and cases where the relevant Rule was the sole and original text governing the question: in the latter case, he suggested, the Court, which has 'an inherent power and duty to ensure the orderly and efficient administration of justice', 'is not rigidly bound by [such] Rules' but 'is free, and indeed obliged, to apply them reasonably and adjust their application to the circumstances of the case'.[6] However, reasonable application and adjustment is one thing; declining to give a litigant the benefit of a rule with which it has complied is another.

It is true that the Court enjoys great freedom in amending its Rules, and probably could add additional conditions on the application of a particular provision (so long as the requirements of the Statute are respected); but that involves an inter-temporal aspect. Most amendments are only applicable to cases instituted after the entry into force of the amendment; this is now indicated in the printed edition of the Rules by a footnote.[7] All that a litigant can be expected to do is comply with the Rules as they stand at the time.

Article 43 paragraph 1 of the Statute provides that 'The procedure shall consist of two parts: written and oral.'[8] This is normally what happens: the parties are naturally anxious to take every opportunity of convincing the Court of the rightness of their cause. But is it mandatory? The Court has dispensed with oral proceedings

[4] See Ch. 8 sect. B.

[5] Judge Weeramantry: *Application of the Genocide Convention* [1997] ICJ Rep 243; Judge ad hoc Lauterpacht, ibid. Rep 284 para. 18. See the discussion of the point in Thirlway, 'Counterclaims Before the International Court of Justice', 12 *LJIL* (1999), 197–229.

[6] Judge Lauterpacht, see n. 5.

[7] This note, attached to the 1978 Rules, reads: 'Any amendments to the Rules of Court, following their adoption by the Court, are now posted on the Court's website, with an indication of the date of their entry into force and a note of any temporal reservations relating to their applicability (for example, whether the application of the amended rule is limited to cases instituted after the date of entry into force of the amendment); they are also published in the Court's *Yearbook*. Articles amended since 1 July 1978 are marked with an asterisk and appear in their amended form.' This seems to imply that some amended Rules may apply to cases already in progress at the time of the amendment: *sed quaere*.

[8] Contrast Art. 9 of the UNIDROIT Principles of International Civil Procedure, which contemplates a three-stage process, the third being one in which 'evidence not already received by the court . . . should be presented in a concentrated final hearing at which the parties should also make their concluding arguments'.

in advisory cases, but this is consistent with Article 68 of the Statute, whereby the Court in advisory proceedings has merely to 'be guided by the provisions of the present Statute which apply in contentious cases to the extent to which it recognizes them to be applicable'. It is suggested that if the parties to a contentious case were agreed to dispense with oral proceedings, for the Court to go along with this would be no breach of the Statute; but the point is probably academic.

B. Terminology and definitions

Some definition of the vocabulary of judicial procedure, in the ICJ context, may be useful at this point.[9]

(1) The Court and the Bench

'The Court' refers to the International Court of Justice, in particular as seen under two aspects. First, when deciding a case or question in a case before it, it is 'the Court' that speaks, not a group of persons in judicial robes, that is to say it is the judicial body set up by the Charter; but for this purpose it includes any judges ad hoc who may be sitting in the case and taking part in the decision. Hence, assuming for example that no judges are absent or disqualified, and that two judges ad hoc are sitting, the Court is composed of seventeen judges, and the majority for a decision is eight judges—whether elected Members or judges ad hoc.

On the other hand, 'the Court' may refer simply to the body of fifteen elected judges: they are referred to as 'Members of the Court', while judges ad hoc are not. Thus according to Article 32 of the Statute, 'Each Member of the Court shall receive an annual salary', while judges ad hoc 'shall receive compensation for each day on which they exercise their functions'.

'The Bench' on the other hand refers to the body of judges, whether Members or judges ad hoc, composing the judicial body that sits and takes the decision or decisions in a particular case. The 'Bench' includes judges ad hoc, if such have been appointed in the case, but does not include any Member of the Court who is for any reason disqualified from sitting under Article 24 of the Statute, or absent through illness under Article 23. Hence the test for the entitlement of a party to appoint a judge ad hoc is that 'the Court includes upon the Bench a judge of the nationality' of the other party (Art. 31, para. 2), or that it does not include a judge of either nationality (para. 3). If the Court includes a judge of that nationality, but he is disqualified from sitting in the specific case, his continuing Membership of the Court is irrelevant to the operation of the rules relating to judges ad hoc.

When a case is being heard by a Chamber of the Court, formed under Articles 26–9 of the Statute, the 'Bench' is composed of the judges elected or appointed to

[9] For the distinction between 'Judgments' and 'Orders', which is more than merely terminological, see Ch. 10 sect. A.

sit in the Chamber; hence the criterion for appointment of a judge ad hoc to sit in a Chamber is whether the *Chamber* includes a Member of the Court of the other party's nationality, or no Member of either nationality.

(2) Cases and phases

a. In general

A case before the Court is a specific operation of judicial activity, regularly set in motion under the Statute of the Court, and destined to be completed by a final judgment or an advisory opinion—destined to be so completed, but not necessarily reaching that stage. A final judgment will normally be a judgment determining the merits of the claim, but it may also be a judgment declining jurisdiction or declaring the case inadmissible, on the basis of a preliminary objection or otherwise; and a merits judgment may leave the consequences, in particular the measure of compensation, to be determined by a subsequent—final—judgment.[10] Similarly, proceedings on a request for advisory opinion may finally result in the Court declining to express its view on the question submitted, but it appears that the form in which a refusal is given will be, nonetheless, an 'advisory opinion'.[11]

Many cases fall into discreet historical and procedural stages,[12] and these are often known for convenience as 'phases' of a case, a term with no statutory authority, but consecrated (apparently for the first time) in Article 33 of the 1978 Rules of Court.[13] A phase is normally completed by a judicial act, generally a judgment or an order of the Court.

A contentious case may involve, for example, one or more successive requests for the indication of provisional measures, each terminating in an Order indicating or refusing measures (or, of course, the request may be withdrawn); one or more preliminary objections, the decision on which (as a group) will be given by a judgement; or an application by a third State (a State not a party to the case) for permission to intervene in the proceedings (see Arts. 62 and 63 of the Statute), settled by an Order. If compensation is reserved for a separate decision, this also results in a separate 'phase'. Two other possible procedural possibilities are a request by a party to the case for interpretation (Art. 60) or for the revision (Art. 61) of the judgment; but since these requests occur (if at all) after the initial case has been closed

[10] See e.g. *Ahmadou Siado Bello*, judgment of 30 November 2010, [2010] ICJ Rep 639 (merits) and judgment of 19 June 2012, [2012-I] ICJ Rep 324 (compensation).

[11] See the advisory opinion of 8 July 1996 on the request of WHO for an opinion on the legality of nuclear weapons, [1996] ICJ Rep 66, where the Court found that 'it cannot . . . give the opinion requested' (84 para. 31).

[12] And see the special case of an application for revision, where the Statute directs division of the proceedings into two phases (though without using that term): Ch. 16 sect. B.

[13] 'Except as provided in Article 17 of these Rules, Members of the Court who have been replaced, in accordance with Article 13, paragraph 3, of the Statute following the expiration of their terms of office, shall discharge the duty imposed upon them by that paragraph by continuing to sit until the completion of any phase of a case in respect of which the Court convenes for the oral proceedings prior to the date of such replacement.'

by a merits judgment, each is treated as opening a new 'case', and concluded by a judgment.[14] It is also possible for the Court to 'join' two separate cases; they then become for procedural purposes a single case, destined to be completed by a single merits judgment.[15]

The distinctive mark of each 'case' is a distinctive name and a number (chronologically consecutive by date of institution) on the Court's General List. This is not provided for in the Statute, but the Registrar is directed by the Rules of Court to keep such a list.[16] The Permanent Court kept its list in separate series, and included the number in the title of the case (e.g. *Eastern Carelia, PCIJ Series B, No. 5*), but the present Court does not do this: the only place the General List number appears is in the margin of the first page of a judgment. Thus whatever the internal convenience of such a numerical list, it remains all but invisible to those who use the Court.

Every case before the Court has, as in courts generally, to be set in motion by a formal step, taken by the person or entity that wishes to press a claim. In contentious cases, this is either an application or a special agreement. A special agreement is essentially a treaty between two States whereby they agree to submit to the Court a specified dispute; an application resembles rather a writ or summons, as it is presented unilaterally by one State, naming the other State with which it claims to have a dispute, and in effect calling on that State to appear and defend its case.

b. Joint proceedings and joinder of cases

Contentious proceedings before the Court are normally brought by one single State against another single State. It is, however, possible for two or more States to bring proceedings as joint applicants against another State; and, at least in theory, for one State to bring proceedings against two other States jointly. It would probably be necessary in such a case for the same jurisdictional basis to be invoked against each respondent, and in the one case that the two Applicants have the same grounds of complaint against the Respondent, and in the other, that the two Respondents are jointly responsible for the injury complained of.[17]

In the first situation, it has in practice been more frequent for two States to bring independent proceedings against the same respondent; and the Court then has

[14] Revision proceedings fall into two phases, each (in accordance with the Statute) to be closed by a judgment; up to the present only that first phase has ever been gone through. See Statute, Art. 61 para. 2.

[15] See further sect. b. Joinder of two advisory cases, that is, two cases originating from two separate requests for opinion, is a highly unlikely scenario, though conceivably possible.

[16] A 'General List of all cases, entered and numbered in the order in which the documents instituting proceedings or requesting an advisory opinion are received in the Registry' (Rules, Art. 26 (1) (*b*). The Registrar was therefore faced with a pretty problem when New Zealand in 1995 filed its 'Request for an Examination of the Situation': was this a 'document instituting proceedings' or a nullity? (See Ch. 8 sect. A.)

[17] A case brought by one State against another may at a later stage acquire an additional party. Through intervention under Art. 62 of the Statute (see Ch. 15 sect. C).

power, if it sees fit, to 'direct that the proceedings . . . be joined' (Rules, Art. 47).[18] The cases are then heard and determined together, by a single judgment; and the Court may 'direct that the written or oral proceedings . . . be in common'. A joinder of this kind was ordered in the two *South West Africa* cases (*Liberia* v *South Africa*; *Ethiopia* v *South Africa*), and in the two *North Sea Continental Shelf* cases (brought by two special agreements: *Denmark/Federal Republic of Germany*; *Netherlands/ Federal Republic of Germany*). Joinder, however, then became less common: it was not ordered in the two *Fisheries Jurisdiction* cases (*UK* v *Iceland*; *FRG* v *Iceland*), or in the two *Nuclear Tests* cases (*Australia* v *France*; *New Zealand* v *France*). Where cases have been brought in parallel in this way, but no formal joinder has been effected, the Court does, for example, hold hearings in quick succession, deliberate on both cases, and issue several judgments on the same day; and the judgments are often identical in much of their reasoning and construction.

In fact, although it is possible for a State to bring proceedings against two or more States as joint respondents, this has never yet occurred. The legal claim of Nauru against Australia in the case of *Certain Phosphate Lands in Nauru* was in fact asserted also against New Zealand and the United Kingdom, who had constituted, jointly with Australia, the administering authority under a UN Trustee Agreement for Nauru; but Nauru did not choose to bring proceedings against all three States, probably because it was uncertain of being able to establish jurisdiction against the other two. The absence of the other two States was in fact raised by Australia as an objection to the admissibility of the claim, but the Court ruled it admissible.[19] In the two cases concerning the *Lockerbie* incident,[20] and the ten *Use of Force* cases brought by Yugoslavia against the NATO States,[21] the contentions against each respondent in each set of cases were virtually identical as regards the merits, but the applicants (Libya and Yugoslavia) nevertheless chose to bring parallel cases, and the Court did not see fit to join them.[22] Since, particularly in the *Use of Force* cases, the jurisdictional titles relied on against each respondent varied considerably, any other technique would probably have encountered procedural obstacles, at least.

A further possibility is of course that proceedings may be brought by State A against State B, and proceedings also be brought by State B against State A,

[18] Rosenne (*Law and Practice*, iii. 1209) suggests that the Court may even join' two or more cases between different parties', i.e. case 1, *Alpha* v *Beta*, and case 2, *Gamma* v *Delta*, but it seems unlikely that such cases would have enough in common; and there might be problems with the extent of the binding effect of the judgment in the combined case.

[19] *Certain Phosphate Lands in Nauru (Nauru* v *Australia)* [1992] ICJ Rep 240, para. 457.

[20] *Questions of Interpretation and Application of the 1971 Montreal Convention arising from the Aerial Incident at Lockerbie (Libya* v *UK, Libya* v *USA).*

[21] *Legality of Use of Force* (*Yugoslavia* v *Belgium, Yugoslavia* v *Canada, Yugoslavia* v *France, Yugoslavia* v *Germany, Yugoslavia* v *Italy, Yugoslavia* v *Netherlands, Yugoslavia* v *Portugal, Yugoslavia* v *Spain, Yugoslavia* v *UK, Yugoslavia* v *USA*).

[22] Similarly, the Court is currently seised of three cases brought by the Marshall Islands against the UK, Pakistan, and India, each concerning *Cessation of the Nuclear Arms Race.* A controversial question is whether the existence of parallel cases which have not been joined affects the right to appoint a judge ad hoc: see the Joint Declaration of Judges Bedjaoui, Guillaume, and Ranjeva in the *Lockerbie* cases, [1998] ICJ Rep 32ff.; and see Ch. 2 sect. B(2).

and that these two cases be joined, provided of course that they relate to the same, or closely related, matters. This was the case when in 2010 Costa Rica brought proceedings against Nicaragua in the case of *Certain Activities Carried Out by Nicaragua in the Border Area* (on the border with Costa Rica), and the following year Nicaragua brought the case of *Construction of a Road Along the San Juan River*, that river forming the border in the same area as was the scene of the 'certain activities' complained of by Costa Rica. Nicaragua was in favour of having the cases joined, and made a request to that effect; Costa Rica opposed a joinder. The Court noted that Article 47 of the Rules, concerning joinder, left it 'a broad margin of discretion'; and that previous exercise of the power to join had been 'in circumstances where joinder was consonant not only with the principle of the sound administration of justice'—a rather slippery criterion[23]—'but also with the need for judicial economy'.[24] It noted that the two cases 'involve the same Parties and relate to the area where the common border between them runs along the right bank of the San Juan River', were both based on facts concerning works being carried out there, and concerned the impact of these on the environment; and both involved allegations of the same treaty provisions. The Court concluded that 'hearing and deciding the two cases together will have significant advantages', since this would 'allow the Court to address simultaneously the totality of the various interrelated and contested issues raised by the Parties, including any questions of fact or law that are common to the disputes presented'.[25] It countered an argument of Costa Rica by confidently asserting that it did not expect 'any undue delay' in giving its judgment.[26]

In the light of, in particular, these dicta in the *Costa Rica/Nicaragua* cases, it might be thought that the consequences of joinder or non-joinder are limited to matters of practical convenience: number and organization of hearings, one judgment or more, etc. There is, however, one more substantial implication of a joinder: it may well affect the composition of the Court, and this could of course affect the outcome, particularly if the Court were narrowly divided on some issue. Theoretically, a judge might be disqualified from sitting, under Article 17 of the Statute, in one of the two cases but not in the other, though in view of the relationship between the cases that would be required to justify joinder, this might seem unlikely.[27]

A particularly significant impact of a joinder may be on the question of appointment of judges ad hoc. Article 31 paragraph 5 of the Statute provides that, for the purposes of entitlement to appoint a judge ad hoc, '[s]hould there be several parties in the same interest, they shall . . . be reckoned as one party only,' that is, they may appoint, jointly, only one judge ad hoc. If two cases are joined, a party to one of

[23] Commented on by Judge Cançado Trindade in a lengthy opinion attached to the Order, which does not, however, seem to elucidate the term further: [2013] ICJ Rep 193–5 paras. 13–18.

[24] Order of 17 April 2013, [2013] ICJ Rep 184, 187 para. 12, citing the PCIJ case of the *Legal Status of the South-Eastern Territory of Greenland* and the *North Sea Continental Shelf* cases.

[25] Order of 17 April 2013, [2013] ICJ Rep 184, 187 para. 17.

[26] Order of 17 April 2013, [2013] ICJ Rep 184, 187–8 para. 18.

[27] Nevertheless it has occurred in the case of a judge ad hoc: see the resignation of judge ad hoc Simma in *Construction of a Road in Costa Rica*, in consequence of the joinder of that case with the *Certain Activities carried out by Nicaragua* case: Order of 18 April 2013, [2013] ICJ Rep 200, 202 para. 8.

them may find itself, in that context, 'in the same interest' as a State that was a party to the other case. Thus, as a result of the joinder of the two *South West Africa* cases, Ethiopia and Liberia were able to appoint only a single judge ad hoc. Had the cases continued separately, there would have been a vote by the Ethiopian judge ad hoc in the one case, and by the Liberian judge in the other, but as the cases were separate, these votes would not have been cumulative. Following the joinder of the two *North Sea Continental Shelf* cases, a single judge ad hoc was appointed jointly by Denmark and the Netherlands. The further complications concerning entitlement to appoint a judge ad hoc have been discussed in Chapter 2.

It is not clear whether a joinder of cases normally requires the consent of the parties to the two cases, or whether it falls within the procedural powers of the Court 'for the good administration of justice' (see Ch. 5 sect. D). In the *Fisheries Jurisdiction* cases, the parties (including Iceland, the non-appearing party) were consulted, and the applicants were not willing to see the cases joined. The Court decided (by 9 votes to 5) not to effect a joinder; in its judgment it notes that it had taken into account 'the fact that while the basic legal issues in each case appeared to be identical, there were differences between the positions of the two Applicants, and between their respective submissions, and that joinder would be contrary to the wishes of the two Applicants'.[28] This suggests that the mere opposition of the applicants (and the lack of stated consent on the part of the absent respondent) was not regarded as in itself sufficient to exclude joinder.[29]

Article 47 also recognizes that procedural convenience may call for common action in relation to two or more cases even if they have not been formally joined: the Court 'may also direct that the written or oral proceedings, including the calling of witnesses, be in common; or . . . without effecting any formal joinder, direct common action in any of these respects'. In the *Lockerbie* cases, for example, at the provisional measures stage a single set of oral proceedings was directed to both cases, the arrangements being adopted '[f]or reasons of convenience, and after consultations with the Governments concerned.'[30] Similarly, in the complicated circumstances of the *Use of Force* cases, oral proceedings to be held 'in common' on preliminary objections were directed by the Court '[a]fter consulting the Governments concerned'.[31]

It is presumably open to the Court to consider that a case brought against two or more Respondents does not really involve an identical claim against each of them, and direct that there be two separate cases; but this has not yet occurred, and there is no provision for it in the Statute and Rules.

[28] *Fisheries Jurisdiction (UK* v *Iceland)*, [1974] ICJ Rep 3, 6 para. 8; *Fisheries Jurisdiction (FRG* v *Iceland)* [1974] ICJ Rep 175, 177 para. 8.

[29] In the *Use of Force* cases the parties were simply informed, shortly before the oral proceedings on the preliminary objections, 'that the Court had decided that the proceedings should not be joined', without indication of reasons: CR 2004/6, 19 April 2004, 6. The respondent States had informed the Court that in their view they 'were not in the same interest', for purposes of Art. 31 para. 5, of the Statute (judges ad hoc): on this aspect see Ch. 2 sect. B(2).

[30] CR 92/2, 26 March 1992, 15.

[31] CR 2004/6, 19 April 2004, 6.

The question whether two advisory cases could be joined has never arisen, and may seem very unlikely to arise. Some identical issues were raised in the two cases concerning nuclear weapons,[32] but the overriding question of the competence of the WHO to make its request required separate treatment—and proved fatal to that request.

3. Parties

a. *In general*

'Only States may be parties in cases before the Court' (Statute, Art. 34 para. 1). The question of what is, and what is not, a State does not usually arise, however, as access is also limited to parties to the Statute, or States qualifying under Security Council resolution 9/1946, so that non-States are already filtered out.[33] It is possible for international organizations, and even individuals, to become involved in a case before the Court, but they cannot be 'parties'; and it is also possible for a State to be involved in a case in a capacity other than that of 'party', through intervention, for example. The most straightforward situation, where there are only two parties before the Court, is that of a case being brought by one State (the Applicant) against one other State (the Respondent). The status of 'party' signifies entitlement to ask the Court to decide in favour of a claim asserted against the other 'party', or, in the case of a Respondent party, to ask the Court to reject such a claim.

A case before the Court may be entirely concerned with a wrong done to an individual; but it is of course the individual's national State that invokes the international responsibility of the State author of the act or acts complained of.[34] Where the case raises issues of human rights, again the treatment of individuals may well be at the heart of the claims, but they still do not have standing before the Court.[35]

Occasionally problems arise in the identification of a party after a case has begun, for example where there has been a splitting up of a State into two or more independent States (or indeed the joining of two States into one). This occurred notably in the two cases concerning *Application of the Genocide Convention*, brought against Serbia (at times known as Yugoslavia) by Bosnia-Herzegovina and by Croatia. After

[32] *Legality of the Use by a State of Nuclear Weapons in Armed Conflict* [1996-I] ICJ Rep 66; *Legality of the Threat or Use of Nuclear Weapons* [1996-I] ICJ Rep 226.

[33] In advisory proceedings (see Ch. 9), Kosovo and Palestine have made their voices heard; and these entities have also taken steps to gain access to arbitrations under the auspices of the Permanent Court of Arbitration: see G. Zyberi, 'Membership in International Treaties of Contested States: The Case of the Permanent Court of Arbitration', *ESIL Reflections* 5:3 (2016).

[34] The Court has also recently reaffirmed the doctrine of the *Barcelona Traction* case [1964] ICJ Rep 6, distinguishing a wrong done to a corporation of private law (limited company) from a wrong done to the individuals owning and directing the corporation, so that only the corporation's national State may make an international claim: *Ahmadou Sadio Diallo* [2010-II] ICJ Rep 674ff.

[35] For a useful account of cases in which the Court has to some extent taken such interests into account when indicating provisional measures, see the separate opinion of Judge Cançado Trindade appended to the Order of 16 July 2013 in the two joined *Costa Rica/Nicaragua* cases, [2013] ICJ Rep 230, 242 paras. 44–8.

the Court had given judgment dismissing preliminary objections in the first of these cases,[36] and while the second case was still in progress, Montenegro, which had up till then formed part of Serbia, declared its independence; Serbia continued its membership in the United Nations, and Montenegro was subsequently admitted as a member.[37] The Court, through the Registrar, invited the States parties to the two cases (Bosnia, Croatia, Serbia, and Montenegro) to indicate their views 'as to the consequences' of these 'developments'.[38]

In the light of the views indicated, the Court ruled, in each of the two cases, that the events described 'clearly show that the Republic of Montenegro does not continue the legal personality of Serbia and Montenegro; it cannot therefore have acquired, on that basis, the status of Respondent in the present case'; and that from Montenegro's reaction to the Registrar's enquiry, it was clear 'that it does not give its consent to the jurisdiction of the Court over it for the purposes of the present dispute'.[39]

An important principle is that of the equality of the parties, which 'must be preserved when they are involved, pursuant to Article 2, paragraph 3, of the [UN] Charter, in the process of settling an international dispute by peaceful means', and the relevant specific rights 'might be derived from the principle of the sovereign equality of States ... reflected in Article 2, paragraph 1, of the Charter'.[40] The principle of the equality of the parties arises in an acute form with regard to access to the Court, in the context of the Court's involvement in the appeal processes for international officials[41] (see Ch. 9 sect. A(4)).

The parties are the two or more States that are conducting the proceedings, and that will be bound by the decision of the Court; it is their dispute that is the focus of the proceedings.[42] They are not necessarily the only parties *to the dispute*, since other States equally involved may choose not to come to court, or may be beyond the reach of jurisdiction.[43] A State becomes a party to a case either by its own choice—by instituting proceedings against another State—or because another State has instituted proceedings against it. Whether these proceedings have a sound jurisdictional basis is immaterial: the State is and remains a party until the case is terminated.[44] The Court cannot impose the status of party on a State, for example

[36] Preliminary objections: [1996-I] ICJ Rep 595; merits: [2007] ICJ Rep 43.

[37] [2008] ICJ Rep 412, 421 paras. 23–5.

[38] [2008] ICJ Rep 412, 421–2, para. 26.

[39] Bosnia case: [2007-I] ICJ Rep 43, 76 para. 76; Croatia case: [2008] ICJ Rep 409, 423 para. 33.

[40] *Seizure and Detention of Certain Documents*, Order of 3 March 2014, [2014] ICJ Rep para. 27.

[41] See e.g. the Court's observations in *Judgment No. 2867 of the ILO Administrative Tribunal* [2012-I] ICJ Rep 10, 25ff., paras. 34ff., particularly para. 39.

[42] And in the past the Court generally arranged its procedure in accordance with their wishes, but this has given way to a more directive approach: R. Higgins, 'Respecting Sovereign States and Running a Tight Courtroom', 50 *ICLQ* (2001), 123, 131.

[43] See e.g. *Certain Phosphate Lands in Nauru* [1992] ICJ Rep 240, where Nauru's claim was against the three States that had administered the territory under UN Trusteeship, but the proceedings were brought only against Australia (probably because it was only against Australia that jurisdiction could be established).

[44] But note the accelerated disposal of two of the *Use of Force* cases, in which no realistic title of jurisdiction was even alleged: *Legality of the Use of Force (Yugoslavia* v *Spain) (Yugoslavia* v *US)* [1999-II] ICJ Rep 763, 916.

by joining it as a party to existing proceedings.[45] In advisory proceedings there are no 'parties', though there are entities that may look rather like them (see Ch. 9 sect. A(1)).

The channel of communication with the Court is the Agent appointed by each party (Statute, Art. 42 para. 1), a system that normally functions smoothly.[46]

b. International organizations

While it is only States that may be parties to cases before the Court, the Statute does take account of the possible interest of public international organizations in the proceedings. Article 34 of the Statute provides for such an organization to 'supply information', being 'information relevant to' a case before the Court, either at the request of the Court,[47] or on the organization's own initiative. Such organizations are not, however, automatically notified of the bringing of a new case, as are the Members of the United Nations and 'any other States entitled to appear before the Court', under Article 40 of the Statute; but an organization is entitled to be notified whenever 'the construction' of its 'constituent instrument ... or of an international convention adoption thereunder is in question in a case' (Art. 34 para. 3).

The position of an organization in these circumstances has been likened to that of an *amicus curiae*;[48] but the parallel is perhaps inexact. It is generally accepted that an *amicus curiae*, in jurisdictions where the concept exists, may (and frequently does) argue for a particular view of the law;[49] but the term 'supply information' would seem to have been intended to exclude any participating organization from arguing the case.[50]

Unlike (for example) the European Court of Justice and the European Court of Human Rights, the ICJ does not recognize the formal participation of NGOs in proceedings before it. However, in advisory proceedings only, under Practice Direction XII, adopted in 2004, written statements and documents submitted by NGOs may be treated as 'publications readily available' (see Ch. 9 sect. A(3)) and

[45] *Land, Island and Maritime Frontier Dispute, Application of Nicaragua to Intervene*, [1990] ICJ Rep 92, 135 para. 99.

[46] For exceptions see *Application of the Genocide Convention (Bosnia* v *Serbia)*, [2007-I] ICJ Rep 43, 52–4 paras. 18–24, and *Certain Questions concerning Diplomatic Relations*, [2010-I] ICJ Rep 303–4.

[47] The Court may decide to receive such information even over the objection of one party: see *Aerial Incident of 3 July 1988, Pleadings*, 639–45, and *Order of 22 February 1996*, [1996-I] ICJ Rep 9.

[48] I. Scobbie, '"All Right, Mr. de Mille, I'm ready for my close-up": Some Critical Reflections on Professor Cassese's "The International Court of Justice: It Is High Time to Restyle the Respected Old Lady"', 23 *EJIL* (2012) 1071, 1084–6.

[49] See e.g. the definition of 'Amicus Curiae Submissions' in Art. 13 of the UNIDROIT Principles of International Civil Procedure. Before the ICJ, a State intervening as a non-party is perhaps in a position closer to that of an *amicus curiae*: see Ch. 15 sect. C.

[50] In the only case in which an organization has taken action under these texts (*Aerial Incident of 3 July 1988)*, the document supplied amounted to no more than an indication of what procedure had been followed within the organization in relation to the matter subsequently brought to the Court: see the Observations of ICAO, *Pleadings*, 617–27.

referred to as such; and for convenience they are placed in a 'designated location in the Peace Palace'.

c. The non-appearing party

In the procedure of the International Court, there is no formal step that might be compared to that of 'entering an appearance' in the courts of the UK, and comparable acts in other jurisdictions. The normal reaction by a respondent State to the notification to it, under Article 38 paragraph 4 of the Rules of Court, that an application has been made instituting proceedings against it, is, however, to appoint an agent to represent it, as required by Article 42 of the Statute. Even if such an appointment is made, the State may yet decide, at any stage, not to participate in the case, and to let it go by default; it is this that is commonly referred to as non-appearance. Article 53 of the Statute does make a distinction, referring to the situation in which 'one of the parties does not appear before the Court' and that in which it 'fails to defend its case', but 'appear' is not defined, and the distinction is of no practical importance. Even a State that decides from the outset to boycott the proceedings normally addresses a communication to the Court to that effect.[51]

If mere non-participation by the respondent sufficed to prevent the Court from proceeding, the whole point of pre-accepted jurisdiction would be lost; thus from the outset the Statute of the Permanent Court contained Article 53, carried over into the Statute of the present Court, enabling the other party in such circumstances 'to decide in favour of its claim'. The Court is authorized to make such a decision, provided that 'before doing so' it 'satisf[ies] itself not only that it has jurisdiction in accordance with Articles 36 and 37 [of the Statute], but also that the claim is well founded in fact and law'.

The institution of proceedings involves, for the Applicant, acquiring voluntarily the status of party, and for the Respondent, acquiring that status involuntarily. States named as Respondents have sometimes asserted that they are not thereby made 'parties' (particularly when they maintain that there is no title of jurisdiction). This is not correct: the proceedings have been regularly begun, and are entered on the Court's General List,[52] with a title indicating the names of the parties; and the 'State which has chosen not to appear remains a party to the case'.[53] It is kept informed of the case, and invited at every stage to exercise its rights as a party.

[51] See e.g. the *Nuclear Tests* cases, in which the French Government addressed a letter to the Court, announcing that it would not appoint an agent, and asking for the case to be struck off the list, but enclosing a lengthy and argumentative Annex: *Pleadings*, ii. 347–57, no. 27.

[52] See Rules of Court, Art. 26 para. 1 (*b*). See, however, the special procedure under Art. 38 para. 5 of the Rules, described in the previous section; while a case of this kind is 'in limbo', as it were, under this provision, is the reluctant State a 'party'? That text carefully refers to it as 'the State against which such application is made', not as 'the Respondent' or 'the respondent party'; but if the procedure has been followed that is provided for in the Statute to cause a State to become a 'party', can this result be averted by a provision in the Rules? Fortunately the point seems to be academic.

[53] *Military and Paramilitary Activities in and against Nicaragua*, [1986] ICJ Rep 24 para. 28.

In 1986, the Court restated '[c]ertain points of principle' in connection with the procedure under Article 53.

A State which decides not to appear must accept the consequences of its decision . . . [it] remains a party to the case and is bound by the eventual judgment. . . . The use of the term 'satisfy itself' in the English text of the Statute . . . implies that the Court must attain the same degree of certainty as in any other case that the claim of the party appearing is sound in law, and, so far as the nature of the case permits, that the facts on which it is based are supported by convincing evidence.[54]

This was in the *Military and Paramilitary Activities* case, in which the United States, having failed to convince the Court on its objections, chose to make no further appearance.

Article 53 of the Statute has proved its effectiveness, in the sense that its application in the *Fisheries Jurisdiction* and *Nuclear Tests* cases in the 1970s demonstrated that there was little or nothing to be gained by a refusal to appear, and the State that did so would have less opportunity to plead its cause and refute the arguments of its opponent, even if the Court took account—as it was bound to do—of informal communications. Whatever the political or 'public relations' advantages of this course, it became apparent that there was nothing legally to be gained, and possibly much potentially lost, by non-appearance, and as a tactic it has since fallen out of favour.[55]

C. Submissions and the rule *ne ultra petita*

The submissions of a party are usually set out as a distinct part of a pleading or speech: they are the formal statement of precisely what it is that the party is asking the Court to decide. According to the general principle of law known as *ne ultra petita* ('not beyond what is asked for'), a court may not go beyond the submissions of the parties and decide something that they have not asked it to decide. The limits of the Court's task are thus set by the claim and the response to it, as contained in the submissions, though it may of course deal with a point not specifically raised if it is necessary to do so in order to decide an issue that has been raised—provided that the point falls within the scope of the jurisdictional instrument on which the case is based.[56] Nor does it have to deal with all the matters raised in the submissions

[54] *Military and Paramilitary Activities in and against Nicaragua*, [1986] ICJ Rep 24 para. 28.

[55] The last case of a complete withdrawal was *Military and Paramilitary Activities in and against Nicaragua*, where the United States, having failed to convince the Court that it lacked jurisdiction, took no further part in the proceedings: see [1986] ICJ Rep 23–6 paras. 26–31. Colombia had a similar reaction to the judgments in *Delimitation of the Continental Shelf between Colombia and Nicaragua beyond 200 miles* and *Alleged Violations of Sovereign Rights and Maritime Spaces in the Caribbean Sea*: see Colombian Press Release, 19 November 2012, cited in S. Yee, 'Article 38 of the Statute and Applicable Law', *ICJ 70th Anniversary Seminar*, to be published shortly in *JIDS*. For the earlier cases, and generally, see Thirlway, *Non-Appearance before the International Court of Justice* (Cambridge: Cambridge University Press, 1985).

[56] The relationship between jurisdiction and the *ne ultra petita* rule is, in a sense, that of the greater to the lesser. A treaty, let us say, confers on the Court jurisdiction to interpret its provisions. A case is

if the decision on one of them disposes of the case; and among a number of possible issues, the Court has 'freedom to select the ground upon which it will base its judgment'.[57]

It has been suggested that the Court might go outside the submissions also if the issues submitted to the Court involve the application of a peremptory norm, a matter of *jus cogens*.[58] The essential characteristic of rules of this kind is that they cannot be contracted out of; and if applicant and respondent were to agree in not recognizing the rule (or in not recognizing its peremptory character), the Court should, it is suggested, refuse to allow itself to be used to enforce a claim that contravenes the rule;[59] but the suggestion, which has been judicially contradicted,[60] is not very convincing.

In some past cases, the parties have, by their submissions, limited the Court's field of enquiry to an extent that some judges or commentators have considered impermissible, but which was accepted by the majority of the Court.[61]

D. Costs and financial support

The International Court does not charge any court fees or costs to UN Member States using it: its expenses are covered entirely by the contributions made by Member States to the budget of the Organization, of which the Court's budget forms part. There were formerly, and theoretically still are, two other groups of States that have access to the Court: Article 35 paragraph 2 of the Statute provides that 'the conditions under which the Court shall be open to other [i.e. non-Member] States shall . . . be laid down by the Security Council'. States may become

brought on this basis, and the submissions ask for an interpretation of Article 10 of the Treaty. The Court can only *decide* the interpretation of Article 10, even though it may discuss, in its reasoning, the meaning of other Articles.

[57] *Application of the Convention of 1902 Governing the Guardianship of Infants*, [1958] ICJ Rep 62, cited in *Oil Platforms*, [2003] ICJ Rep 161, 180 para. 37.

[58] By A. Orakhlashvili, *Peremptory Norms in International Law* (Oxford: Oxford University Press, 2006), 492ff. For the significance of peremptory norms, see Ch. 3 sect. D.

[59] And even that the Court therefore should always check whether there are any such rules that might impinge on its decision: Orakhlashvili (see n. 58), with reference to the considerations of environmental law in the *Gabčíkovo/Nagymaros* case. He reads the decision in the *Oil Platforms* case [2003] ICJ Rep 161 as applying the *jus cogens* rule on the use of force to override the US/Iran treaty, but the text does not seem to support this: the Court refused to enforce the US security exception (Article XX, paragraph 1 *(d)* of the treaty), not because a peremptory norm (barring unlawful use of force) overrode it, but because the article was interpreted as itself intended to be subject to general law on the unlawful use of force: [2003] ICJ Rep 182 para. 41.

[60] Judge Buergenthal in his separate opinion in the *Oil Platforms* case, [2003] ICJ Rep 270, 279 para. 23.

[61] See e.g. the *Oscar Chinn* case: the PCIJ ruled on a dispute arising under the bilateral Treaty of Saint-Germain, which, it was suggested, amounted to a bilateral modification of the regime of the multilateral Treaty of Berlin, which could only be modified by general accord of the parties. See in particular the dissenting opinions of Judges van Eysinga, *PCIJ Series A/B, No. 63*, 131, 136, and Schücking, ibid. 148–50. Cf. also *Land and Maritime Boundary between Cameroon and Nigeria*, [2002] ICJ Rep 303, 400 paras. 194–5.

parties to the Statute without becoming Members of the Organization (Art. 93 of the Charter); and other States, not parties either to the Charter or to the Statute of the Court, may also have access by virtue of Article 35 paragraph 2 of the Statute and Security Resolution 9 (1946). The conditions of access are determined by the General Assembly on the recommendation of the Security Council; if the State is not already 'bearing a share of the expenses of the Court', as it will be if it is a party to the Statute, then an appropriate contribution to the expenses of the Court is to be fixed by the Court on each occasion.[62]

International litigation is nevertheless expensive, involving fees to counsel and advisers, translation and printing costs, etc., and for smaller States with limited resources this is a greater burden than for their larger and more affluent neighbours. To go some way to meet this problem, in 1989 the UN Secretary-General set up a Trust Fund, to provide assistance where needed to enable a State to have access to the Court for resolving the dispute.[63] The Court has power under Article 64 of the Statute to make an order for costs, but to date it has never done so. In one case in which a party had committed breaches of an order indicating provisional measures, and had acted in such a way that the other party was obliged to come back to the Court for a further order, some judges indicated that in their view the Court should have made an order for costs against the peccant party.[64]

Even more unbalanced is the position when the proceedings before the Court involve an individual's search for justice. This is not so much a problem in cases such as *Ahmadou Siado Diallo*, where it is the national State of the individual that is exercising diplomatic protection, presumably at its own expense. But in the cases involving appeals from administrative tribunals, the individual appellant, though not entitled to be a party before the Court, is very much involved, and the employment of counsel, with the attendant expense, is unavoidable. This was a matter of concern to Judge Greenwood in the case of *Judgment No. 2867 of the ILO Administrative Tribunal*; in a declaration appended to the advisory opinion, he pointed out that 'In substance ... if not in form, the proceedings before the Court are proceedings between the Organization requesting the Opinion and the staff member' since 'the Court's opinion will determine whether or not the staff member continues to be entitled to the compensation awarded to her'. He considered that the staff member could have asked the Court to make an order for costs under Article 64 of the Statute (as applied in advisory proceedings by virtue of Art. 68), and he would have directed that IFAD pay at least part of her costs.[65]

[62] The only example appears to be that of the Federal Republic of Germany when it was a party to the *North Sea Continental Shelf* case in 1969.

[63] For an account of this, and comparison with the similar fund set up later to provide assistance in cases before ITLOS, see D. Anderson, 'Trust Funds in International Litigation', in N. Ando et al. (eds.), *Liber Amicorum Judge Shigeru Oda* (Kluwer: Springer, 2002), ii. 799.

[64] *Certain Activities Carried Out by Nicaragua in the Border Area (Costa Rica* v *Nicaragua)*, Judgment of 16 December 2015, Joint Declaration of Judges Tomka, Greenwood, and Sebutinde and Judge ad hoc Dugard; see Ch. 13 sect. D.

[65] *Judgment No. 2867 of the ILO Administrative Tribunal*, Declaration of Judge Greenwood, [2012-I] ICJ Rep 94, 95–6.

8

The Procedure in a Contentious Case

A. Institution of proceedings

The proceedings in contentious cases are set in motion in one of two ways. If the parties have concluded an agreement (*compromis* or special agreement) to bring the dispute before the Court, the case begins with the notification of this to the Court. If not, one State may file an application instituting proceedings against another State, and the Registrar communicates this to the State so named.[1]

Article 39 of the Statute of the Court provides that 'The official languages of the Court shall be French and English', but continues with provision for authorization by the Court for another language to be used 'at the request of any party' (para. 3).[2] A formal problem with reliance on this text to justify *instituting* proceedings in another language is that, until the proceedings have been instituted, there is no 'party' to make the request; the almost universal employment of counsel or advisers speaking one or both languages, however, means that the problem is no more than theoretical.

Whether the case is instituted by a special agreement or by application, all other States entitled to appear before the Court are notified; the primary purpose of this is to enable each State to be aware of the existence and nature of the proceedings, in case these are such that it might wish to intervene.[3] Thus it is not only for the Court's benefit that Article 40 paragraph 1 of the Statute states that, whether the case is brought by application or by notification of a special agreement, 'the subject of the dispute and the parties shall be indicated'. This requirement is elaborated in the Rules of Court: Article 38 provides that an application is to 'specify as far as possible the legal grounds upon which the jurisdiction of the Court is said to be based; it shall also specify the precise nature of the claim, together with a succinct

[1] See Part III, Sect. C subsect. 1 of the Rules of Court (Arts. 38–43).

[2] See Ch. 1 sect. A. This power has been used almost exclusively for the oral proceedings, so that counsel may be employed who are not anglo- or francophone: cf. the case of *Barcelona Traction, Light and Power Co.*, where Spanish was extensively used, for this reason, and for reasons of linguistic prestige.

[3] Rules, Art. 42, and see Ch. 15. If the case appears to involve the interpretation of a convention, Arts. 63 and 43 of the Rules of the Statute provide that any other States party to it are to be specially notified, as they may be entitled to intervene in the proceedings under that Article. In the case of the UN Charter, this notification has been ruled otiose, in view of the notification of the institution of proceedings under Art. 40 para. 3. See Schwebel, dissenting opinion, *Military and Paramilitary Activities in and against Nicaragua*, Order of 4 October 1984, [1984] ICJ Rep 223, 233–4.

statement of the facts and grounds on which the claim is based. There is no parallel requirement when the case is brought by special agreement, since the agreement itself constitutes the basis of jurisdiction, and will also define the claim. The words 'as far as possible' will be noted; the Statute contains no requirement that a title of jurisdiction be specified at the outset, and it may be doubted whether the Court, in the exercise of its rule-making power, may impose an absolute requirement which is not provided for in the Statute. Thus the possibility of *forum prorogatum* (as discussed in Ch. 5 sect. A(3)) is left open; and it does not appear that a State named as Respondent could argue for the nullity of the application by endeavouring to demonstrate that it would have been perfectly 'possible' for the Applicant to give details of jurisdiction at that stage. In practice, a ground of jurisdiction is usually specified, but one or more other grounds may well be added later,[4] and may prove to be more substantial, or may be chosen by the Court as basis for its competence in preference to the original ground advanced.

Mention has already been made of the exceptional case of the *Request for an Examination of the Situation* submitted by New Zealand in 1995.[5] In its judgment against France in the *Nuclear Tests* cases in 1974, the Court had noted that France had agreed to cease the testing activity complained of, but that the treaty forming the basis of jurisdiction there relied on had been denounced during the proceedings. It therefore indicated that 'if the basis of the Judgment were to be affected' (i.e. if France went back on its commitment to cease testing), 'the Applicant could request an examination of the situation' and the denunciation of the treaty would be no bar to this.[6] When France resumed testing (though underground) New Zealand therefore endeavoured to reopen the matter by submitting a 'Request for the Examination of the Situation'; this was however, despite the title, an application instituting proceedings. Yet the Court in effect found that there was no case before it, rather than that there was no jurisdictional basis.[7]

Where there is a shared will to achieve a settlement of a legal dispute, the possibility contemplated by Article 38 paragraph 5 of the Rules, of beginning proceedings with an invitation to accept jurisdiction, may be valuable, as explained in Chapter 5 section A(3), on the basis of the doctrine of *forum prorogatum*. In the case of *Certain Questions of Mutual Assistance in Criminal Matters*, for example, Djibouti brought proceedings on this basis against France, and France agreed to accept jurisdiction, and defended the case.[8]

[4] Provided this is not left so late in the proceedings that the Respondent does not have a proper opportunity to contest the existence of such jurisdiction: cf. *Use of Force (Yugoslavia* v *Belgium)* [1999-I] ICJ Rep 124, 139 para. 44. Note also that the Court may decline to consider an added title of jurisdiction, either for the merits or for the purpose of provisional measures proceedings: *Application of the Genocide Convention (Bosnia* v *Yugoslavia)* [1996-II] ICJ Rep 621 para. 41; *Use of Force (Yugoslavia* v *Belgium)* ibid.

[5] Ch. 4 sect. A, text and n. 6.

[6] [1974] ICJ Rep 457, 477 para. 63. See the discussion in Thirlway, *Law and Procedure*, ii. 1764–5.

[7] *Request for an Examination of the Situation in Accordance with Paragraph 63 of the Court's Judgment of 20 December 1994 in the* Nuclear Tests (New Zealand *v* France) *Case*, [1995] ICJ Rep 288.

[8] Judgment of 4 June 2008, [2008] ICJ Rep 177.

The Statute and Rules contain no provision for an application, once filed, to be amended; but it appears that this is possible, subject the right of the respondent to object.[9]

When proceedings are instituted by notification to the Court of a special agreement, the agreement itself will necessarily indicate the parties to the dispute, and will afford the necessary jurisdiction; it will usually specify very precisely the subject of the dispute, but *ex abundante cautela* the Rules (Art. 39 para. 2) specify that '[t]he notification [to the Court of the special agreement] shall also, in so far as this is not already apparent from the agreement, indicate the precise subject of the dispute and identify the parties to it.'

The Statute does not indicate what should be the contents of an application, or indeed of a special agreement, but Article 38 paragraph 2 of the Rules of Court states that: 'The application shall specify as far as possible the legal grounds upon which the jurisdiction of the Court is said to be based; it shall also specify the precise nature of the claim, together with a succinct statement of the facts and grounds on which the claim is based.' Where the applicant is relying on a future consent to jurisdiction, by way of *forum prorogatum*, this will of course replace the indication of an existing basis of jurisdiction. The specification of the claim is essential, although it will be elaborated subsequently in the formal submissions of the applicant.[10]

The Statute and Rules do not specify the precise action to be taken by the State named as respondent on receipt of the application; but Article 42 of the Statute (and Art. 40 para. 1 of the Rules) requires that all procedural steps be taken by the parties be taken by agents, so that a first step is the appointment of an agent. At one time States reluctant to see a particular matter litigated tried simply to boycott the proceedings; they refused to appoint an agent, or to co-operate in any way. However, Article 53 of the Statute enables the Court to decide in favour of the claim in the respondent's absence, provided that it is satisfied on jurisdiction and that the claim is 'well founded in fact and law'. Non-appearance thus proved to be ineffective, and often unwise.[11]

[9] *Land and Maritime Boundary beteween Cameroon and Nigeria*, Order of 16 June 1994, [1994] ICJ Rep 105, 106; and see E. Lauterpacht, '"Partial" Judgments and the Inherent Jurisdiction of the International Court of Justice', in V. Lowe and M. Fitzmaurice (eds.), *Fifty Years of the International Court of Justice (Jennings Festschrift)* (Cambridge: Cambridge University Press, 1996), 465, 475–6. Art. 52 para. 3 of the Rules provides for the correction of 'a slip or error in any document filed', but in context this appears to refer only to pleadings and annexes thereto, not to an application or special agreement.

[10] See Section C below.

[11] See Thirlway, *Non-Appearance before the International Court of Justice* (Cambridge: Cambridge University Press, 1985), and the cases there discussed; Alessandra Zanobetti, *La non comparazione davanti alla Corte internazionale di giustizia* (Bologna: Guiffrè, 1996). The same policy is currently that of China before an arbitration tribunal established under ITLOS, with, it seems, similar lack of success: see PCA Case No. 2013-19, *Republic of the Philippines* v *Republic of China*, citing ITLOS, Annex VII, Art. 9.

B. The written proceedings

The procedure before the Court represents something of a blend of, on the one hand, the Continental system of extensive written pleadings, and on the other the Anglo-American common law system in which the pleadings are confined to fairly formal statements of the issues and the parties' contentions on each, and the hearing, the 'day in court', is the essential element. Article 43 paragraph 2 of the Statute provides that 'The written proceedings shall consist of the communication to the Court and to the parties of memorials, counter-memorials and, if necessary replies; also all papers and documents in support.' An essential principle is here unobtrusively stated; that everything that one party communicates to the Court in connection with the case must be communicated to the other party. In the case of pleadings, in the technical sense, a certified copy of the pleading destined for the other party must be supplied to the Registry at the time of the deposit of the original pleading, and is then transmitted by the Registrar to that party.[12] When one party addresses a letter to the Court, for example in connection with some pending question of procedure, the Registrar forwards a copy to the other party; in practice the letter will quite often already have been copied to the other party by its author.

Article 43 of the Statute is supplemented by Articles 44–53 of the Rules of Court. The present work is not intended as a guide to the conduct of a case, so only a few salient points will be noted here.

The parties exchange written pleadings, within time-limits fixed by the Court (Memorial by the applicant, Counter-Memorial by the respondent). Sometimes, particularly in special agreement cases, the same time-limit is fixed for the pleading of each party, and these may thus be exchanged simultaneously. However, the more common practice is for the dates fixed to follow each other, so that (e.g.) the respondent when preparing its Counter-Memorial knows what are the allegations and arguments it has to answer. Pleadings are always in English or French; under Article 39 paragraph 3 of the Statute, a party might be authorized to file a pleading in another language, but if so, it would have to provide a translation into an official language, so it is generally simpler to file the translation as the pleading, thus needing no special authorization.

While only States may be parties to cases, under Article 34 of the Statute public international organizations may be requested by the Court to supply 'information relevant to' a case, or may present such information 'on their own initiative'. For this purpose, '[w]henever the construction of the constituent instrument of a public international organization or of an international convention adopted thereunder is in question in a case', the organization is to be notified by the Registrar, and supplied with copies of the written proceedings. The procedure for this is specified in Article 43 of the Rules (which was amended in 2005 to be more specific).

12 Rules, Art. 52 (1).

A question that has arisen on a number of occasions relates to the principle that the respondent must be informed of the exact claims of the applicant, and have the opportunity to respond to them; this signifies that, while the applicant may not be able to spell out its allegations fully and precisely at the very outset, it cannot keep supplementing and adding to the claims already presented without injustice to the respondent. The Court's jurisprudence was summarized and applied in its 2010 judgment in the *Ahmadou Sadio Diallo* case. The Court there cited Article 40 paragraph 1 of the Statute and Articles 38 paragraph 2 and 49 paragraph 1 of the Rules, and indicated that '[f]rom these provisions, the Court has concluded that additional claims formulated in the course of proceedings are inadmissible if they would result, were they to be entertained, in transforming "the subject of the dispute originally brought before [the Court] under the terms of the Application" '.[13] However, what looks like a new claim may have been 'included in the original claim in substance', so that 'a new claim is not inadmissible *ipso facto*; the decisive consideration is the nature of the connection between that claim and the one formulated in the Application instituting proceedings'.[14] The Court 'formulated two alternative tests. Either the additional claim must be implicit in the Application . . . or it must arise directly out of the question which is the subject-matter of the Application.'[15] There is evidently here still much material for counsel to argue in any given case, but the question probably does not lend itself to more precise formulation.

In the same case, the Court also made some observations on the question of the burden of proof. It restated the general rule, 'based on the maxim *onus probandi incumbit actori*', to the effect that 'it is for the party which alleges a fact in support of its claims to prove the existence of the fact'.[16] The Court added some remarks in the context of the particular case, relating to the acts or omissions of a public authority.

The Statute provides for the written proceedings to consist of 'memorials, counter-memorials and, *if necessary*, replies' (Art. 43 para. 2). The present trend, encouraged by the Court, has been for one exchange of pleadings only, often with the agreement of the parties; for a recent case where one party asked for, and was refused, a second pleading, see *Whaling in the Antarctic*, particularly the separate opinion of Judge Greenwood explaining the reasons for this.[17]

The closure of the written proceedings occurs when the last pleading is filed, or on the date when it should have been filed, as the case may be. After this date, no further documents may be submitted to the court by either party, except with

[13] *Ahmadou Sadio Bello* [2010-II] ICJ Rep 639, 656 para. 39, citing *Territorial and Maritime Dispute between Nicaragua and Honduras in the Caribbean Sea* [2007-II] ICJ Rep 695 para. 108.

[14] [2010-II] ICJ Rep 639, 656–7 paras. 40, 41.

[15] [2010-II] ICJ Rep 639, 657 para. 41, citing *Temple of Preah Vihear* [1962] 36, and *Territorial and Maritime Dispute between Nicaragua and Honduras in the Caribbean Sea* [2007-II] ICJ Rep 695 para. 108.

[16] [2010-II] ICJ Rep 639, 660 para. 54, citing *Pulp Mills on the River Uruguay* [2010-I] ICJ Rep 14, 71 para. 162. As cited, the Latin phrase lays the burden on the plaintiff (*actor*); it is often completed with *in excipiendo reus fit actor*, so that the burden is transferred in certain circumstances to the respondent. Another version corresponding more closely to the Court's reading is *onus probandi incumbit ei qui dicit, non qui negat.* On evidence and proof generally, see further at sect. E below.

[17] [2014] ICJ Rep 405, 418–19 paras. 32–8.

the consent of the other party, or in accordance with the procedure laid down in Article 56 of the Rules. This involves the Court giving the other party the opportunity to object, and then deciding whether it 'considers the document necessary'. This date is also the cut-off date for an international organization to volunteer information under Article 34 of the Statute (as mentioned above); the Court may, however, request such information at any time up to the closure of the oral proceedings.[18]

C. Counter-claims

The concept of a counter-claim implies some relationship between the claims made by the one State and those made by the other. The mere existence of an existing procedural nexus between the two States, constituted so that the claim of the applicant may be handled, should not mean that some totally independent ground of complaint asserted by the respondent may be grafted on to the proceedings. In the international context, with the need for specific jurisdictional bases for all claims, this is particularly so if that other ground of complaint is one which the respondent could not have pressed by independent proceedings, for lack of a jurisdictional link.

The Statute of the Court has nothing to say on the matter; however, Article 80 paragraph 1 of the Rules of Court provides that 'The Court may entertain a counter-claim only if it comes within the jurisdiction of the Court and is directly connected with the subject-matter of the claim of the other party.'[19]

But what exactly is a counter-claim? The only source of interpretation available is the interpretation of this text given in successive cases by the Court and by its predecessor. The Permanent Court was faced with counter-claims only in three cases: *Factory at Chorzów*, *Diversion of Water from the Meuse*, and *Panevezys-Saldutiskis Railway*. Before the ICJ, the earlier years included the cases of *Asylum* and *Rights of US Nationals in Morocco*. More useful jurisprudence is to be found in *Application of the Genocide Convention (Bosnia* v *Yugoslavia)*, *Oil Platforms*,[20] *Land and Maritime Boundary between Cameroon and Nigeria*,[21] *Jurisdictional Immunities of the State*,[22] and the combined cases of *Certain Activities* and *Construction of a Road (Costa Rica/Nicaragua)*.

In the *Genocide Convention* case between Bosnia and Yugoslavia, Yugoslavia (Serbia) submitted what it asserted was a counter-claim: essentially it was an allegation that in the course of the events following the break-up of the original

[18] Art. 69 of the Rules.

[19] Text as amended in 2001: the original 1978 version stated essentially the same conditions, but began 'A counter-claim may be presented provided that . . .' The change was probably directed to meeting the criticism of Judge Kreća in the *Genocide (Bosnia* v *Serbia)* case, [1997] ICJ Rep 264–5. For a full discussion of the significance of the two conditions stated, see Thirlway, 'Counterclaims before the International Court of Justice: The *Genocide Convention* and *Oil Platforms* Decisions', 12 *LJIL* (1999), 197, 201–9.

[20] *Order of 10 March 1998*, [1998] ICJ Rep.

[21] *Order of 30 June 1999*, [1999-II] ICJ Rep 983.

[22] *Order of 6 July 2010*, [2010-I] ICJ Rep 310.

Yugoslavia, breaches of the Genocide Convention had occurred on both sides, so that it was entitled to make the same claims against Bosnia as the latter had made against Serbia. Bosnia objected that the

so-called counter-claim is not really one at all: in submitting its counter-claim the other Party does not counter the initial claim, but formulates a second, autonomous dispute relating to other facts, the settlement of which could in no way influence the solution of the first dispute . . .[23]

The Court favoured such a distinction, but preferred a different formulation:

[A] counter-claim has a dual character in relation to the claim of the other party . . . [it] is independent of the principal claim in so far as it constitutes a separate 'claim' [*demande*], that is to say an autonomous legal act the object of which is to submit a new claim [*prétention*] to the Court . . . at the same time it is linked to the principal claim, in so far as, formulated as a 'counter' claim, it reacts to it . . . the thrust of a counter-claim is thus to widen the original subject-matter of the dispute by pursuing objectives other than the mere dismissal of the claim of the Applicant . . . for example that a finding be made against the Applicant . . . in this respect, the counter-claim is distinguishable from a defence on the merits.[24]

The Court there held the counterclaims to be 'admissible as such', the purpose being 'to achieve a procedural economy whilst enabling the Court to have an overview of the respective claims of the parties and to decide them more consistently'.[25] In the *Oil Platforms* and *Land and Maritime Boundary* cases it was not disputed that the counterclaim was procedurally valid as such, but in the latter case the Court examined the question of 'direct connection'.[26]

The close relationship between a counter-claim and an original claim was better illustrated in the most recent relevant decision, in the two joined cases, one brought by Costa Rica against Nicaragua, and one by Nicaragua against Costa Rica. Nicaragua had filed certain counter-claims in the first case; one of these proved to be the same as Nicaragua's principal claims in the second case, and as a result of the joinder, became otiose: the Court therefore found it to be 'without object'.[27]

Particularly in situations in which the two parties are engaged to some degree in exchanges of hostile or injurious acts, a claim based on such acts by the respondent

[23] *Application of the Genocide Convention, Bosnia* v *Yugoslavia*, Order of 17 December 1997 [1997] ICJ Rep 243, 253 para. 14. It should not be overlooked that the claim was of genocide, and that the nature of that concept is that commission of it on one side cannot justify the commission of it on the other. That is why the settlement of the one dispute is irrelevant to the settlement of the other.

[24] Ibid. ICJ Rep 243, 256 para. 27.

[25] Ibid. ICJ Rep 243, 257 para. 30; cited by Judge Guillaume in *Certain Activities* and *Construction of a Road (Costa Rica/Nicaragua), Order of 18 April 2013*, [2013] ICJ Rep 217. The reference to consistency presumably implies recognition that the Court will not necessarily decide the same point, of law or fact, in the same way on two different occasions, which is probably true even if legal theory asserts the contrary!

[26] On these cases, and generally, see Thirlway, 'Counterclaims before the International Court of Justice: The *Genocide Convention* and *Oil Platforms* Cases', 12 *LJIL* (1999) 197–229; Kolb, 658–63.

[27] *Certain Activities* and *Construction of a Road (Costa Rica/Nicaragua), Order of 18 April 2013*, [2013] ICJ Rep 200, 209 para. 24.

may be met by a purported counter-claim that is no more than a *tu quoque*: a claim that the applicant is guilty of acts of the same kind, and to the same degree. Does this fall within the definition of a counterclaim for purposes of the procedure of the Court? This was a central issue not only in the *Application of the Genocide Convention* case between Bosnia and Serbia, already mentioned, but also in the case of the *Land and Maritime Boundary between Cameroon and Nigeria*. In the latter case, following, in effect, its decision in the *Genocide Convention* case, the Court was satisfied that there was a 'direct connection' between claim and counter-claim: it mentioned that the two 'related to facts of the same nature' (the use of force), and related to a conflict between two neighbouring States; that they 'form part of the same factual complex'; and that the two parties were asserting each other's responsibility on the same legal bases, and 'thus pursuing the same legal aims'.[28] These conditions must, it would seem, be read together: if, for example, each State is exercising diplomatic protection for one of its citizens, but the actions complained of on each side are entirely separate, it is not enough that the two States are 'pursuing the same legal aims'.

Nevertheless, the test of 'direct connection' looks less exigent in the light of the jurisprudence than the original text of the Rule might have suggested. In the most recent case where the Rule has been applied, a distinction was made between the counter-claims as to their admissibility, two of them being ruled inadmissible,[29] and it was suggested that this might be because the Court might 'have wanted to move its case law in a restrictive direction'.[30]

There is some suggestion in the *Genocide Convention* case that if the claim *could* be presented independently, this should 'normally' be the course adopted, but that 'it is permitted for certain types of claims to be set out . . . within the context of a case which is already in progress';[31] the 'types of claims' are presumably those where there is the 'direct connection' required by the Rules. If both parties invoke the same treaty text as jurisdictional basis for claim and counter-claim, in particular if it is a specialized treaty and not a general settlement convention, this would seem to be exactly what the Rule requires. But there may be differences as to which provisions of the treaty are invoked as imposing the *substantive* obligations alleged to have been breached; this was a complication of the *Oil Platforms* case, in which Judge Higgins raised the question whether 'the *very identical* jurisdictional nexus must be established by a counter-claimant'.[32]

The jurisdictional requirement of Article 80 has already been mentioned, and is at first sight more straightforward: if the subject-matter of the counterclaim could not have been brought before the Court by independent proceedings, for lack of a

[28] *Armed Activities on the Territory of the Congo (DRC* v *Uganda)*, Order of 29 November 2001, [2001] ICJ Rep 679 para. 40.

[29] Order of 18 April 2013, *Construction of a Road in Costa Rica along the San Juan River*, [2013] ICJ Rep 200, 215–16 para. 41(B) and (C).

[30] Declaration of Judge ad hoc Guillaume, Order of 18 April 2013, *Construction of a Road in Costa Rica along the San Juan River*, [2013] ICJ Rep 221 para. 17.

[31] Order of 17 December 1997, [1997] ICJ Rep 243, 247 para. 30.

[32] *Oil Platforms*, separate opinion, [1998] ICJ Rep 217, 218.

jurisdictional basis, then it is not admissible as a counter-claim.[33] (Although this is a specific requirement of the Rules, it would seem that it could be waived by an applicant, on the basis that consent, being the basis of jurisdiction, cures defects in jurisdiction.[34]) In many cases the requirement will be satisfied inasmuch as it is the same conventional basis of jurisdiction for the one claim as for the other.[35]

If objection is taken to the presentation of a counter-claim, the Court decides (Art. 80 para. 3 of the Rules); its task at that stage is 'only to verify whether or not the requirements laid down by Article 80 of the Rules of Court [are] satisfied', namely jurisdiction and 'direct connection', and it cannot be taken to have addressed 'any other question relating to jurisdiction and admissibility, not directly linked to Article 80 . . .'[36]

What legal or practical difference does it make whether a claim by a State that is already a respondent in a case before the Court is handled as a counter-claim (assuming it qualifies as such) or by a subsequent judgment in a separate case? Apart from the delay of resolution of the respondent's claim, and consequent staggering of the Court's decisions (which might be relevant, for example, to set-off of compensation obligations), there may, however, be what might be called 'political justice'. Commenting on the problem in the *Genocide Convention* case, the present writer observed that 'to make the atrocities committed on one side the subject of a judicial condemnation, while declining on purely procedural grounds even to examine the allegations of atrocities on the other, would not inspire confidence in international justice'.[37]

D. The oral proceedings and the role of counsel

The hearings usually take several days (at one time these could even take several weeks!), during which the parties address their arguments to the Court in the same order: a presentation by the applicant, followed by a presentation by the respondent, and a much briefer 'second round' devoted to refutation by each party of its opponent's contentions.[38] When the case is brought jointly by special agreement,

[33] This was the reason for the rejection of the Italian counter-claim in the case brought by Germany concerning *Jurisdictional Immunities of the State*: Order of 6 July 2010, [2010-I] ICJ Rep 310, 320–1 paras. 30–1.

[34] And note that the Court has excluded from the category of counter-claims 'claims which exceed the limits of its jurisdiction *as recognized by the parties*' (emphasis added): Order of 17 December 1997, *Application of the Genocide Convention*, [1997] ICJ Rep 257–8 para. 31.

[35] Even if this is so, however, there may be a jurisdictional problem: cf. *Jurisdictional Immunities of the State*, Order of 6 July 2010 [2010-I] ICJ Rep 310, 320–1 paras. 29–31, where the facts relied on as basis of the counter-claim fell outside the temporal application of the convention relied on by both parties to found jurisdiction, while the facts relied on as basis of the claim fell within it.

[36] *Oil Platforms*, [2003] ICJ Rep 161, 210 para. 105. It is therefore possible for the respondent to raise other questions of jurisdiction at a later stage (ibid.)

[37] Thirlway, 'Counterclaims before the International Court of Justice', (n. 25 above), 197, 228.

[38] When the hearings are being held in the context of a request for provisional measures, or of a preliminary objection, it is in principle the party requesting the measures, or the party raising the objection, that speaks first (*in excipiendo reus fit actor*). See Chs. 13 and 14.

rather than by a unilateral application filed by one State against another, neither party is, strictly speaking, in the position of applicant or respondent; the order of speaking is determined by the Court, taking into account the views of the parties. The hearing is open to the public; the Court has power to hold a closed hearing (Statute, Art. 46), but has done so only on two occasions.[39] The grounds on which a closed hearing might be ordered are not indicated, except in so far as the Article refers to the possibility that the parties may 'demand that the public be not admitted': the term 'demand' in the English text suggests that the Court must accede to such a demand if made jointly. In the two cases in which the article was applied, the participation of one or more judges had been challenged; but since there was no question of, for example, moral turpitude asserted, the matter being simply the application of the disqualification provision of Article 17 of the Statute, the Court's attitude seems to have been over-cautious. On two occasions the Court convened in private session, without invoking Article 46, in order to view a film (which at the time was not feasible in the courtroom).[40]

It is at the oral stage that the role of counsel appearing on behalf of the parties becomes evident, though they will of course already have been active in advising, and in drafting pleadings and correspondence with the Court. There is no closed bar at the Court; it is for the parties to say who should appear and address it on their behalf, and to take such account as they see fit of the presence or absence of their representatives' right of audience before national tribunals. Conduct and professional standards are thus not regulated by the Court itself.[41] In 2010, a Study Group of the International Law Association produced a document entitled 'The Hague Principles on Ethical Standards for Counsel Appearing before International Courts and Tribunals',[42] which is admirable as a guide but has no legal force.

The closure of the oral proceedings is marked by a declaration of the President to that effect, normally at a public sitting, 'when, subject to the control of the Court, the agents, counsel and advocates [on both sides] have completed their presentation of the case' (Art. 54 of the Statute), and the Court then 'withdraws', that is, goes into private session, 'to consider its judgment'. The closure is significant inasmuch as, according to the terms of Article 69 of the Rules, the Court cannot thereafter invite information from public international organizations under Article 34 of the Statute. Article 54 itself implies that no further argument can be made after that

[39] *South West Africa, Pleadings, Oral Arguments, Documents*, viii. 4; *Legal Consequences for States of the Continued Presence of South Africa in Namibia (South West Africa) Notwithstanding Security Council Resolution 276 (1970) Pleadings, Oral Arguments, Documents*, ii. 3. In the latter case, the verbatim record of the closed sitting was later made public (ibid. and 672 no. 90.). See further in sect. F.

[40] *Temple of Preah Vihear* [1962] ICJ Rep 9; *Continental Shelf (Tunisia* v. *Libya)* [1982] ICJ Rep 25, para. 12.

[41] The President however may call counsel to order if anything improper should occur: it has been known for counsel on one side to complain of insulting language used by his opponent, and for the President to intervene (personal recollection).

[42] Reproduced in R. Wolfrum and I. Gätzschmann (eds.), *International Dispute Settlement: Room for Innovations?*, Max-Planck Institut (Heidelburg: Springer, 2012), 136–42; see also the paper by Philippe Sands in the same volume, and the comments of Antony Aust thereon.

date (unless the hearings are formally reopened); but the Court can invite a party to reply to a question, or to submit evidence or an explanation, 'at any time' (Art. 62 of the Rules), and such reply, evidence, or explanation may be received after the oral proceedings have closed (Art. 72 of the Rules).

E. Evidence

The subject of evidence before the Court will be discussed only briefly here; while a proper handling of evidence is, of course, essential to the attainment of a just decision, the principles that apply are not peculiar to the Court. Reference should be made to more specialized studies of the subject.[43]

As in courts generally, evidence may be submitted in the form of documents, including statements by witnesses, physical objects (or more commonly photographs of these), or statements made in open court by witnesses. Provision in the Statute for evidence is very brief and general. Article 43 provides for written pleadings to be accompanied by 'all papers and documents in support'; and Article 49 indicates that the Court 'may even before the hearing begins call upon the agents to produce any document or to supply any explanation'. Article 51 states that '[d]uring the hearing any relevant questions are to be put to the witnesses and experts,' and adds 'under the conditions laid down by the Court' in the Rules of Court.

These, as might be expected, deal with evidence more fully. Article 50 deals with documents attached to the pleadings, and Article 56 with documents that a party may seek to submit after the closure of the written proceedings. Articles 63–5 deal with the examination of witnesses during the oral proceedings.

The provision that has probably caused the most argument between parties is Article 56. The principle there stated is that '[a]fter the closure of the written proceedings, no further documents may be submitted to the Court by either party except with the consent of the other party' or, in the absence of consent, if the Court 'after hearing the parties . . . considers the document necessary'. Needless to say, a party is often reluctant to consent to the other party having the opportunity to improve its case at this late stage. In that event, the problem that may arise for the Court is to determine whether or not the document is 'necessary', initially without seeing it; and if it needs to see the document to make the decision, then, it may be argued that the document has effectively been 'submitted', making any objection pointless.

Paragraph 6 (1) of the Hague Principles, mentioned in section D above, states that 'Counsel shall . . . refrain from presenting or otherwise relying upon evidence

[43] In particular, A. Riddell and B. Plant, *Evidence before the International Court of Justice*, (London: BIICL, 2009); see also the entry by R. Wolfrum and M. Möldner in the *Max Planck Encyclopedia of Public International Law* on 'International Courts and Tribunals, Evidence; the article by C. J. Tams on 'Evidentiary Issues' in Zimmermann et al., *Commentary*; also the valuable recent study by L. Malintoppi, 'Fact Finding and Evidence (Notably in Scientific-Related Disputes)', *ICJ 70th Anniversary Seminar* (2016), to be published shortly in *JIDS*.

that he or she knows or has reason to believe to be false or misleading.' It has been suggested that there is an increasing tendency of States to make use of false evidence before international courts, including the ICJ, and if this is so counsel are not fulfilling their professional duty. As long ago as 1986, Judge Schwebel drew attention in his dissenting opinion in the *Military and Paramilitary Activities* case to what he was satisfied were false statements on behalf of Nicaragua;[44] and in the *Qatar/Bahrain* case a number of historical documents were presented to the Court which were shown to be forgeries (and withdrawn without any admission or comment). The question has been raised whether international courts have a duty to do more 'to police the honesty of States and their representatives'; and if so, how this could be done.[45]

F. Public nature of the proceedings

Unlike the proceedings in most international arbitrations, the proceedings before the International Court are for the most part open to other States, in the first place, and to the public in general, in the second.

Article 46 of the Court's Statute provides that 'The hearing in Court shall be public, unless the Court shall decide otherwise, or unless the parties demand that the public be not admitted.' Similarly, Article 71 paragraph 6 of the Rules of Court states that 'The minutes (*procès-verbal*) of public hearings shall be printed and published by the Court'; the term 'minutes' is slightly misleading, as in fact the *procès-verbal* consists of a complete transcript of what has been said in court during a hearing.

The pleadings, that is to say the *pièces de la procédure écrite*,[46] are initially reserved for the eyes of the judges alone, and the Statute does not expressly provide for their publication. Under Article 53 paragraph 1 of the Rules of Court, however, the Court may decide, after ascertaining the views of the parties, to make copies available to any State entitled to appear before the Court that has requested them. States frequently make such requests when it appears possible that the subject-matter of the case may affect their interests, and such a request is sometimes a preliminary to an application for permission to intervene under Article 62 of the Statute. The Court may, however, decide not to grant the request, particularly if it is opposed by the parties; the difficulties that may result from a refusal, for the State considering intervention, were a feature of the case of *Sovereignty over Pulau Ligitan and Pulau*

[44] [1986] ICJ Rep 259ff., in particular 276–7 paras. 24–7 and the 'Factual Annex', Sections G and H, 410–509.

[45] W. M. Reisman and C. P. Skinner, *Fraudulent Evidence before Public International Tribunals: The Dirty Stories of International Law* (Cambridge: Cambridge University Press, 2014), 199; a pioneering study, presenting a number of other examples and thought-provoking discussion. For the discreet—if that is the word—manner in which the Court dealt with the forged documents in *Qatar/Bahrain*, see [2001] ICJ Rep 40, 46 paras. 15–16.

[46] See above, sect. B.

Sipadan, discussed in Chapter 15, Section C. In that case, the Court found no support for the view that 'there exists an inextricable link' between the procedure of requesting copies of the pleadings and that of intervention,[47] so that delay in filing an application to intervene could not necessarily be excused by the lack of access to the pleadings.

Under paragraph 2 of the same Article, the Court (again, after ascertaining the views of the parties) may decide that copies of the pleadings 'shall be made accessible to the public on or after the opening of the oral proceedings'. This has virtually always been done, and nowadays they are placed on the Court's website (www.icj-cij.org). An exception was the case concerning *Application of the Genocide Convention (Croatia* v *Serbia)*, where making public copies of the pleadings was delayed 'as more information was required by the Court before deciding exactly which documents should be redacted (and to what extent) or withheld from publication altogether',[48] in the interests of protection of witnesses.

On a more long-term basis, the decisions of the Court (judgments, advisory opinions, orders) are published in the Court's *ICJ Reports* series, as individual fascicles and later as bound annual volumes.[49] The pleadings and the records of hearings are in principle published in the printed series *Pleadings, Oral Arguments, Documents*, but the need for this series has been enormously reduced by the use of the internet;[50] the Court's *Yearbook* continues to list these volumes under the heading of each case, but for cases dealt with over the last fifteen years or so, these are marked 'Not yet published', and there is no indication when (if ever) they will appear.

As noted above, the Court has the power under Article 46 of the Statute to hold oral proceedings *in camera*. Its discretion in this respect is unfettered, except when the parties agree to 'demand' that the public be not admitted.[51] The history and *travaux préparatoires* of the Statute give no indication of the reasons for the provision; the emphasis in the drafting seems to have been on the generally public nature of the oral proceedings, so that the exception may have been included 'just in case', with no very clear idea of the circumstances that might justify a hearing behind closed doors.[52] One obvious possibility, though less probable before the

[47] *Sovereignty over Palau Ligitan and Pulau Sipidan (Indonesia/Malaysia), Application to Intervene*, [2001] ICJ Rep 575, 585 para. 22.

[48] [2015] ICJ Rep p. 16 of advance text, para. 39.

[49] There is nowadays often a substantial time-lag between the pronouncement of a decision and its appearance in print. The reason for this is that time is needed for translation. The actual decision is always adopted at the close of the deliberation in both its English and French texts; at one time, the appended separate and dissenting opinions were also available in both languages by the date of delivery of the decision, and attached to the text of the decision. The practice now is that any opinions short enough to be translated quickly may be issued with the decision in both languages, but longer opinions (of which there are many, some extravagantly long) are issued at that stage only in the original language, the translation appearing in the printed edition.

[50] This, of course, requires that they be scanned, unless they are already in digital form; but the work involved is immensely less that that involved in preparation of the documents for print.

[51] The French text of Art. 46 uses the verb *demander*, which means no more than 'request': it is possible that 'demand' in the English text is an inadequate translation. Even so, the mere fact of the joint request appears to exclude the Court's discretion.

[52] von Schorlemer (*Max-Planck Commentary*, art. 46 para. 7) suggests that secret proceedings 'bear the risk of not guaranteeing a fair trial for the parties'; but such a risk would surely only attach to secret

Court than in a domestic court, would be protection of witnesses: a witness giving evidence against the repressive regime of his own State might be protected by anonymity and a closed hearing—or part of a hearing, a possibility specifically contemplated by Article 59 paragraph 2 of the Rules of Court. This possibility was realized in the case of *Application of the Genocide Convention (Croatia* v *Serbia)*, as described below.

The power has very rarely been used; and in most cases the record of the closed hearing has been made public subsequently. On two occasions, the power appears to have been used merely for practical convenience in completely uncontentious circumstances.[53]

In the *South West Africa* case, an application was made just before the opening of the oral proceedings 'concerning the composition of the Court', and the Court decided to hear the parties on the matter in closed hearings, in accordance with Article 46. The application was dismissed, and only the formal record, indicating that closed hearings were held, was published.[54] In the *Namibia* case closed hearings were held; the sensitive aspect resulted from a claim by South Africa to the right to appoint a judge ad hoc, on the basis that the request related to 'a legal question actually pending between two or more States'; this might involve a contention that certain Members of the Court had to be regarded as though they were nationals of the 'other party' for purposes of Article 31 of the Statute.[55] The application was rejected, but (unlike in the *South West Africa* case), the matter was discussed in the judgment, and the record of the closed hearing published.[56]

The thinking behind the decision to hold closed hearings in these cases is difficult to assess, particularly where the nature of the issue is unknown. So far as it related to the position of individual Members of the Court, it can hardly have been feared that representatives of a State would indulge in wild unproven allegations, or scurrilous abuse; and if there was any doubt about the impartiality of a judge, it would seem better that this be investigated in public.

meetings between the Court and one party, to which Article 46 would not apply. Another suggested reason is 'to protect judges from interference from outside'; again, this seems rather beside the point.

[53] For the viewing of a film showing the place in dispute (with commentary), or the maritime areas involved: see *Temple of Preah Vihear* [1962] ICJ Rep 6, 9; *Continental Shelf (Tunisia/Libya)* [1982] ICJ Rep 18, 25. This would today be perfectly possible in the Great Hall of Justice, but was probably less so in 1962, or even 1982.

[54] See *South West Africa, Pleadings, Oral Arguments, Documents*, vii. 4–5: Order of 18 March 1965, [1965] ICJ Rep 3; Judgment of 18 July 1966, [1966] ICJ Rep 6, 9. Von Schorlermer states (*Max-Planck Commentary*, art. 46 para. 22) that this was '[w]ith the consent of the parties', but this is not stated in the Order. It is known that the proceedings concerned the participation of one Member of the Court: T. M. Franck (*Fairness in the International Legal and Institutional System*, RCADI 240 (1993-III), 310) states that this was in the absence of the judge concerned; but see *South West Africa, Pleadings*, viii. 3.4, showing the same composition as the public sittings.

[55] Objection had already been taken in South Africa's written statement, specifically to the participation of three Members of the Court (see the three Orders of 26 January 1971, [1971] ICJ Rep 3, 6, 9). In fact, at the closed sitting, counsel for South Africa dealt with the other requirements of the Statute and Rules, but trod very delicately around this particular issue (Mr de Villiers, *Namibia, Pleadings, Oral Arguments, Documents*, ii. 19–22).

[56] Order of 29 January 1971, 12; Judgment [1971] ICJ Rep 16, 19 paras. 10–11; 25–7 paras. 36–9.

In the case of *Application of the Genocide Convention (Croatia* v. *Serbia)*, for the first time closed hearings were held for the protection of witnesses.

With regard to the protective measures requested for two of the witnesses, the Parties were informed that the Court had agreed to the use of pseudonyms when addressing these witnesses or referring to them; it had also agreed that these witnesses would be heard in closed session, with only Registry staff and members of the official delegations permitted to be present during their examination, and that two separate sets of documents would be produced (one reserved for confidential use by the Court and the Parties, and the other to be made public, with any information that might lead to the identification of the protected witnesses having been deleted.[57]

Even with regard to the other witnesses, the Court prescribed a sort of semi-closure of the hearings at which they would give evidence; it directed that

the public could attend the examinations (except the closed sittings), but would be requested not to divulge the content of the testimony/statements until the oral proceedings had closed; the same would apply to the media, who would have to subscribe to a code of conduct under the terms of which they would be allowed to take photographs and make sound recordings, on the express condition that they did not make public the content of the testimony/statements before the oral proceedings had closed.[58]

These arrangements were duly carried out, as recorded in the judgment in the case;[59] but it appears that while the anonymity of witnesses was respected, their testimony was such as could be published.[60]

G. Termination of the proceedings: decision or discontinuance

The normal conclusion to the proceedings in a case is a judgment, in most cases a judgment on the merits. Alternatively there may be a judgment upholding one or more preliminary objections (see Ch. 14), and finding either that the Court has no jurisdiction in the case, or that the claim is, for whatever reason inadmissible. Such a finding may also be made in the absence of a formal preliminary objection. There have in addition been a small number of judgments, to be considered in Chapter 10 section B, each of which disposed of the case in the sense that no more proceedings would be possible, but did not resolve the legal or factual issues raised by the case.[61] This section is, however, concerned with cases in which no judgment at all is ever given, primarily because the parties have agreed not to go on with the case, or because the applicant decides not to proceed; this is the process known as

[57] [2015] ICJ Rep p. 14 of advance text, para. 33.

[58] [2015] ICJ Rep p. 15 of advance text, para. 33. The judgment makes no specific reference to Art. 46 of the Statute or to Art. 59 of the Rules of Court.

[59] [2015] ICJ Rep p. 18 of advance text, para. 46.

[60] See [2015] ICJ Rep [p. 19 of advance text], para. 48, in fine.

[61] See e.g. *Monetary Gold removed from Rome in 1943* [1954] ICJ Rep 19 (absence of necessary party); *Northern Cameroons* [1963] ICJ Rep 15 (judgment could have no practical effect), etc.

discontinuance; there is no provision in the Statute for it, and it is regulated by Articles 88 and 89 of the Rules.

The first of these texts deals with cases in which the two parties are agreed to discontinue the proceedings 'at any time before final judgment on the merits has been delivered'.[62] Reference is made to the agreement of 'the parties'; this presumably would include a State admitted to intervene as a party, but not a State permitted to intervene on a non-party basis (see Ch. 15 sect. C). A non-party intervenor is not bound by the judgment in the case, and cannot invoke it against the parties,[63] so it seems consistent to suppose that such a State does not have any right to say whether there shall be such a judgment at all. The procedure is straightforward, simply involving the issuing of 'an order recording the discontinuance and directing that the case be removed from the list' (that is, the General List kept by the Registrar under Art. 26 (1) (*b*) of the Rules). If the discontinuance is the result of a settlement of the dispute, the parties may ask the Court to record this fact in the order.

Proceedings instituted by an application may also be discontinued by the applicant unilaterally (Art. 89 of the Rules). If at the date when it so notifies the Court, 'the respondent has not yet taken any step in the proceedings', the Court 'shall make an order officially recording the discontinuance'; the case is removed from the list, and the respondent notified. This is something that happens fairly frequently; the applicant usually does not say why it is discontinuing, but one may speculate that the other party has convinced it that negotiation would be a better means of settlement, or it has come to have doubts about the strength of its case, or the Court's jurisdiction. Sometimes it is apparent on the face of the original application that it was made as a means of pressure, and was never likely to proceed further. If the respondent has taken a step in the proceedings, it is invited to say (within a set time-limit) whether it opposes the discontinuance, and if it does not, or does not reply within the time-limit, the Court makes a discontinuance order.[64]

Mention has been made of the applications filed from time to time in the earlier years of the Court directed against States whose attitude to the Court was such that they had made no acceptance of jurisdiction, and that it was virtually certain that they would not make one. The applicant had no particular incentive to discontinue, and see the cases disappear from sight, and the respondent was (legally, at least) going to ignore them. On the basis of informal communications from the States named as respondents asserting that there was no jurisdiction, the Court, having passed these communications to the applicant, made orders removing the cases from the list. It made no reference in these orders to Article 53 of the Statute, governing non-appearance, but simply to Article 36 and 48.[65]

[62] Discontinuance after that time would obviously be meaningless, since there are no proceedings left to discontinue; but the emphasis is probably on 'at any time'—the Court might even be told of the agreement to discontinue just before the sitting for delivery of the judgment!

[63] *Land, Island and Maritime Frontier Dispute* [1992] ICJ Rep 351, 609–10 paras. 421–4.

[64] For a recent example, see *Jurisdiction and Enforcement of Judgments in Civil and Commercial Matters (Belgium* v *Switzerland)*, Order of 5 April 2011, [2011-I] ICJ Rep 341; unusually the reason for the discontinuance was stated by the applicant, and recorded in the order.

[65] See e.g. *Aerial Incident of 10 March 1953 (USA* v *Czechoslovakia)*, Order of 14 March 1956, [1956] ICJ Rep 6; *Antarctica (UK* v *Argentina)*, Order of 16 March 1956, [1956] ICJ Rep 15.

In these few early cases, it was the Court that ultimately took the initiative to bring the proceedings to an end, though after inviting an informal denial of jurisdiction by the State named as respondent, inasmuch as it was clear that they were not going anywhere; otherwise, a decision to this effect is reserved for the parties, or for the active party if the other is effectively absent from the proceedings. Altogether exceptional were two linked cases in which the Court of its own motion decided that further proceedings were unnecessary, and brought them to an end: the *Nuclear Tests* cases. The Court there asserted an inherent jurisdiction sufficiently extensive and empowering to permit it to 'decline to give judgment'.[66] It noted that it would have been open to the Applicants, if they had considered 'that the case had in effect been concluded, to discontinue the proceedings in accordance with the Rules'. But if they had not done so, 'this does not prevent the Court from making its own independent finding on the subject'.[67] So much may be conceded; but it is one thing to form a view, and another to act on it, and to act in a manner that would be irrevocable. Furthermore, the general relationship between the Court and the parties before it would seem to require that before taking such a step, one normally reserved for the parties at their option, the Court should consult them. This was not done.[68]

[66] [1974] ICJ Rep 253, 271 para. 58. [67] [1974] ICJ Rep 253, 270 para. 54.

[68] It is probably not over-cynical to suspect that the Court was aware, or had reason to suppose, that the two applicants would *not* be satisfied with what the cases had achieved up to that time, and would have pressed for them being allowed to continue.

IV

ADVISORY PROCEEDINGS

9

Procedure in Advisory Cases

A. Participation

(1) Are there are 'parties' in advisory cases?

A question that is perhaps more than purely procedural is whether any State or other entity participating in advisory proceedings has the status of a 'party', or an equivalent status; this has relevance particularly with regard to the operation, in the advisory context, of the system of judges ad hoc.

In contentious cases, the *dramatis personae*, as explained in Chapter 7 section B, are primarily the States in the roles of applicant and respondent, who have necessarily the status of 'parties', and in addition third States admitted to intervene, who may or may not have party status. The advisory procedure makes possible the participation, at least potentially, of all United Nations Member States: do any of them thus have the status of party, or a status comparable to that status?

The fact that advisory proceedings are brought by an international body, not a State, and that no State is obliged to become involved, in itself suggests that there are no 'parties'. Furthermore, no State (or organization) is bound by the decision, except in a few situations where a particular treaty text, on the basis of which an opinion is requested, provides that the opinion so given shall be binding, that is to say binding on the parties to the treaty.[1] What then of a status comparable to that of a party?

At the stage of the decision to request the opinion, made by the General Assembly or whatever other authorized body may be concerned, no State, even the parties to any underlying dispute, has any special right to be consulted, nor is their consent required.[2]

A particular category of States is, however, defined, for the purpose of advisory proceedings, in Article 66 of the Statute. When a request for an advisory opinion

[1] e.g. Sect. 30 of the Convention on the Privileges and Immunities of the United Nations, discussed in the 'Mazilu' case: *Applicability of the Obligation to Arbitrate under Section 21 of the United Nations Headquarters Agreement of 26 June 1947* [1988] ICJ Rep 12, 188ff., paras. 29ff. In that case, Romania had purported to exclude Sect, 30 by reservation to the Convention; the Court was not called upon to rule on this point.

[2] It might nevertheless be sought, of course: when the Council of the League obtained legal advice from a Commission of Jurists on the *Aaland Islands question*, this was with the consent of Finland and Sweden, the disputing parties (Council of the League, 12 July 1920).

is received, notice of this to be given in two ways: first (para. 1), the Registrar gives notice of the request to all States entitled to appear before the Court.[3] The text then continues (para. 2):

> The Registrar shall also, by means of a special and direct communication, notify any state entitled to appear before the Court or international organization considered by the Court, or, should it not be sitting, by the President, as likely to be able to furnish information on the question, that the Court will be prepared to receive, within a time-limit to be fixed by the President, written statements, or to hear, at a public sitting to be held for the purpose, oral statements relating to the question.[4]

There is no suggestion that the States 'likely to be able to furnish information' have any further special status, analogous to that of parties to contentious proceedings.

It is, however, recognized impliedly by the Statute and explicitly by the Rules, that there may be some States that have a more direct interest in the question submitted for opinion than have other States. Article 68 of the Statute, it may be recalled, provides that 'In the exercise of its advisory functions the Court shall further be guided by the provisions of the present Statute which apply in contentious cases to the extent to which it recognizes them to be applicable.'

Article 102 paragraph 2 of the Rules implements this: having repeated the terms of Article 68, the text continues: 'For this purpose, it shall above all consider whether the request for the advisory opinion relates to a legal question actually pending between two or more States.' Article 102 then continues that when the opinion is requested on such a 'question actually pending', Article 31 of the Statute (and the appropriate provisions of the Rules concerning judges ad hoc) is to apply.

A distinct category of States therefore exists, or may come to exist, analogous to that, in the contentious context, of States parties; these are then quasi-parties. Since Article 102 carefully avoids, perhaps as too restrictive, the term 'dispute', one has to define this category as that of States between whom a legal question is pending, such that the request for opinion may be said to relate to it. But just as not all parties to a dispute are necessarily all parties to a contentious case in which the dispute is submitted to the Court, so the States in the category just defined may or may not choose to involve themselves in the advisory proceedings.[5]

The States in the category of 'pending between', just explained, will almost certainly have been regarded as 'likely to be able to furnish information', in so far as the Court can identify them at this early stage, but the two categories are conceptually distinct.

[3] Statute, Art. 66 para. 1; this parallels the notification of an application instituting contentious proceedings under Art. 40 para. 3 of the Statute.

[4] Para. 3 entitles any State entitled to appear but not so notified (presumably on the basis that it was not 'considered likely to be able to furnish information') to apply to be treated in the same way.

[5] Though many do: in the *Kosovo* case there were written statements by thirty-six States, and in the *Palestine Wall* case, forty-nine (including on behalf of the Euopean Union and the Islamic Conference).

(2) Appointment of judges ad hoc in advisory cases

Article 68 of the Statute, quoted above, is interpreted by the Rules as having (*inter alia*) the result that if in an advisory case a State can claim to be, if not a 'party', at least one having a status analogous to that of 'party', for the purposes of Article 68, then Article 31, paragraphs 2–5 of the Statute come into play, and that State may appoint a judge ad hoc. Although Article 102 of the Rules is not part of the Statute, but only a gloss upon it made by the Court in the exercise of its rule-making power, the Court necessarily treats it as the defining text for this purpose.

Practice has shown that the implementation of these texts in specific cases in relation to the appointment of judges ad hoc is not always straightforward. In a contentious case, the right to appoint a judge ad hoc appertains to a party, and there is normally no doubt who are the parties;[6] and the question whether there is or is not a judge of that State's nationality 'on the Bench' is also usually a simple one. Even in that context, however, once a claim to the appointment of a judge ad hoc has been made, the Court would not be properly constituted to take any decisions in the case until the issue had been disposed of; and in advisory proceedings the determination of the validity of such a claim may not be a simple matter. As the Court stated in the *Namibia* case, 'the question whether a judge ad hoc should be appointed is of course a matter concerning the composition of the Bench and possesses . . . absolute legal priority. It has to be settled prior to the opening of the oral proceedings, and indeed before any further issues, even of procedure, can be decided.'[7] Yet, as that case showed, the question of entitlement to appoint a judge ad hoc may be linked with other questions, which may be compromised by the early decision on the judge ad hoc. South Africa had a very special interest in the proceedings, since its conduct in the administration of South West Africa (later Namibia) was what the case was all about; and in view of the general attitude of other UN Member States towards it on this point, it could claim that there was a 'legal question actually pending' between itself and nearly every other State. Yet in the event it was not authorized to appoint a judge ad hoc. The decision was made in an Order at a fairly early stage in the case,[8] which gave no reasons. The matter was then addressed in the eventual advisory opinion, but the reasoning on the point is not impressive,[9] and the political context undoubtedly weighed heavily.

In the *Western Sahara* case, Morocco and Mauritania each claimed the existence of special legal ties with the territory, and contested the arguments of Spain,

[6] Except in the case of an intervention: see further Ch. 15.

[7] *Legal Consequences for States of the Continued Presence of South Africa in Namibia (South West Africa)*, [1971] ICJ Rep 16, 25 para. 36. The Court had already dealt with other issues, but since these also affected the composition of the Bench (challenges to the propriety of three judges sitting), this was appropriate.

[8] *Legal Consequences for States of the Continued Presence of South Africa in Namibia (South West Africa), Order of 29 January 1971* [1971] ICJ Rep 12.

[9] A fine distinction was drawn, for example, between a question that was also a dispute, and a question answering which would involve the Court in deciding 'legal and factual issues which are actually in dispute between South Africa and other States': *Legal Consequences for States of the Continued Presence of South Africa in Namibia (South West Africa)* [1971] ICJ Rep 16, 24 para. 34.

the former colonial power: there was, as it happened, a regular judge of Spanish nationality on the Bench. Morocco was permitted to appoint a judge ad hoc, but Mauritania was not.[10] The reason given was that the Court saw a difference in the position of the two claimant States, such that in the one case there was a 'legal dispute' with Spain, but in the other there was not; a different view might have been taken on the facts, but legally the decision is impeccable, but also striking as using the existence of a *dispute* as criterion, not merely a 'legal question actually pending'.

In the *Palestine Wall* case one of the parties to the dispute (Israel) chose not to participate in the proceedings, and thus did not assert the right to a judge ad hoc; another (Palestine) was not a State for the purposes of the Statute; the implications of this are discussed in Section A(3). It was, nevertheless, enabled to participate as 'furnishing information', but there was no question of it appointing a judge ad hoc.[11]

(3) Non-State entities

As already emphasized, Article 34 paragraph 1 of the Statute provides that '[o]nly States may be parties before the Court'; and in the context of contentious cases this excludes both individuals and corporate bodies of private law, and international organizations. In advisory proceedings, however, there are no 'parties'; and the whole purpose of the proceedings may be to resolve a legal problem affecting the role or the operation of an international organization.[12] There is of course a role for the organ requesting the opinion and thus for the organization of which it is an organ; both States and international organizations, not merely the requesting organization, are given an equal opportunity to participate in the proceedings. This does not apply to non-governmental organizations, but in practice bodies of this kind not infrequently transmit statements to the Court commenting on the subject of advisory proceedings. Practice Direction XII provides for these: they acquire no formal status in the proceedings, but are to be 'treated as publications readily available', and may thus be referred to 'in the same manner as documents in the public domain'. The expression 'publication readily available' is borrowed from Article 56 of the Rules; a document of this kind may be referred to in the oral proceedings even if it has not been formally produced under Article 43 of the Statute, or Article 56 itself.[13]

[10] *Western Sahara, Order of 22 May 1975*, [1975] ICJ Rep 6.

[11] See the Separate Opinion of Judge Owada, *Legal Consequences of the Construction of a Wall in the Occupied Palestinian Territory*, [2004-I] ICJ Rep 136, 267 para. 19. The problem remained hypothetical, as Israel, consistently with its aloof attitude, did not claim the right to appoint a judge ad hoc, so that whether or not Palestine could, had it been a State, have appointed a judge ad hoc, there was no need to 'balance' an Israel-appointed one.

[12] Even in the contentious context, however, as mentioned in Ch. 7 sect. B(3), international organizations may supply 'information' if requested to do so, or indeed may volunteer information, under Art. 34 of the Statute.

[13] This text in terms refers to oral proceedings in contentious cases, but affords 'guidance' in advisory cases under Art. 102 of the Rules.

In two recent cases the problem has arisen that there were non-State entities, or at least entities not falling within the category of States entitled to appear before the Court, that nevertheless appeared eminently 'likely to be able to furnish information' on the subject of the request for opinion. In the *Wall* case, it was Palestine that fell into that category. Accordingly, by an Order of 19 December 2003, the Court decided *inter alia* that:

In the light of resolution ES-10/14 and the report of the Secretary-General transmitted with the request, and taking into account the fact that the General Assembly had granted Palestine a special status of observer and that the latter was co-sponsor of the draft resolution requesting the advisory opinion, Palestine might also submit a written statement on the question . . .[14]

Palestine was also authorized to make an oral statement, along with the other suppliers of 'information'.

In the case concerning *Accordance with international law of the unilateral declaration of independence in respect of Kosovo*, the Court, in its Order deciding what States might be considered able to 'furnish information', added the following:

Decides further that, taking account of the fact that the unilateral declaration of independence by the Provisional Institutions of Self-Government of Kosovo of 17 February 2008 is the subject of the question submitted to the Court for an advisory opinion, the authors of the above declaration are considered likely to be able to furnish information on the question; and *decides* therefore to invite them to make written contributions to the Court within the above time-limits . . .

Each of these is an exercise of judicial creativity—particularly the second, as the authors of the declaration certainly did not constitute an international organization; and whether they collectively constituted a State was, if not the question submitted to the Court, one intricately related to it. It was, however, such a sensible step to take if the advisory process was to be meaningful that objections to it would seem pedantic—and apparently there were none.

(4) Individuals: the staff appeal cases

In general, neither the purpose of advisory proceedings nor the governing texts make it appropriate for individuals to have any role. However, when the General Assembly established a system of appeals by staff members to an Appeal Tribunal against decisions affecting their employment and their rights, provision was made for the possible review of decisions of the Tribunal.[15] This was entrusted to a

[14] [2008] ICJ Rep 409, 410 para. 4.

[15] A similar provision that already existed, and is still in operation, is Article XII of the Annex to the Statute of the Administrative Tribunal of the International Labour Organization; this is applicable in relation to a number of other organizations that have accepted the jurisdiction of that Tribunal. In certain circumstances the Permanent Court, and now the ICJ, can be asked for an advisory opinion on specified grounds: broadly, jurisdictional defects or defects in judicial process. See *Judgment No. 2867 of the Administrative Tribunal of the International Labour Organization upon a Complaint Filed against the International Fund for Agricultural Development, Advisory Opinion*, [2012] ICJ Rep 10, 19–20 para. 19.

Committee on Applications for Review of Administrative Tribunal Judgments; but it was envisaged that the final appeal body should in effect be the ICJ.[16] Since no inter-State dispute would be involved, this was to be by means of an advisory opinion, and the Committee was empowered to request such an opinion, under Article 96 paragraph 2 of the Charter: this was the effect of a new Article 11 introduced into the Statute of the Administrative Tribunal in 1955.[17] When the first such reference to the Court was made in the *Fasla* case in 1972, one problem that was immediately evident was that while the Organization (the employer, and one party to the Tribunal's decision) was able to make representations to the Court, the individual staff member directly the subject of the Tribunal decision could not. However, Article 11 paragraph 4 of the Tribunal's Statute provided that the Secretary-General should attach a statement by the staff member concerned to the Secretary-General's statement on behalf of the Organization, and this was done in the *Fasla* case.[18] It had been foreseen at the time that Article 11 was adopted that a difficulty, rather less easily overcome, was that the individual staff member would not be able to take part in the oral proceedings. The best that could be done to meet this problem was a provision in the General Assembly resolution adopting Article 11, 'recommending' that the Secretary-General and Member States should not make oral statements to the Court in proceedings resulting from Article 11. In the *Fasla* case (and subsequent cases), the Court took the initiative of deciding that there should be no oral proceedings (or rather that 'it was not contemplated' that there would be such).[19] It further observed that '[i]n advisory proceedings . . . it lies within the entire discretion of the Court to decide whether to obtain oral in addition to written statements', and that it was 'satisfied' that 'the interested parties' had the appropriate opportunity to express their views, and that it had 'adequate information to enable it to administer justice'.[20] The problem now arises only in the context of appeals from the ILO Administrative Tribunal, which are, perhaps fortunately, infrequent. In the most recent of these the Court noted that 'questions may now properly be asked whether the system established in 1946 meets the present-day principle of equality of access to courts and tribunals'; it noted that it was 'not in a position to reform this system', but it could 'attempt to ensure, so far as possible, that there is equality in the proceedings before it'.[21]

[16] A number of legal problems arose out of this arrangement; here only the question of participation by the staff member is examined, the others being considered elsewhere.

[17] The Court had already been asked, in 1953, for an advisory opinion on the *Effect of Awards of Compensation Made by the United Nations Administrative Tribunal*, [1954] ICJ Rep 47; and it was also asked, in 1955, for an opinion on *Judgments of the Administrative Tribunal of the ILO upon Complaints Made against Unesco*, [1956] ICJ Rep 77.

[18] Though there was some doubt at first whether it had been properly done: see [1973] ICJ Rep 166, 168 para. 7.

[19] [1973] ICJ Rep 166, 168 para. 6.

[20] [1973] ICJ Rep 166, 182 para. 38.

[21] *Judgment No. 2867 of the ILO Administrative Tribunal*, [2012] ICJ Rep 10, 29–30, para. 44. See further in Ch. 11.

B. Procedure

The main theoretical difference between the procedure in a contentious case and that in proceedings on a request for an advisory opinion is that in contentious proceedings the States concerned aim, by the submission of evidence and by argument, to convince the Court of the validity of their respective claims; while in an advisory case, the role of the requesting organization, and of States taking part in the proceedings, is—at least theoretically—to assist the Court at arriving at a clear and well-founded statement of the law. In fact, of course, individual States may have very definite interests of their own in the matter, and the requesting organization may also be seeking or hoping for an opinion aligned with a particular standpoint. Be that as it may, the procedure laid down in the Statute and Rules contains some element of the *contradictoire*, reflecting the rule of Article 68 of the Statute, already cited, whereby in advisory cases the Court is to be 'guided by' the provisions of the Statute applicable in contentious cases.

This is perhaps particularly marked where the subject-matter of the request involves considerations of fact. The purpose of the advisory procedure being to settle a disputed or unsettled legal question, the cases to which it is most suited are those in which the facts are established or agreed. In its general judicial, dispute-settling, capacity, the Court is of course expected, and equipped, to determine factual issues also, to the extent necessary to settle the legal dispute laid before it. The procedure for giving advisory opinions is, however, less well-fitted than is the contentious procedure to factual determination. First, the parties to any underlying dispute are not under any obligation to appear in the proceedings to make their respective cases; and while the Court, on the basis of the principle *jura novit curia*,[22] does not need their help to arrive at a conclusion of law, any factual findings it may need to make as basis for its legal conclusions must be based on evidence, which it is for the parties to provide.[23] Secondly, in contentious proceedings, the rule is *onus probandi incumbit actori*, it is for the party making a claim to prove it; which carries the important consequence that if it does not succeed in doing so, the claim is rejected.[24] In advisory proceedings there is, however, no 'claim' to be upheld or rejected; and the Court may have to indicate that it is

[22] See Ch. 3 sect. E. As there mentioned, there may also be an absence of a legal rule covering the point at issue, as shown in the advisory case of the *Legality of the Threat or Use of Nuclear Weapons*, where the Court was obliged to conclude that it '[could] not reach a definitive conclusion as to the legality or illegality of nuclear weapons' in certain circumstances: [1996-I] ICJ Rep 226, 263 para. 97.

[23] It is true that, on the basis of Art. 53 of the Statute, a contentious case may proceed even if the Respondent declines to appear, and the Court in such case still has to be satisfied that 'the claim is well founded in fact *and law*'; but in an advisory context the Court does not even have the guidance of a specific claim submitted to it by an Applicant. On the non-appearing party and the procedure under Art. 53, see Ch. 7 sect. B(3).

[24] Otherwise expressed in the adage *in dubio pro reo*: it is the respondent that enjoys the benefit of any doubt.

insufficiently supplied with factual evidence to respond, and perhaps decline to give an opinion altogether.[25]

(1) The request for opinion

The request to the Court for an advisory opinion generally differs from an application instituting contentious proceedings as regards its drafting history. While an application is usually carefully prepared by a single party, to present to the Court a dispute that will probably have been clearly defined by previous diplomatic exchanges, a request for opinion is often the outcome of political bargaining, sometimes under pressure in a session of the requesting body, and involving more than one hand in its drafting. It is not surprising therefore that the Court has asserted a power to revise the terms of the request to enable it to give a legal answer, and one that will meet the needs of the requesting organ, as seen by the Court. This process is most visible in the *Interpretation of the Agreement of 25 March 1951 between the WHO and Egypt*: in order to give 'a pertinent and effectual reply', the Court found it necessary to 'ascertain the meaning and full implications of the question in the light of the actual framework of fact and law in which it falls for consideration'.[26] How far this involved a rewriting may be seen by comparing the simple terms of Question 1 in that case with the relevant complex paragraph of the operative clause of the opinion (itself incorporating by reference a long paragraph of the reasoning).[27] The Court may thus to some extent 'second-guess' the requesting body's intentions, but nevertheless 'it is not for the Court to decide whether or not an advisory opinion is needed' by the requesting body.[28] A more complex issue was raised in the *Kosovo* case, where the reformulation of the question involved the identification of the authorship of the declaration of independence of Kosovo; the matter was complex and controversial, and need not be gone into here.[29]

(2) The written proceedings

As there are no parties, there are thus no pleadings in the strict sense; the written material before the Court will consist first and foremost of a dossier of documents supplied by the UN Secretary-General, or chief executive officer of the requesting organization, under Article 65 paragraph 2 of the Statute. This is in principle, as implied by its title, simply a collection of documents from which the Members of the

[25] This is one interpretation of the PCIJ's refusal of an opinion in the *Eastern Carelia* case (1923), *PCIJ Series B, No. 5*.

[26] [1980] ICJ Rep 67, 76 para. 10.

[27] See [1980] ICJ Rep 67, 76 para. 10 and 97 para. 51 (2), referring to 95–6 para. 49. This is perhaps an extreme example.

[28] *Legality of the Threat or Use of Nuclear Weapons* [1996-I] ICJ Rep 226, 237 para. 16.

[29] See *Accordance with International Law of the Unilateral Declaration of Independence in respect of Kosovo*, [2010-I] ICJ Rep 403, 443ff. paras. 102–9, and C. Greenwood, 'Judicial Integrity and the Advisory Jurisdiction of the International Court of Justice', in G. Gaja and J. Grote Stoutenberg (eds.), *Enhancing the Rule of Law through the International Court of Justice* (Leiden: Brill, 2014).

Court can grasp what the problem is on which the Court is asked to advise. It is, however, normal for the dossier to contain, or have attached to it, a document of a more argumentative, or contentious, nature, particularly when the general motivation of the request is to have the Court endorse a particular view of the law taken by the organization, or by the majority of States in the organ submitting the request. More closely resembling pleadings are the written statements submitted under Article 66 paragraph 2 of the Statute. All States entitled to appear before the Court are informed that the request has been made (Art. 66 para. 1); but the Registrar is required by paragraph 2 to address a 'special and direct communication' to such of those States (and any international organization) that is considered 'as likely to be able to furnish information on the question', inviting them to submit a written statement or an oral statement at the eventual hearings.[30] 'Likely to be able to furnish information' is a diplomatic way of saying 'Likely to want to put its views forward', since in most cases there is not likely to be any factual information needed that is not already in the Secretary-General's dossier. The Statute indicates in general terms that those States (and organizations) that have filed statements are to be able to comment on the other statements submitted (Art. 66 para. 4). In practice, this results in a procedure which amounts to a multilateral exchange of argument parallel to the bilateral exchange which constitutes contentious procedure: general exchange of written statements (Memorials, as it were); general exchange of comments (Counter-Memorials); oral argument by each participant; oral reply by each participant.[31]

The principle of the public nature of the Court's proceedings is preserved, for the written stage of advisory cases, by Article 106 of the Rules; as with contentious pleadings, the Court (or the President) may decide that these be 'made accessible to the public'. However, the States involved in a 'legal question actually pending' have first to be consulted, in the same way as parties to a contentious case are consulted under Article 53 of the Rules.

(3) The oral proceedings

In the *Fasla* case, already mentioned, the Court observed that

> when under Article 66, paragraph 2, of its Statute, written statements have been presented to the Court in advisory proceedings, the further procedure in the case, and in particular the holding of public hearings for the purpose of receiving oral statements, is a matter within the discretion of the Court. In exercising that discretion, the Court will have regard both to the provisions of its Statute and to the requirements of its judicial character.[32]

The reasons for the omission of oral proceedings in that case, and in subsequent staff appeal cases, have been dealt with already. Earlier, in the case concerning *Voting Procedure on Questions Relating to Reports and Petitions Concerning the Territory of*

[30] If an eligible State has not received the communication, it can ask the Court to permit it to submit a statement: Statute, Art. 66 para. 3.

[31] In practice of course not every participating State wishes to take advantage of every one of these opportunities of making its views known.

[32] [1973] ICJ Rep 166, 181 para. 36.

South West Africa, when the Court announced the date fixed for the hearings, no State requested to be heard, and the Court accordingly held no oral proceedings.[33]

The organization of the hearings in an advisory case may be more complex than in a contentious case. First, there may be many more than two States exercising the right to speak; and this also means that it is not a matter of hearing one side of the case, then the other. In the two cases concerning the legality of nuclear weapons the Court heard, in addition to the representative of WHO, the representatives of twenty-one States.[34] What is important, however, is that at least the principle of argument and counter-argument has to be respected, so that so far as possible every argument may be exposed to the stated criticism of those holding the opposite, or a different, view.

Article 46 of the Statute, concerning the public nature of the oral proceedings, is presumably to be applied, on the basis of the general assimilation of advisory to contentious procedure in Article 68. As noted in Chapter 8 section F, Article 46 apparently gives the parties to a contentious case the right to 'demand' that the public be not admitted to the hearings; it must be doubtful whether this right extends to the States concerned with a 'pending legal question', as quasi-parties, but the Court would no doubt give considerable weight to a joint request by all the States in that category.

(4) Delivery of the opinion

Article 107 paragraph 2 of the Rules gives a summary indication of what is to be contained in an advisory opinion. The process of preparation and drafting of an opinion differs little from that of a judgment (examined in Ch. 10 sects. A and C).

The public delivery of the advisory opinion is the subject of a specific article of the Statute (Art. 67), rather than being left to the operation of Article 58, on delivery of judgments, coupled with Article 68; it is also required by Article 107 paragraph 1 of the Rules. Notice has to be given to the 'representatives of Members of the United Nations, of other States and of international organizations immediately concerned', presumably those that have been actively involved in the proceedings, and any others in the category of 'legal question pending States'. Specific provision is made for notification of the UN Secretary-General; this is read to include also the corresponding officer of such bodies as ILO or WHO when it is one of these that has requested the opinion.[35]

An advisory opinion is by definition not binding; this aspect of the subject is considered in Chapter 11 section B.

[33] [1955] ICJ Rep 67, 70. It appears that if even one State does wish to be heard, oral proceedings will be held: cf. *Admissibility of Hearing of Petitioners by the Committee on South West Africa*, where the UK representative was the only speaker: *Pleadings*, pp. 40–1.

[34] [1996-I] ICJ Rep 69–71 and 230–2. Admittedly, these did not represent 21 totally diverging views, but fell to some extent into groups.

[35] See e.g. *Constitution of the Maritime Safety Committee of IMCO, Pleadings* 471, nos. 70 and 71.

V

THE DECISION

10

Form, Content, and Preparation of Decisions

A. Judgments and orders

The principal decisions discussed in this chapter may be judgments or advisory opinions; in many respects, especially as regards their form and the process of their preparation, these do not greatly differ. The Court also embodies its decisions for certain purposes in what are termed 'Orders': for the most part these decisions are directed to comparatively minor matters, such as the fixing and prolongation of time-limits, and the question whether they are 'binding' (Statute, Art. 59) does not really arise. However, this is also the form used for the joinder of proceedings (Rules, Art. 47), admission of counter-claims (Rules, Art. 80), and—of great importance in practice—the indication (or refusal) of provisional measures (Statute, Art. 41; Rules, Arts. 73–8). The logic of the distinction is apparently that a judgment embodies either the final disposition of the case, resolving the dispute, or at least the final decision of a disputed legal aspect such as the existence of jurisdiction or the admissibility of a claim: matters that form the subject of preliminary objections. The matters dealt with by orders may be classified as adjectival rather than going to the substantive dispute;[1] another way of viewing the distinction may be that a decision takes the form of a judgment if it puts an end to the case, or is capable of putting an end to it. Thus both a decision to uphold a preliminary objection and a decision to reject any such objection, opening the way to a continuation of the proceedings on the merits, take that form.

Some decisions, particularly those regulating some procedural incident arising in the course of a case are expressed simply in a letter from the Registrar to the parties to the case,[2] sometimes indicating that this is on the direction of the President. Again, the question whether these are 'binding' does not really arise, as they affect

[1] Orders are commonly expressed, following French judicial style, as a single sentence, the reasoning paragraphs being each introduced by 'Whereas' (Fr. *considérant*), and the operative clause ultimately containing the main verb. For provisional measures Orders, which tend to be rather long, this practice has been abandoned. Kolb (p. 988) suggests that for Orders the participation of judges ad hoc is not required: *sed quaere.*

[2] For an example of this method of communication to convey a radical change in the procedure in progress, see *Legality of the Use of Force* (Yugoslavia *v* Belgium), [2004] ICJ Rep 279, 287 para. 18. Up to that time the parties to the several *Use of Force* cases had understood that each of them having no national judge 'on the Bench' would be entitled to appoint a judge ad hoc; at the last minute before the hearings this procedure was radically altered. See further in Ch. 2 sect. B(2).

matters that must necessarily be settled by the Court for the orderly process of the case concerned.

B. Deciding not to decide: the role of *non liquet*

Deciding such contentious cases as are submitted to him is both the privilege and the duty of the judge. A refusal to judge will in many situations (though not all) be a silent and unreasoned favouring of the respondent, since it is the object of the applicant to obtain redress, that is, usually to alter at least the factual situation in his favour, so as to correspond with the true legal situation. It may be said to be a general principle of law that a court must give a decision in any dispute submitted over which it has jurisdiction,[3] provided the claim is admissible; these two latter aspects will be dealt with in Chapter 14 (under the heading of Preliminary Objections). And the decision must be a reasoned decision: Article 56 of the ICJ Statute, in requiring that '[t]he judgment shall state the reasons on which it is based,' states a similar principle,[4] though the degree of elaboration of the reasons will vary according to the kind and importance of the decision.

Does this principle admit of exceptions? In most legal and judicial systems, there exists at least a theoretical concept of *non liquet*, the name given to a decision not to decide; such decisions being not the exercise of an unfettered discretion, but based on considerations of principle. Strictly, the term (which means 'it is not clear') refers to the situation where there is a lacuna in the law, so that there is no rule to be applied; or possibly that the law *may* apply to the situation presented, but it is not possible to establish precisely what the applicable rule indicates in respect of this situation.[5] Does this possibility exist at the international level, and specifically in relation to the International Court of Justice?[6] There are certain cases that suggest that this may be so, or at least that the Court has acted consistently with an approach of this kind; a brief survey of these will indicate the possible bases and limits of a *non liquet* at this level.

[3] In fact the issue in the *Northern Cameroons* case, discussed below in the context of *non liquet*, was raised in that case by the United Kingdom as a preliminary objection, but an objection to jurisdiction: [1963] ICJ Rep 20. The Court regarded the case as one in which it 'finds that it has jurisdiction', but is 'not obliged to exercise it' and should refuse to do so: ibid. p. 37.

[4] The position taken by the Court in *Continental Shelf (Libya/Malta), Application of Italy to Intervene*, of offering two alternative views of the law and declining to choose between them since, in the instant case, the result would be the same ([1984] ICJ Rep 3, 24 para. 38, must be regarded as exceptional; its consistency with the principle of reasoned decisions is perhaps questionable.

[5] For an excellent study of the whole concept, see Kati Kulovesi, 'Legality or Otherwise? Nuclear Weapons and the Strategy of *Non Liquet*', X *Finnish Yearbook of International Law* (1999), 55, particularly 62–70.

[6] It is a tenable view that a *non liquet* is impossible in international law, either because that law is, by definition, complete, on the basis that whatever is not forbidden is permitted (the so-called '*Lotus* doctrine'), or on the basis that, as the law develops, any lacunae that exist automatically become filled: for a discussion of these theses, see Weil, '"The Court cannot conclude definitively . . .": *Non Liquet* Revisited', 36 *Columbia Journal of International Law* (1997) 109.

The ICJ case that is generally regarded as exemplifying a *non liquet*, or constituting the nearest thing to such, is the advisory case of *Legality of the Threat or Use of Nuclear Weapons*.[7] It might seem that the question of the possibility of declaring a *non liquet* would not arise in the context of an advisory opinion, since it is well established that the Court is free to decline to give such an opinion.[8] This power, or freedom, discussed in Chapter 6 section E, is to be distinguished from a possible power to declare a *non liquet*, however, inasmuch as its exercise involves a decision by the Court that no opinion should be given at all (for good and sufficient reason). The Court in such a case might never reach the stage of examining the facts and arguments that the requesting organ, and other interested parties, seek to lay before it as relevant to the decision sought. As the *Nuclear Weapons* case demonstrates, quite distinct from this is a finding, *after* examination of all the relevant material, that the Court *cannot*, or perhaps *should not*, give a decision, in the sense of declaring what is in its view the true legal position.

The relevant passage in the *Nuclear Weapons* opinion is as follows: the Court found that

> the threat or use of nuclear weapons would generally be contrary to the rules of international law applicable in armed conflict, and in particular the principles and rules of humanitarian law;
>
> However, in view of the current state of international law, and of the elements of fact at its disposal, the Court cannot conclude definitively whether the threat or use of nuclear weapons would be lawful or unlawful in an extreme circumstance of self-defence, in which the very survival of a State would be at stake;[9]

The reference to 'the current state of international law' indicates that this is not merely a case of insufficient evidence, which in a contentious context could be dealt with by holding that the claim, not having been sufficiently proved, would have to be dismissed. That would not amount to a *non liquet*, nor would a parallel finding in advisory proceedings. However, the 'elements of fact at [the Court's] disposal' were not the facts showing that such-and-such an act had or had not been committed: it is clear that the Court was referring to the facts that might amount to an indication of the state of customary law on the issue. Theoretically international law has all the answers, and the Court is its interpreter; but here international law gives no answer: it has none to give.[10]

One aspect of the controversial question of *non liquet* is this: if the Court finds that the issue in dispute is not covered by any existing rule of law, an evident question that arises is whether or not the Court (or indeed any international court) may make law to fill the gap. To some extent this filling-in happens fairly

[7] [1996-I] ICJ Rep 226. [8] See on this Ch. 6.

[9] ICJ Rep [1996-I] 226, 263 para. 97.

[10] A distinction has been suggested between two kinds of *non liquet*: ontological and epistemological. The first would be where there exists no rule of international law on the point; the second where the court seised of the matter cannot determine what the rule is (see D. M. Bodansky, '*Non Liquet*', in R. Wolfrum et al. (eds.), *Max Planck Encyclopedia of International Law*, vii. 698 para. 4). The passage quoted from the *Nuclear Tests* opinion seems to rely on both kinds.

frequently, when a rule that applies to one situation is applied by analogy to a similar one. In the *Nuclear Weapons* case, the Court found that 'in view of the present state of international law viewed as a whole . . . it cannot reach a definitive conclusion' on the central legal issue; but since this was not an appropriate case for argument from analogy, it is perhaps hardly surprising that that the Court was not willing to go beyond this finding, since the issue was controversial in the highest degree.[11] In the past, and in less controversial circumstances, the Court was more ready to sketch out the law as, in its view, it ought to be. At the time of the *North Sea Continental Shelf* cases in 1969, the claims of coastal States to rights over the continental shelf areas off their shores were becoming more frequent, but had not attained a degree of widespread consistency such that an incipient custom could be discerned; and while a Convention had been prepared to establish a consistent legal regime,[12] it had not been ratified by the parties to the case, nor by sufficient States generally for the Convention itself to be regarded as showing or embodying a customary rule.

The *North Sea* case was unusual in that the parties, when instituting proceedings, had not made defined claims against each other which the Court was asked to uphold or dismiss: by their Special Agreement they had asked the Court to answer a carefully defined question of law, namely 'What principles and rules of international law are applicable to the delimitation between the Parties of the areas of continental shelf in the North Sea which appertain to each of them . . .?' The only rule that had been suggested that would not depend, for its application, on subjective considerations, was the rule of equidistance; and the Court held that this was not 'a mandatory rule of customary law'. Nevertheless, 'it is not the fact . . . that rules are lacking', or that 'if the equidistance principle is not a rule of law, there has to be as an alternative some other single equivalent rule'.[13] The Court therefore went on to develop its own theory of application of 'equitable principles', and a concept of 'natural prolongation of the land territory'.[14] The parties do not appear to have been inspired by this approach when concluding delimitation agreements subsequently; and the general law on continental shelf delimitation has seen the triumph of the equidistance principle.[15]

Two other refusals to decide, in contentious cases, and on rather different grounds, have already been noted (ch. 5, sect. C), but may usefully be recalled here. In the case of *Monetary Gold Removed from Rome in 1943*, the Court was asked to determine which of the four States before it (Italy, France, the UK, and the US) was entitled to the gold; it had already been decided by an

[11] [1996-I] ICJ Rep 226, 263 para. 97. It is ironic that earlier in its decision in that case the Court, when rejecting the argument that it should refuse an opinion because to give one would require it to legislate, to make law, rejected the 'supposition that the present *corpus juris* is devoid of relevant rules in this matter': ibid. 237 para. 18.

[12] The 1958 Geneva Convention on the Continental Shelf.

[13] [1969] ICJ Rep 4, para. 83.

[14] [1969] ICJ Rep 53 para. 101 (C).

[15] This is not of course to say that the Court was wrong in rejecting that principle as customary law, simply that at the time the case was brought it had not yet attained customary law status. For a useful account of the development of the law in this respect, see Y. Tanaka, *The International Law of the Sea* (Cambridge: Cambridge University Press, 2012), 192–8.

arbitrator that the gold belonged to Albania, but the UK (for example) claimed it in settlement of the reparations owed to it in the *Corfu Channel* case. The Court found that, although its decision would only be binding on the four States before it, not on Albania, it could not decide a case in which 'Albania's legal interests would not only be affected by a decision, but would form the very subject-matter of the decision'.[16] The *Northern Cameroons* case was brought after the UN Trusteeship Agreement for the Territory of the Northern Cameroons had been terminated, in 1961; a plebiscite had been held, and the inhabitants of part of the Territory had voted to join the Federation of Nigeria, and those of the other part had voted to join the Republic of Cameroon; a General Assembly resolution of 21 April 1961 gave effect to these wishes. The Republic of Cameroon, however, thought that the vote in favour of Nigeria had resulted from unlawful actions of the United Kingdom as Trustee during the Trusteeship, and brought proceedings against the UK, not seeking to reverse the decision of the Assembly, but simply a legal declaration on these lines. The Court recognized to grant such a declaration was a possibility, but observed that if it was 'satisfied, whatever the nature of the relief claimed, that to adjudicate on the merits of an Application would be inconsistent with the judicial function, it should refuse to do so'.[17] It pointed out that there was no 'retrospective or prospective action or avoidance of action, which would constitute a compliance with the Court's judgment', and that adjudication would be 'devoid of purpose'.[18] This was referred to by Judge Fitzmaurice as 'the dismissal of a claim on what are essentially issues of propriety'.[19]

C. Deliberation and the drafting of the decision

The deliberations of the Court 'shall take place in private and remain secret' (Statute, Art. 54 para. 3); this is repeated, and elaborated upon, in Article 21 of the Rules. There is one known example of this rule being violated: the number of votes in favour of, and against, the decision on provisional measures in one of the *Nuclear Tests* cases became known to the applicant government, and was indiscreetly (and perhaps inadvertently) publicized before the decision was read in public sitting.[20] Neither the Statute nor the Rules make any further provision for how the deliberation is to be conducted, but the matter is referred, by Article 19 of the Rules, to 'resolutions on the subject adopted by the Court'. The current *Resolution concerning the Internal Judicial Practice of the Court* (a public document) was adopted on 12 April 1976.[21]

[16] [1954] ICJ Rep 19, 32. [17] [1963] ICJ Rep 37. [18] [1963] ICJ Rep 38.

[19] Separate opinion. [1963] ICJ Rep 106.

[20] See the declaration of President Lachs in [1974] ICJ Rep 273; and for the details of the incident, and the enquiry by the Registry, see the Report reproduced in *ICJ Pleadings, Nuclear Tests*, ii. 386ff., No. 104.

[21] Some indications of how this is applied in practice will be found in Thirlway, 'The Drafting of ICJ Decisions: Some Personal Recollections and Observations', *ChJIL* (2006), 15–28.

A judgment or advisory opinion of the Court is normally composed of three distinct sections. Preceding these, but not treated as a part of the decision, is the Headnote, a series of key phrases referring to the various arguments set out in the decision, in the order in which they appear. When it was suggested that the headnote to a judgment established the correct interpretation of a frontier line, the Court ruled that

> [u]nder Article 95, paragraph 1, of the Rules of Court (Article 74, Paragraph 1, of the Rules of Court of 1946 applicable in 1962), the headnote is not one of the elements of the Judgment and it does not form part thereof. Moreover, the purpose of the headnote is only to give the reader a general indication of the points examined in a judgment; it does not constitute an authoritative summary of what the Court has actually decided.[22]

The first section of a decision, traditionally entitled the *qualités*, comprises essentially the procedural history of the case: how it was brought and when, the sequence of written and oral proceedings, and mention of such procedural incidents as appointments of judges ad hoc, applications to intervene and their consequences, etc. This section normally contains no reasoning: any necessary explanations of earlier procedural steps will normally have been given at the time, in many cases in an order. If such explanation is required in the final decision, this will found in the next (substantive) section of the decision.[23]

There follows the reasoning section, in which each of the issues is taken in turn and the various arguments analysed, leading to an indication of how the Court will be deciding on each. In many decisions the first part of this section is made up of a brief—sometimes not so brief—summary of the parties' arguments, without any assessment of their validity; this can be (and probably usually is) prepared by the Registry in advance. However, in the main body of the reasoning, the draftsman may well find it necessary to explain each argument, and this leads to duplication, sometimes considerable. Furthermore, the Court's decision on one disputed point may make it unnecessary to reach any decision on another; and if so, any formal summary of the parties' contentions on the latter point will become superfluous.[24]

The final section of the decision is the 'operative clause' (*dispositif*). The form of this is very much dictated, in a contentious case, by the shaping of the formal

[22] *Request for Interpretation in the 'Temple of Preah Vihear' Case*, [2013] ICJ Rep 281, 307 para. 73.

[23] Compare e.g. the explanation in the *Namibia* advisory opinion of the reasons for the rejection of South Africa's contention that the Court should not give an opinion, and the handling of its application to appoint a judge ad hoc: [1971] ICJ Rep 16, 20 paras. 14–15 and 23, paras. 28–9; ibid. 19 paras. 10–11, and the Order of 29 January 1971, [1971] ICJ Rep 12.

[24] In many recent cases, the parties' arguments are recited at great length, first those exchanged in the written proceedings, and then those from the oral argument, in chronological order. This distinction seems to be quite unnecessary, unless there is some procedural or other issue raised by the fact that a given contention was made only at the oral stage. For a recent example see the Order of 16 July 2008 in *Avena and other Mexican Nationals (Interpretation)*, [2008] ICJ Rep 311. For a case in which reproducing the arguments presented on all points was particularly inappropriate as the decision was on a preliminary point, see the Order of 15 October 2008, *Application of the Racial Discrimination Convention (Georgia* v *Russia)*, [2008] ICJ Rep 353 etc.

submissions presented by the parties. However, even if a judgment upholds a claim, the Court is not obliged to cast its decision in the exact form of the submission. For example, in the recent case of *Dispute regarding Navigational and Related Rights (Nicaragua* v *Costa Rica)*, the Court found that Nicaragua had breached certain obligations owed to Costa Rica, and Costa Rica had asked (*inter alia*) that the Court 'order Nicaragua to cease all the breaches of its obligations which have a continuing character'. The Court however declined to cast its decision in that form, noting that

> [The] obligation to cease wrongful conduct derives both from the general obligation of each State to conduct itself in accordance with international law and from the specific obligation upon States parties to disputes before the Court to comply with its judgments, pursuant to Article 59 of its Statute.
>
> It is not necessary, and it serves no useful purpose as a general rule, for the Court to recall the existence of this obligation in the operative paragraphs of the judgments it renders: the obligation incumbent on the State concerned to cease such conduct derives by operation of law from the very fact that the Court establishes the existence of a violation of a continuing character.[25]

Similarly, it declined to direct Nicaragua to give guarantees and assurances of non-repetition of unlawful conduct: the Court would

> only do so if the circumstances so warrant, which it is for the Court to assess. As a general rule, there is no reason to suppose that a State whose act or conduct has been declared wrongful by the Court will repeat that act or conduct in the future, since its good faith must be presumed.[26]

Strictly speaking, the Court cannot, even at the request of the parties, give a provisional or conditional judgment (though it can give a declaratory judgment, confined, for example, to certain aspects of a dispute). Parties to a case before the Permanent Court of International Justice once requested the Court to give an informal and non-binding indication of how it was minded to decide, so that they could negotiate a settlement on that basis; but the Court declined, on the basis that it had no power to give a ruling of this kind, which would be dependent for its implementation on the wishes of the parties.[27] A more modern case, however, concerned a treaty contemplating a complex project, which had not been completed, each party asserting breach of the treaty by the other; the Court decided (*inter alia*) that the parties 'must negotiate in good faith in the light of the prevailing situation, and must take all necessary measures to ensure achievement of the objectives' of the

[25] [2009] ICJ Rep 213, 266–7 paras. 147, 148.

[26] [2009] ICJ Rep 213, 267 para. 150, citing *Factory at Chorzów, PCIJ Series A, No. 17*, 63; *Nuclear Tests (Australia* v *France)*, [1974] ICJ Rep 272 para. 60; *Nuclear Tests (New Zealand* v *France)*, [1974] ICJ Rep 477 para. 63; and *Military and Paramilitary Activities in and against Nicaragua*, [1984] ICJ Rep 437 para. 101.

[27] *Free Zones of Upper Savoy and the District of Gex, Order of 6 December 1930, PCIJ Series A, No. 24*, 14.

treaty.[28] In any event, a judgment is always in some sense 'dependent for its implementation on the wishes of the parties' in the sense that if the parties are agreed in not liking the Court's solution of the dispute, they may always agree to substitute a solution of their own.[29]

When a judgment of the Court stops short of dealing with all the issues raised by the parties, it sometimes nevertheless comments on one of those left aside. This tends to occur particularly when, usually because of a finding of lack of jurisdiction, the merits (or an aspect of them) cannot be determined by the Court. A particularly striking, if not flagrant, example, is this, from the judgment in *Armed Activities (DRC* v *Rwanda)*; the Court had found that there was no basis whatever for jurisdiction, and continued:

> The Court is precluded by its Statute from taking any position on the merits of the claims made by the DRC. However, as the Court has stated on numerous previous occasions, there is a fundamental distinction between the question of the acceptance by States of the Court's jurisdiction and the conformity of their acts with international law. Whether or not States have accepted the jurisdiction of the Court, they are required to fulfil their obligations under the United Nations Charter and the other rules of international law, including international humanitarian and human rights law, and they remain responsible for acts attributable to them which are contrary to international law.[30]

The first sentence of this passage is correct, and is also the reason why the rest of the paragraph is inappropriate; although it is expressed in wide general terms, it cannot but be seen as a comment on the issues raised in the case.[31] It is moreover not the only example of extra-judicial admonitions of this kind.[32]

[28] *Gabčíkovo/Nagymaros Project*, [1997] ICJ Rep 7, 83 para. 155 (2) (c).

[29] Always reserving, of course, the possibility that the judgment states a rule of *jus cogens*. For an example of the parties diverging by agreement, to a limited extent, from the very precise terms of a maritime delimitation decision, see *Maritime Delimitation in the Area between Jan Mayen and Greenland*, where, by the Agreement between the parties of 18 December 1995, three out of the four points indicated by the Court as defining the line were modified: see C. Schulte, *Compliance with Decisions of the International Court of Justice* (Oxford: Oxford University Press, 2004), 223–4.

[30] [2006] ICJ Rep 6, 52–3 para. 127.

[31] It may be—though this is merely a hypothesis—that this passage and other similar ones could have resulted from attempts to secure the most substantial majority possible, that a judge hesitating, but inclined to favour upholding jurisdiction in order to deal with the merits, might be more inclined to join the majority if something of this kind could be said. This however is speculation (and not based on any incident known to the writer).

[32] e.g. the Court's criticism of the ill-fated attempt to rescue the hostages in *United States Diplomatic and Consular Staff in Tehran*, [1980] ICJ Rep 3, 43–4 paras. 93–4; the penultimate paragraph of the judgment declining jurisdiction in the *Armed Activities (DRC* v *Rwanda)* case: [2006] ICJ Rep 6, 52–3 para. 127; the 'reminder' to the parties of their duty to comply with the Racial Discrimination Convention, in the Order of 15 October 2008, *Application of the Racial Discrimination Convention (Georgia* v *Russia)*, [2008] ICJ Rep 353, 398 para. 149; etc. In favour of this practice, see J. d'Aspremont, 'The Recommendations Made by the International Court of Justice', (2007) 56 *ICLQ* 185–98, and the present writer's response, 'The Recommendations Made by the International Court of Justice: A Sceptical View', (2009) 58 *ICLQ* 160. See also Ch. 4, text and n. 11, and Ch. 16, text and n. 28.

D. Adoption of the decision: voting

Article 55 paragraph 1 of the Statute provides that '[a]ll questions shall be decided by a majority of the judges present' and paragraph 2 gives a casting vote to 'the President or the judge who acts in his place'. The need for this is infrequent, since the question arises only if the Court is composed of an even number of judges (e.g. because there is only one judge ad hoc, or as a result of sickness or disqualification of a judge).[33] There may be judges who are not sitting in the case, and therefore automatically excluded from being present, and thus from voting. This may be because they are disqualified from the case under Articles 17 or 24 of the Statute; or have been granted periodic leave under Article 23 paragraph 2 of the Statute; because they have been 'dispensed from sitting' under Article 25 paragraph 2 of the Statute;[34] or because they became Members of the Court after the opening of the oral proceedings, and are thus not sitting in the case.

Absence for any other reason (e.g. illness) from the meeting at which the decision is taken also excludes the judge concerned.[35] The Resolution Concerning the Internal Judicial Practice of the Court (Art. 9 (ii)) contains provisions intended to avoid the exclusion of a judge 'because of physical incapacity or other compelling reason'; while in principle '[a] judge who is qualified to participate in the final vote must record his vote in person', arrangements may be made for the planned meeting for the vote to be postponed; or for the Court to 'convene elsewhere than at its normal meeting place', e.g. beside a judge's hospital bed. Except where these provisions apply, the vote of a judge absent from The Hague (or simply from the meeting) cannot be recorded. The minimum number of judges required to constitute the Court (the quorum) is nine (Statute, Art. 25 para. 3). In the earlier years of the Court, it might sometimes be necessary to convene in the absence of one or more judges from remote countries; and a meeting with a limited number of judges might still sometimes be necessary in urgent cases, for example on a request for provisional measures in a death-penalty case. However, not only has international travel become speedier, but the Court now spends so much of the year in session that such a request is much less likely to be presented at a time when most of the judges are absent.

[33] The only final decisions so adopted have been the PCIJ decision in the *S.S. Lotus* case, *PCIJ Series A, No. 1, South West Africa* [1966] ICJ Rep 51 para. 100; one issue in the *Nuclear Weapons* advisory opinion [1996] ICJ Rep 266 para. 105 (2) E; and on Colombia's Third Preliminary Objection in *Delimitation of the Continental Shelf between Nicaragua and Colombia* [2016] ICJ Rep para. 126 (1)(*b*).

[34] The article states that the Rules of the Court 'may provide for allowing one or more judges, according to circumstances and in rotation', to be so dispensed; this is distinct from 'periodic leave' under Art. 23. In fact the present Rules do not make any such provision, so an absence for this reason remains no more than theoretical or potential.

[35] Article 23 paragraph 2 of the Statute confers on Members of the Court an entitlement on periodic leave, which of course would justify a judge's absence; but with the increased workload of the Court this text has become something of a dead letter; the Court adjourns as a body periodically (e.g. at Christmas, and in the summer) to the extent that its calendar permits.

A principle generally recognized is that a judge may not abstain, but must vote in the affirmative or negative on every question; this is, in fact, nowhere stated in the Statute or Rules of Court, but is provided for in the Judicial Practice Resolution (Art. 8 (iv)). Apart from the risk that, if abstention were permitted, it might be impossible to form a majority in favour of any solution, so far as questions of law are concerned, it is the essence of judicial duty to form a view and thus to decide. As to controverted questions of fact, in contentious cases, the judge is assisted by the rule as to burden of proof: if a judge finds it difficult to say whether or not he is convinced on a particular point, he may conclude that, for him, the burden of proof has not been discharged, and he can reject the claim on that point with a good conscience.

A judge may agree with the result, but for reasons other than those set out in the decision, which will have been drafted to reflect the views of the majority; his proper course is then to vote in favour of the *dispositif* (the operative clause), and—if he wishes—to add an opinion explaining his position.[36] The judgment itself does not distinguish between judges who endorse it and judges who merely agree with the result.[37]

Cases before the International Court are rarely simple; in many, there are a number of issues or questions, some of which arise only if a particular previous question is resolved in a particular sense. The most obvious example is where jurisdiction is disputed; if it is found that there is no jurisdiction, then the Court is not called upon to decide any of the other issues raised. It would seem to go without saying that an individual judge who disagrees with a decision on a preliminary issue is nevertheless bound by his colleagues' decision, to the extent that the decision forms an essential step in the argument towards the final decision of the case. If the Court rejects a preliminary objection to jurisdiction, and the case continues, the dissenting judge may not refuse to participate in the decision on the merits, on the ground that his view continues to be that the Court lacks jurisdiction. This is equally so if the decision on jurisdiction and that on the merits are taken in one and the same judgment. As Judge Onyeama observed, when he found himself in this position, Members of the Court may express their dissent in opinions, but '[h]aving expressed their separate opinions, they should then approach the rest of the case on the footing that the Court's decision on jurisdiction is the right one.'[38]

The position may be less simple in advisory cases. Here again, if the Court decides (contrary to some arguments submitted to it) that it has jurisdiction to give the opinion, a judge who took the opposite view must nevertheless participate in the formulation of the opinion given, and vote upon the points in the operative clause. However, it may be recalled that the Court, even if it has jurisdiction to give a particular advisory opinion, has the discretion to refuse to give it. If the Court, having

[36] On judges' separate or dissenting opinions generally, see Ch. 12.

[37] An unexplained exception to this is the 1970 judgment in the *Barcelona Traction, Light & Power Co.* case, which rejected the Belgian claim 'by fifteen votes to one, twelve votes of the majority being based on the reasons set out in the present Judgment': [1970] ICJ Rep 3, 51 para. 103.

[38] *Application for Review of UNAT Judgment No. 158*, [1973] ICJ Rep 223.

considered whether, in the exercise of its discretion, it should give the opinion or decline to give it, decides to give the opinion, does the principle just mentioned require that any judge who voted for a refusal of the opinion should nevertheless participate fully in the decision as to the content of the opinion to be given?

This was the problem facing Judge Buergenthal in the *Wall* case. He explained his thinking in a declaration to the Court's opinion, to the following effect:

> Since I believe that the Court should have exercised its discretion and declined to render the requested advisory opinion, I dissent from its decision to hear the case. My negative votes with regard to the remaining items of the *dispositif* [i.e. those other than the decision to give the opinion] should not be seen as reflecting my view that the construction of the wall by Israel in the Occupied Palestinian Territory does not raise serious questions as a matter of international law. I believe it does, and there is much in the opinion with which I agree. However, I am compelled to vote against the Court's findings on the merits because the Court did not have before it the requisite factual bases for its sweeping findings; it should therefore have declined to hear the case.[39]

While one may sympathize with Judge Buergenthal's dilemma, this position inspires doubts. If the reason for his view, that the opinion should be refused, had been, let us say, that to give the opinion would in effect amount to deciding an inter-State dispute contrary to the wishes of the States concerned, then seemingly he should have accepted that the majority was correct in thinking otherwise, and examined the request on its merits, following the Onyeama formula. But his position went beyond saying that it would not be proper for the Court to give the opinion; his view was that it was not *possible* for it to do so, for lack of factual evidence; and this was an advisory case where there was no *onus probandi* to come to the rescue.

It is nevertheless suggested that the proper course for a judge in this position is, having endeavoured, but failed, to convince his colleagues that the factual material as a whole was inadequate for an opinion to be given, then to argue on each factual finding,[40] and vote on each part of the *dispositif* on its own merits.

[39] *Legal Consequences of the Construction of a Wall in the Occupied Palestinian Territory*, declaration, [2004-I] ICJ Rep 240.

[40] Which Judge Buergenthal may of course have done, this being covered by the secret of the deliberations. Whether he could have called for a separate vote on each such issue depends on the interpretation of Art. 8 (ii) of the *Resolution concerning the Internal Judicial Practice of the Court.*

11

The Effect of the Decision and its Enforcement

A. Judgments

Article 59 of the Statute states that '[t]he decision of the Court has no binding force except between the parties and in respect of that particular case.' The effect of this is to protect third States: a State that has gained a judgment against one particular respondent stating, it may be, a particular legal rule, cannot validly assert that that rule is equally and automatically applicable to its relations with a third State, so that the third State is bound by it. The distinction between this and the recognized value of ICJ judgments as precedents may sometimes be a fine one, but it is essential.

Where problems have arisen in connection with the application of Article 59, these have not concerned judicial statement of legal rules so much as the effect of the judgment 'on the ground'. In the *Frontier Dispute* between Burkina Faso and Mali, the Court had to consider whether it could indicate a land frontier line between the two parties in a region where a third State might have sovereignty over certain areas. The relevant passage from the decision[1] is cited in Chapter 5 section C: essentially the argument is that, as a result of Article 59, a judgment defining a frontier between two States has no more impact on a neighbouring third State than would have a frontier agreement concluded between the first two States. Nevertheless, in its decision in *Land and Maritime Boundary between Cameroon and Nigeria*, when dealing with maritime boundaries, the Court distinguished the earlier decision as inappropriate outside a land-boundary context. It considered that 'in particular in the case of maritime delimitation where the maritime areas of several States are involved, the protection afforded by Article 59 of the Statute may not always be sufficient'; and the Article might 'not sufficiently protect' a named third State 'from the effects—even if only indirect—of a judgment affecting their legal rights'.[2] Quite how this could occur is not specified: and there is a certain *petitio principii* involved in defining the decision as one 'affecting their legal rights'.[3]

Since Article 59 provides that 'The decision of the Court has no binding force except between the parties and in respect of that particular case', it necessarily implies *a contrario* that, between the parties and in respect of the particular case, it is

[1] [1986] ICJ Rep 554, 577 para. 46. [2] [2002] ICJ Rep 303, 421 para. 238.

[3] The point may be that land boundaries are usually based on historical fact, while maritime boundaries may be based on proportions, so that if there is an unknown in the equation, injustice to the absent State can only be avoided by limiting the scope of the decision.

binding. Furthermore, under Article 94 paragraph 1 of the Charter, 'Each Member of the United Nations undertakes to comply with the decision of the International Court of Justice in any case to which it is a party.'[4] What is the significance of this 'binding force', and to what extent do Court decisions have a role as precedents? First, as to the scope of the provision, which clearly applies to a judgment, are Orders also binding?[5] Orders of a procedural nature must be, within the procedural context; even a time-limit Order must be respected, on pain of, for example, a pleading submitted out of time not being included in the case-file.[6] If proceedings in two cases are joined, or a counter-claim is admitted, by means of an Order, the decision is, as it were, self-executing, so that the question of compliance with it does not arise. Orders indicating provisional measures are a special case: whether or not such measures are 'binding' on the parties was for long a controversial question, finally settled by the decision in the *LaGrand* case.[7] The measures do thus constitute a binding obligation on the party or parties to whom they are addressed; but this is a direct consequence of Article 41 of the Statute, as interpreted in *LaGrand*, and the procedural form (an Order) in which they are couched is irrelevant. A judgment would in fact not be the appropriate form for provisional measures, as no part of the dispute is finally decided, as indeed the term 'provisional measures' indicates.

By virtue of the Charter, there is a clear obligation of treaty law to treat a judgment of the Court as binding and to comply with it. In legal theory, however, the judgments of the Court are in principle declaratory of the rights and obligations of the parties, not creative of new rights and obligations.[8] If therefore the Court decides, for example, that under a provision in a treaty, the correct interpretation of which is disputed, one of the parties is under a particular obligation, that obligation results from the treaty (as authoritatively interpreted), but is backed by the obligation to

[4] This commitment does not, as such, apply to parties to the Statute that are not UN members, or to States admitted to appear without being parties to the Statute. However, when the General Assembly admits a State, under Art. 93 of the Charter, to become a party to the Statute, it always attaches as a condition 'Acceptance of all the obligations of a Member of the United Nations under Article 94 of the Charter' (see GA Res 91 (I), 11 December 1946 (Switzerland); 3 GA Res 63 (IV), 1 December 1949 (Liechtenstein); GA Res 806).

[5] Arts. 56, 57, 58, 60, and 61 all refer to the 'judgment' of the Court: Art. 59 (and Art. 62, on intervention) refers to the 'decision'. This may simply result from the drafting history: what became Art. 59 of the PCIJ Statute was proposed separately from the other texts (see C. Brown in Zimmermann et al., *Commentary*, Art. 59 para. 5 pp. 1418–20.

[6] There seem to be no instances where delay has gone so far, and the Court would certainly be very reluctant to ignore a document actually submitted merely on the ground that it was out of time. Usually a request is made for an extension of time, sometimes at the last possible moment. There have been cases where a respondent State has chosen not to take part in the proceedings at all, or to withdraw its participation, and therefore has allowed the time-limit for a pleading to pass without taking any action: see for example *Corfu Channel*, where Albania contended in a letter that the Court had no jurisdiction to assess the compensation due to the United Kingdom, and therefore filed no pleading in that phase of the proceedings: [1949] ICJ Rep 246; *United States Diplomatic and Consular Staff in Tehran*, [1980] ICJ Rep 5 paras. 4–5; *Military and Paramilitary Activities in and Against Nicaragua* [1986] ICJ Rep 17 para. 11.

[7] *LaGrand (Germany* v *USA)* [2001] ICJ Rep 506 para. 100; see further Ch. 13 sect. A. The fact that doubt subsisted, while measures were always indicated in an Order, suggest that that form has never been regarded as conferring binding force on its content.

[8] With the possible exception of Orders indicating provisional measures: see Ch. 13 sect. A.

comply with the judgment. The only special status that the existence of the judgment confers on the original obligation is confirmation that it exists, in the sense that no alternative interpretation of the treaty provision is legally possible.[9] Similarly for an obligation of customary law declared by a judgment, which is taken to have existed before the judgment and independently of it.

However, the fact that the judgment is binding on the parties is expressed in the principle that *res judicata pro veritate habetur*. That principle was the subject of much discussion in a recent case, in which the Court declared that 'the principle of *res judicata*, as reflected in Articles 59 and 60 of [the Court's] Statute, is a general principle of law which protects, at the same time, the judicial function of a court or tribunal and the parties to a case which has led to a judgment that is final and without appeal'.[10] The principle implies that the legal situation is as declared by the Court, and not otherwise, specifically not as contended by the party whose arguments have not been upheld. When the case concerns the conduct of one of the parties, if 'the Court has found that the conduct of [that] State is of a wrongful nature, and in the event that this conduct persists on the date of the judgment, the State concerned is obliged to cease it immediately'.[11] As a matter of ICJ practice, the Court explained that '[i]t is not necessary, and it serves no useful purpose as a general rule, for the Court to recall the existence of this obligation in the operative paragraphs of the judgments it renders . . . The Court may consider it appropriate, in special circumstances, to mention that obligation expressly in the operative part of its judgment.'[12] Article 59 does not of course oblige the parties to comply with the judgment if, after it has been given, they agree on some other course of action or solution to the dispute. In maritime delimitation disputes, the Court has sometimes been asked to draw a very precise line or give very precise indications as to how it should be drawn, but the parties have sometimes modified such prescriptions between themselves.[13] Cases of this kind also show that the parties

[9] Note the special case of an interpretation of the Statute of the Court (which is first and foremost a treaty) in the *LaGrand* case, and the subsequent finding, in the *Genocide Convention* case ([2007-I] ICJ Rep 43, 230 para. 453), that the interpretation there given had always been the correct interpretation: discussed in Ch. 13.

[10] *Delimitation of the Continental Shelf between Nicaragua and Colombia beyond 200 nautical miles* [2016] ICJ Rep para. 58. See also the discussion of the principle in the Joint Dissenting Opinion of Vice-President Yusuf, Judges Cançado Trindade, Xue, Gaja, Bandhari, Robinson, and Judge ad hoc Brouwer. Although the question was related to an issue on which the Court was completely divided, there was no real disagreement over the significance of the principle itself, but simply over what the judgment alleged to have created *res judicata* had in fact decided.

[11] *Dispute regarding Navigational and Related Rights (Nicaragua* v *Costa Rica)*, [2009] ICJ Rep 267 para. 148. The Court explained that this obligation 'derives both from the general obligation of each State to conduct itself in accordance with international law and from the specific obligation upon States parties to disputes before the Court to comply with its judgments, pursuant to Article 59 of its Statute' (ibid.).

[12] Ibid.

[13] See e.g. the *Greenland/Jan Mayen* case: in the Agreement of 18 December 1995 drawing the delimitation lines between fisheries zones and the continental shelf, the parties adjusted three of four points indicated by the ICJ in its decision, thus partly modifying the ICJ judgment by agreement. See C. Schulte, *Compliance with Decisions of the International Court of Justice* (Oxford: Oxford University Press, 2004), 223–4; Report by Anderson in J. I. Charney and L. M. Alexander (eds.), *International*

are not obliged to conform to their rights and duties as declared in the Court's judgment: except in matters of *jus cogens*, they may by agreement adjust their mutual conduct to a different view of the applicable law. A rule of law from which States may depart by agreement does not become more intangible merely by being declared in a judgment.

The significance of Article 59 of the statute is that no judgment of the Court operates as binding precedent of general application. There is, however, a sense in which a judgment of the Court is also binding on the Court itself; not as a precedent in a similar or analogous case, but within the confines of the case itself (subject to the possibility of revision, examined in Ch. 16 sect. B). Setting aside that possibility, and that of a request for interpretation, there is, of course, no reason why a judgment on the merits of a case should ever come before the Court again for consideration.

However, as a result in particular of the system of preliminary objections, there may be two (or even more) judgments given in the same case; and between the dates of two such judgments there may have been such changes in the composition of the Court as to influence what would be, or might be, the majority view. Clearly, the new majority, composed of judges who take the view, shall we say, that the Court was mistaken in holding that it had jurisdiction, cannot just substitute for the expected judgment on the merits a new judgment with a negative finding on jurisdiction. The *South West Africa* cases are illuminating in this respect. In 1962, the Court held, by a majority of eight votes to seven, that it had 'jurisdiction to adjudicate on the merits of the case'.[14] By the time it came to give a decision on the merits, in 1966, the composition of the Court had undergone a marked change, and it appears that the supporters of jurisdiction had become fewer.[15] Contrary to all expectations, the Court did not give a judgment on the merits in 1966: the text was headed 'Second Phase', and it decided, 'by the President's casting vote, the votes being equally divided', to reject the claims of the applicants, not on their substance, but on the 'preliminary' point that they had not established that they possessed any 'right or interest' of the kind protected by the jurisdictional clause relied on. Whatever the legal validity of this finding, the decision was widely regarded as 'the revenge of the 1962 minority', a de facto reversal of the finding in favour of jurisdiction. The device adopted—if it was a device, since the bona fides of the 1966 majority need not be questioned—did not involve any infringement of the legal validity of the 1962 judgment; the 1966 decision merely argued that an issue not dealt with in 1962 was as fatal to the Court's power to decide the merits as was (according to the respondents and the 1962 minority) the jurisdictional objection.

A judgment may be relied on in argument in a later case, but neither the findings of fact nor the reasoning in law have any compelling force for the Court in the

Maritime Boundary (Dordrecht: Nijhoff, 1993), ii. 2517 and 2519. (I owe this example to Professor Yoshifumi Tanaka.)

[14] [1962] ICJ Rep 319, 347.

[15] At this time the Court did not indicate the names of the judges voting each way (this was an innovation in the 1978 Rules of Court), but the separate and dissenting opinions filed give clues to the distribution of votes.

later case: that is the essence of Article 59 of the Statute. In the case of the *Land and Maritime Frontier between Cambodia and Nigeria*,[16] counsel for Nigeria endeavoured to convince the Court that a previous decision,[17] on a point of interpretation of the Statute, should be departed from in the case before it. It was submitted that the earlier case was one of 'first impression', that 'the Judgment given is outdated, and that it is an isolated one; that international law, especially as it relates to good faith, has evolved since and that in accordance with Article 59 of the Statute, that Judgment only has the force of *res judicata* between the parties and in respect of that case'.[18] The Court rejected this submission, and in effect repeated the argument that had been adopted in the earlier decision. It observed that, on the basis of Article 59, '[t]here can be no question of holding Nigeria to decisions reached by the Court in previous cases. The real question is whether, in this case, there is cause not to follow the reasoning and conclusions of earlier cases.'[19] It then examined, and dismissed, Nigeria's arguments that the law had moved on since 1960, either as regarding the law of treaties or in relation to the role of good faith, taking the view that there had been no significant change in this respect. It thereby implicitly recognized, as it could hardly fail to do, that if a previous decision can be shown to have been based on law that has been modified by subsequent developments, this would be a reason *not* to 'follow the reasoning and conclusions of earlier cases'.

More difficult is the question that arises when the Court is asked, in two or more separate cases, to consider the same historical set of facts: the evident example is afforded by the events in the former Yugoslavia examined in the two cases concerning *Application of the Genocide Convention*.[20] In the later of these two decisions, the Court said:

> While some of the facts and the legal issues dealt with in those cases arise also in the present case, none of those decisions were given in proceedings between the two Parties to the present case (Croatia and Serbia), so that, as the Parties recognize, no question of *res judicata* arises (Article 59 of the Statute of the Court). To the extent that the decisions contain findings of law, the Court will treat them as it treats all previous decisions: that is to say that, while those decisions are in no way binding on the Court, it will not depart from its settled jurisprudence unless it finds very particular reasons to do so.[21]

Despite the reference to the 'facts' at the beginning of this passage, the Court did not go on to consider whether or not, in principle, it could take account of factual findings in the earlier case. However, such an examination would have been premature, as the 2008 judgment was addressed solely to preliminary objections to jurisdiction. At the stage of the merits, the Court noted that the parties agreed that 'the

[16] Preliminary Objections, [1998] ICJ Rep 275.

[17] *Right of Passage over Indian Territory*, [1960] ICJ Rep 6. The question was whether an optional-clause declaration can be relied on if the other party was, when proceedings were instituted, unaware that it had been made: see Ch. 5 sect. A(3).

[18] [1998] ICJ Rep 275, 290 para. 24.

[19] [1998] ICJ Rep 275, 292 para. 28.

[20] *Bosnia* v *Serbia*, [2007] ICJ Rep 43; *Croatia* v *Serbia*, [2008] ICJ Rep 412. Cf. also the various cases concerning *Armed Activities on the Territory of the Congo*.

[21] [2008] ICJ Rep 412, 428 para. 53.

standard of proof, laid down by the Court in its 2007 Judgment in the proceedings between Bosnia and Herzegovina and Serbia is applicable in the present case',[22] but did not in fact rely on any of the same evidence.

One field in which the Court tends to give practically automatic respect to previous decisions of its own is that of its own procedure; there is much to be said for consistency in this respect. Matters of this kind tend to be resolved on successive occasions with a reference to previous cases, the list of citations in support tends thus to get longer and longer!

A wider question is whether or to what extent a judgment of the Court contributes to international law on the questions with which it deals.[23] Article 38 of the Statute gives to 'judicial decisions and the teachings of the most highly qualified publicists' the status merely of 'subsidiary means for the determination of rules of law', and it is generally understood that the decisions referred to include those of the Court itself. Nevertheless, the Court is not alone in adopting the approach that its own decisions can be treated as precedents, to a much greater extent than Articles 38 and 59 of the Statute would suggest. This is a much-debated field, which will not be fully explored here.[24]

If the party against which a judgment has been given fails to comply with it, what steps are open to the successful party? Sometimes, of course, a judgment is purely declaratory of the rights of the parties, and there is nothing further required to be done. Complete non-observance of a duty, for example of reparation,[25] is something that has not frequently occurred, though the most marked example was the very first case heard by the post-War Court, the *Corfu Channel* case. It was forty-five years before Albania, the losing party, paid the indemnities ordered by the Court's judgment to be paid to the United Kingdom; in the interim, the United Kingdom endeavoured to compensate itself by intercepting monetary gold belonging to Albania (see the *Monetary Gold* case discussed in Ch. 10 sect. B). This was, of course, an extra-Statute remedy, on the simple basis that Albania owed a debt and the origin of the debt was irrelevant.

There is no provision in the Statute for what might be termed enforcement of a judgment, but this is provided for in the Charter. As mentioned earlier in this section, Article 94 contains an undertaking by the Members to comply with decisions of the Court, and the article continues: 'If any party to a case fails to perform the obligations on it under a judgment rendered by the Court, the other party may have

[22] Judgment of 3 February 2015, [2015] ICJ Rep para. 177.

[23] The extent to which national courts recognize ICJ decisions as authoritative definitions of the law varies: German courts apparently regard such decisions as persuasive 'even in cases in which Germany was not a party': see B. Simma and C. Hoppe, 'The *LaGrand* Case: A Story of Many Miscommunications', in J. Noyes et al. (eds.), *International Stories* (New York: Foundation, 2007), 371, 402–3, citing the Bundesverfassungsgerichtshof, 2 BvR 2115/01 para. 62.

[24] For an excellent study of the matter in relation specifically to the Court, see M. Byers, *Custom, Power and the Power of Rules* (Cambridge: Cambridge University Press, 1999), 120–4 (the theory of 'legitimate expectation'); also Thirlway, *The Sources of International Law* (Oxford: Oxford University Press, 2014), 120–6.

[25] As distinct from repudiating the legal position stated in a judgment, as did, e.g. the US in the *Armed Activities* case: that case was withdrawn before the Court ruled on compensation.

recourse to the Security Council, which may, if it deems necessary, make recommendations or decide upon measures to be taken to give effect to the judgment.' Very little use has been made of this faculty,[26] which does not confer any additional powers on the Security Council; the political implications of any attempt to enforce a judgment by this means need not be gone into here.

Two requests in recent years for the interpretation of a judgment under Article 60 of the Statute may be seen as, in effect, attempts to enforce the judgment: that of Mexico in relation to the *Avena* case, and that of Cambodia in relation to the *Temple of Preah Vihear*. These cases are considered in Chapter 16. In 2015 Nicaragua brought a totally independent new case in an endeavour to enforce a judgment given in a case between itself and Colombia, with which Colombia had allegedly refused to comply. One of the grounds of jurisdiction asserted was, in effect, that the earlier case was still continuing, that the subject-matter of its Application 'remained' within the Court's jurisdiction, because in its earlier judgment 'the Court did not definitively determine the question—of which it was seised—of the delimitation of the continental shelf . . .'[27] The Court found that it had jurisdiction on a different ground, and therefore did not rule on this assertion.[28]

B. Advisory opinions

The essence of an advisory opinion is that it is advisory, not determinative: it expresses the view of the Court as to the relevant international legal principles and rules, but does not oblige any State, not even the body that asked for the opinion, to take or refrain from any action. The distinction, clear in theory, is less so in practice: if the Court advises, for example, that a certain obligation exists, the State upon which it is said to rest has not bound itself to accept the Court's finding, but it will be in a weak position if it seeks to argue that the considered opinion of the Court does not represent a correct view of the law. Thus the advisory procedure may be used to bring pressure to bear on a State that is out of step with the general view of States on a legal question that particularly concerns that State: for example, South Africa in relation to Namibia;[29] and Israel and its supporters in relation to Palestine.[30]

[26] The United Kingdom made some attempt to enforce the Order indicating provisional measures in the *Anglo-Iranian Oil Co.* case, [1951] ICJ Rep 89, but without success. Nicaragua endeavoured by this means to enforce the judgment in the *Military and Paramilitary Activities* case ([1986] ICJ Rep 14) against the United States, but the negative vote of the US on the draft resolution submitted was treated as an exercise of the veto, so that the resolution was not adopted; for the arguments on whether this is a correct interpretation of the Charter, see B. Simma et al. (eds.), *The Charter of the United Nations: A Commentary*, ii. 1177–8, *sub* Art. 94 para. 13.

[27] *Delimitation of the Continental Shelf between Nicaragua and Colombia beyond 200 nautical miles*, [2016] ICJ Rep para. 14.

[28] Ibid. paras. 91–4.

[29] See *Legal Consequences of the Continued Presence of South Africa in Namibia (South West Africa) notwithstanding Security Council resolution 276 (1970)*, [1971] ICJ Rep 16.

[30] See *Legal Consequences of the Construction of a Wall in the Occupied Palestine Territory* [2004-I] ICJ Rep 136.

The essentially non-binding character of an advisory opinion has in the past given rise to some doubts as to the legal effect of a treaty commitment whereby an opinion of the Court is to be accepted, by the parties to the treaty, as binding. One field in which treaty provisions of this kind have proved useful is the relations between international organizations, particularly the United Nations itself, and States. Since an international organization cannot be a party to proceedings before the Court, a dispute between an organization and a State cannot be settled by contentious proceedings.

A device that has been used to meet the difficulty is to provide in a convention (e.g. the 1946 Convention on the Privileges and Immunities of the United Nations) that, in the event of a dispute of this kind, the General Assembly (or other organ concerned) will ask the Court for an advisory opinion on the point at issue, and that it is agreed in advance that the Court's opinion will be accepted as 'decisive' by the State and the organization. It is established that since the essentially non-binding character of the opinion itself is not affected, there is no legal obstacle to the conclusion of an agreement of this kind. Nor is such a provision essential for the Court to be able to give an advisory opinion on a legal question arising out of such a Convention. In a case where the State involved in a difference with an organ of the United Nations as to the application of a Convention had made a reservation to the article of the Convention giving 'decisive' effect to an opinion, the Court was asked for an opinion without reference to that article. The Court found that since the request for opinion made no reference to that article, the reservation was irrelevant; it observed, however, that if the request had been made 'under' the Convention article, the Court 'would of course have to consider any reservation which a party to the dispute had made' to it; the effect might have been found to be that the reservation could 'act as a bar to the operation of the request for advisory opinion, or merely ... deprive any opinion given of the decisive effect attributed to such opinions' by the Convention.[31]

Another field in which it has been found useful to employ the advisory process, in order to obtain an opinion recognized in advance by those concerned as 'binding', is that of appeals mechanisms for the staff of international bodies in disputes affecting their terms of service. The United Nations had from the beginning its own Administrative Tribunal; and as mentioned (Ch. 9 sect. A(4)), between 1955 and 1995 its Statutes provided for a review process, which could be set in motion by the staff member and not solely by the administration, that could lead to an advisory opinion of the Court. Three advisory opinions were given on the basis of this system; it was found, however, in 1995 not to have been 'a constructive or useful element in the adjudication of staff disputes within the Organization', and abolished.[32] In 2009 the UN Administrative Tribunal as such was abolished, and replaced by a two-tier system of a United Nations Dispute Tribunal and a United

[31] *Applicability of Article VI, Section 22, of the Convention on the Privileges and Immunities of the United Nations* [1989] ICJ Rep 177, 190 para. 34.

[32] GA resolution 50/54 of 11 December 1995, preamble.

Nations Appeals Tribunal.[33] The Court no longer has any formal role in the staff appeal system, and these Tribunals are not bodies authorized to request advisory opinions (though presumably the General Assembly could ask the Court to review their decisions in an opinion).

Although the old system for the UN itself has thus been abolished, the parallel system still exists for the ILO Tribunal;[34] and a few points of principle arising under the old UN system may also be mentioned. On the first occasion when the advisory opinion procedure was resorted to in relation to a staff dispute, concerning the ILO Tribunal, doubts were raised as to the legality of the process,[35] but the Court upheld its competence in the matter. It had already given an advisory opinion on the general issue whether the General Assembly could refuse to give effect to an award of compensation made by the UN Administrative Tribunal, and in those proceedings no suggestion was made that the matter was inappropriate for the use of the advisory function of the Court.[36] Nevertheless the question came to be raised whether, even on the basis that there was no legal or constitutional obstacle to giving an advisory opinion to review a UNAT judgment, the Court might better exercise its discretion, under Article 65 of the Statute, to decline to do so. A number of reasons why this might be so: some were related to the procedure for staff appeals, and since the system has since been abolished, they do not need to be examined. Others, however, went to the role of the Court itself.

First, it was suggested that there was an inherent inequality under the Statute between the staff member on the one hand, and his nominal opponent, the Secretary-General, and the Member States on the other. The same point had been raised in connection with the review of decisions of the ILO Tribunal, and the view was then taken that 'any absence of equality' of this kind, 'inherent in the terms of Article 66 of the Statute' was 'capable of being cured by the adoption of appropriate procedures which ensure actual equality in the particular proceedings'.[37] In relation to the case before it, the Court was satisfied that this had been done.[38] Secondly, it was objected that an advisory opinion is by definition non-binding; but under Article 11 paragraph 3 of the Statute of UNAT, the opinion was to have 'a conclusive effect with respect to the matters in litigation'; however, as the previous experience of the ILO Tribunal case showed, since the binding effect resulted 'not from the advisory opinion itself, but from the provisions of an autonomous instrument

[33] See GA resolutions 61/261 of 4 April 2007, 62/228 of 22 December 2007, and 63/253 of 24 December 2008.

[34] For the Court's broad hint that the whole staff appeal system is, as regards the Court, antiquated and should be abandoned or reformed, see *Judgment No. 2867 of the Administrative Tribunal of the International Labour Organization upon a Complaint Filed against the International Fund for Agricultural Development, Advisory Opinion*, [2012] ICJ Rep 10, 28 para. 44.

[35] *Judgments of the Administrative Tribunal of the ILO upon Complaints Made against Unesco*, [1956] ICJ Rep 77.

[36] *Effect of Awards of Compensation made by UNAT*, [1954] 47; this point was adverted to in the first application for review case: *Application for Review of UNAT Judgment No. 158* [1973] ICJ Rep 166, 171–2 para. 14.

[37] *Application for Review of UNAT Judgment No. 158*, [1973] ICJ Rep 166, 180 para. 35.

[38] Ibid. 182 para. 38.

having the force of law', this circumstance furnished no reason for refusing an opinion.[39] (If it had been upheld, this objection would presumably have struck down by implication also the provisions in treaties, having nothing to do with staff matters (e.g. the Headquarters Agreement, or the Privileges and Immunities Convention), that employed the advisory opinion procedure as a means of settling disputes between the Organization and its Members.[40])

[39] Ibid. 182–3 para. 39.

[40] See e.g. *Applicability of the Obligation to Arbitrate under Section 21 of the UN Headquarters Agreement*, [1988] ICJ Rep 12; *Applicability of Article VI, Section 22, of the Convention on Privileges and Immunities of the UN* [1989] ICJ Rep 177.

12

Judges' Separate and Dissenting Opinions

As indicated in Chapter 10, the decision of the Court is adopted by majority vote, the President of the Court (or the judge presiding in the case) having a casting vote in the event of a tie (Statute, Art. 55 para. 2). Although it is not specifically so stated in the Statute, it is understood that every judge who has participated in the case is under a legal duty to cast his vote on each of the questions stated in the operative clause of the decision: there is no possibility of abstention.[1] Consistently with this, or in consequence, a judge who has dissented from a decision finding that the Court has jurisdiction over a particular dispute, if still sitting when the Court considers the merits, is obliged to examine the merits and cast his vote even though he may still be of the opinion that the Court is acting without jurisdiction.[2]

Under Article 57 of the Statute, every judge has the right to append to the decision an individual statement of his views; this is not an obligation, nor is there any reward other than intellectual satisfaction.[3] The Article in fact refers simply to 'a separate opinion', but the practice of the two successive Courts has been that the judge entitles his opinion a 'separate opinion' if he agrees with the decision, or a 'dissenting opinion' if he does not.[4] The non-statutory term 'declaration' is also used: according to the Rules of Court, this is intended for the situation where the judge 'wishes to record his concurrence or dissent without stating his reasons', but in practice it has come to be used as a sort of catch-all title for brief statements or opinions that are not clearly either the one thing or the other. The purpose of a declaration as stated in the Rules has in fact become obsolete: until 1978, the way in which a judge had voted would not become public unless he chose to attach such a statement (or an opinion); but the revised Rules of Court adopted in that year

[1] See Ch. 10 sect. D, above. Nor would it be easy to evade the duty to participate, one way or the other, in the final vote. The *Resolution Concerning the Internal Judicial Practice of the Court* makes elaborate provision for the taking of the vote of a judge who 'is otherwise in a fit condition to record his vote', but unable 'because of physical incapacity to attend the meeting': Art. 9 para. (ii). There have, however, been cases in which it has simply been announced that judges had been unable to participate in a decision by reason of illness, e.g. President Lachs and Judge Dillard in the decisions on provisional measures in the *Nuclear Tests* cases (Public Sitting of 22 June 1973, *Pleadings*, 245).

[2] See Ch. 10 sect. F.

[3] Unlike in Homeric times, where the custom was to reward (with 2 talents of gold) the judge who best expounded the law: see Maine's *Ancient Law*, 405, and *Iliad*, Σ. 497–508 (shield of Achilles).

[4] These terms are not used in the English text of the Rules of Court, which refers to 'his individual opinion' (Art. 95 para. 2); the sentence is differently constructed in the French text, and does use the terms 'son opinion individuelle ou dissidente'.

provided that in future the decision would indicate not only the numbers of the votes on each side, but also the names of the judges.[5]

Generally, the purpose of an opinion is indicated by the title given to it. A dissenting opinion indicates principally the reasons why the author of the opinion was unable to support the adoption of one or more of the operative clauses of the decision. The choice of a separate opinion generally indicates that its author voted in favour of the decision (or the relevant part of it), but would have wished the reasoning to be fuller or different, or for certain matters to be treated which the majority considered it unnecessary or inappropriate to go into. The more neutral term 'declaration' is often used when what is discussed is a minor matter or side-issue, or when the opinion is 'in part dissenting'.[6]

As was well stated by Judge Higgins in the *Oil Platforms* case, 'The function served by a separate or dissenting opinion is to allow a judge to explain why she or he disagrees with part or all of the *dispositif* or the reasoning. It is not the occasion for writing an alternative judgment.'[7]

Some judges treat the right of attaching an opinion as an excuse for publishing a lengthy discursus or lecture on some or all of the legal issues they see as raised in the case, sometimes duplicating the arguments employed in the decision without substantively adding anything useful, and sometimes ranging far and wide beyond the confines of the case. The practice was defended as long ago as 1961 by Fitzmaurice, who considered it justified for a judge in this way 'to make general pronouncements of law and principle that may enrich and develop the law', but he added 'while not unduly straying outside the four corners of the case'.[8] Whatever objections there may be of principle to this practice,[9] it is understood to be unpopular with the other Members of the Court, in view of the extra time required for the preparation of such a document, and the consequent delay in the preparation and finalizing of the decision.[10]

[5] Interestingly, the legality of this change seems nowhere to have been questioned, even though it deprived each judge of the right (if it was a right) not to reveal which way he had voted. The practice of some national courts (e.g. the UK Supreme Court and Court of Appeal) is that every judge states whether he is or is not in favour of the decision, with as much in the way of opinion as he cares to add. Others (e.g. the French *Cour de cassation*) give a decision of the Court, with no indication of the distribution of votes.

[6] Some opinions in the past have in fact carried the title 'Separate opinion (in part dissenting) of Judge X', but this indication is rarely used now.

[7] [2003] ICJ Rep 233 para. 29.

[8] 'Hersch Lauterpacht—the Scholar as Judge', 37 *BYIL* (1961) 14–15. See also the present writer's study, 'Judicial Activism and the International Court of Justice', in N. Ando et al. (eds.), *Liber Amicorum Judge Shigeru Oda* (The Hague: Kluwer, 2002), 75–105. The procedure has been defended by some judges, e.g. Judge Ammoun in *Barcelona Traction* [1970] ICJ Rep 287.

[9] See e.g. the criticism of G. I. Hernández, *The International Court and the Judicial Function* (Oxford: Oxford University Press, 2014), 114–17, naming Judge Cançado Trindade in particular. The record for length of an opinion is probably still held by Judge Schwebel, whose dissent in *Military and Paramilitary Activities* runs to 379 pages of the Reports: [1986] ICJ Rep 259–527; but Judge Schwebel's opinion is focused on the case (particularly the facts), and is not one of the irrelevant discourses offered by some judges in other cases.

[10] At least theoretically, all Members of the Court should be able to read their colleagues' opinions before the final vote on the decision, and in the language of their choice (cf. *Resolution Concerning the Internal Judicial Practice of the Court*, art. 7 (2)). In the modern practice, the translations of many of the

The problem of the scope of judges' opinions arose in an acute form as long ago as the *South West Africa* case in 1966. Since the Court was very divided, the controversial decision being adopted only by the President's casting vote, numerous judges were anxious to indicate in opinions how they would have decided the merits. President Sir Percy Spender did not consider this a proper exercise of the right, and attached to the judgment a Declaration discussing the issue. Briefly, his view was that, while the right of attaching an opinion is 'an important right which must be safeguarded', it is not the case that 'there are no limits to the scope and extent of the exercise of this right by any individual judge'.[11] Citing the records of the drafting of the PCIJ Statute, and the views of President Huber, he considered that at least the 'main purpose' of the right was 'to enable the view of the dissenting judge or judges on particular questions of law dealt with in the Court's judgment to be seen side by side with the views of the Court on those questions';[12] the implication thus being that if the Court had seen fit to be silent on a point, then the judge was also bound to keep his views to himself. Spender noted that 'if a dissenting judge is free to state his opinion on matters which are not directly connected with the Court's judgment', then so may a concurring judge in a separate opinion, which would lead to confusion 'destructive of the Court's authority'.[13] In terms that seem to cover also opinions written as irrelevant pontifications (as described above), he concluded that '[t]he mere fact that a judgment (or opinion) of the Court has been given does not afford justification for an expression of views at large on matters which entirely exceed the limits and intended scope of the judgment (or opinion).'[14] Subsequent practice has contradicted Spender on the specific issue of opinions on matters that, though they have been argued, the Court has decided it cannot or should not deal with; but there is much merit in his observations in relation to purely academic disquisitions entitled 'opinions'. Unfortunately, it does not seem possible to regulate the matter by amending either the Rules or the Resolution Concerning the Internal Judicial Practice of the Court; too specific a restriction would be objectionable as fettering the right of a judge to indicate in what respects he disagrees (or agrees) with the judgment; and a mere recommendation would undoubtedly be ignored.

opinions do not appear until some considerable time after the decision has been given (which is why the printed text of the decision is only then available). The translation and printing costs of lengthy opinions have a measurable effect on the Court's budget.

[11] [1966] ICJ Rep 52 para. 7. [12] [1966] ICJ Rep 53 para. 12.

[13] [1966] ICJ Rep 54 paras. 19–20. This is an unexpected approach by a judge from a common-law tradition, in which it has long been the practice that every member of a multi-judge court may explain his reasons for his vote; as a result, there will be a majority (or even unanimity) as to *what* is decided, but there may be several different stated explanations *why*. Finding the *ratio decidendi* is then something of a puzzle.

[14] [1966] ICJ Rep 55 para. 24.

VI

INCIDENTAL PROCEEDINGS

13
Provisional Measures

Provisional measures in international judicial proceedings are indications, by the court seised of the matter, of action to be taken, or not to be taken, by one or both of the parties during the period leading up to the decision. Their precise justification in ICJ jurisprudence will be examined below, but their purpose may be said to be to prevent one party pre-empting the settlement of the dispute by unilateral action, thus rendering the eventual judgment ineffective; or, more broadly, to prevent unilateral action that might make it more difficult to achieve a settlement. The French term *mesures conservatoires* conveys this meaning better than the English term 'provisional'; and the expression, formerly used in the English text of the Rules of Court, 'interim protection' (1946 Rules Art. 61) was, from this viewpoint, also perhaps more appropriate.

So long as international dispute settlement was on the basis of ad hoc agreement between the parties to the dispute to accept the decision of an arbitrator or arbitral body, such measures were generally unlikely to be needed; since if the parties were agreed that the best way of resolving the dispute was by an independent arbitral or judicial decision, it was not to be expected that they would deliberately frustrate the decision. The need for a power to indicate measures was linked with the development of instruments establishing blanket agreement in advance to the settlement of disputes (or particular categories of disputes), since when one party came to implement such an agreement, the other party might no longer be of the same mind.

A. Binding effect of measures

It may seem illogical to begin this study of provisional measures by considering their effect, but it is their effect that defines their nature. Most, if not all, higher municipal courts have the power to issue binding interim injunctions, that is to say, directives requiring or prohibiting certain action pending settlement of the case before the court, backed by penalties for non-compliance. Is an analogous power also a necessary and essential part of the armoury of international courts, and of the International Court of Justice in particular? The Statute of the Court provides (in Art. 41) that the Court may 'indicate, if it considers that circumstances so require, any provisional measures which ought to be taken to preserve the respective rights of either party', but is silent on the consequences if such measures are not complied with. The text of Article 41 thus does not in terms say that measures indicated impose a binding obligation on the State concerned, and at first sight the word 'indicate' (Fr. *indiquer*), rather than 'order', and the words 'ought to be taken' (Fr. *doivent être prises*) rather than 'must be taken' may be significant; nor—on the assumption that measures are binding—does the article say what would be the result of a breach of that obligation.

Under Article 94 of the Charter, '[e]ach Member of the United Nations undertakes to comply with the decision of the International Court of Justice in any case to which it is a party', but paragraph 2 continues by contemplating the case where a party 'fails to perform the obligations incumbent upon it under a judgment rendered by the Court'; the article therefore clearly applies primarily, if not uniquely, to the final decision on the merits. Measures are always indicated, not by a 'judgment', but by an Order, as is appropriate for an interlocutory act; and is the indication of provisional measures a 'decision'? This text also thus does not unequivocally support the thesis that measures indicated are binding; but neither does it unequivocally state the opposite. Appeal has been made to, inter alia, the existence of the power at the national level as of similar significance; or the parallel afforded by the power of a court to determine its own jurisdiction, in support of an interpretation of Article 41 as authorizing the imposition of a binding obligation;[1] but this too is not conclusive.

The question long remained unsettled, with the Court showing apparent reluctance to treat measures it had granted as having such a binding legal effect;[2] but in the *LaGrand* case in 2001 the Court decided that provisional measures addressed to the United States, which had not been complied with, had created a legal obligation, of which the US (which had not been able to comply, due to internal constitutional arrangements) was therefore in breach.[3] It did not, however, base this conclusion on any general principle, analogous to that of the *compétence de la compétence*, but on an interpretation of Article 41 as having been intended to achieve that result.[4] As to Article 94 of the Charter, the Court considered whether that text 'precludes attributing binding effect to orders indicating provisional measures'. It concluded, perhaps unsurprisingly, that it did not, since of the two possible interpretations of Article 94, one would confirm that possibility, and the other would 'not preclude it'.[5]

[1] It has been suggested that the power to indicate measures is an inherent power in international tribunals, even in the absence of textual provisions, on the basis of a 'general principle of law': Chester Brown, *A Common Law of International Adjudication* (New York: Oxford University Press, 2007), 126–7. The variation between the scope of such a power as exercised by different tribunals is one reason, among others, for doubting this proposition.

[2] See e.g. *Military and Paramilitary Activities*, where measures were indicated, and Nicaragua specifically drew the Court's attention to the fact that they had not been complied with, but the Court took no action: [1986] ICJ Rep 14, 144 para. 287.

[3] *LaGrand (Germany* v *United States of America)*, [2001] ICJ Rep 466, 516 para. 128 (5).

[4] In the light of the *travaux préparatoires* and of the general trend of interpretation of the text in practice, this view of Art. 41 may be regarded as somewhat revolutionary: see Thirlway, *Law and Procedure*, i. 114ff. *contra*, Kolb, 646–60.

[5] [2001] ICJ Rep 466, 505–6 para. 108. A question the Court carefully did not put to itself was whether, if the overall intention of the drafters had been that measures should be binding, the words 'decision' and 'judgment' would have been used in Art. 94.

One implication of this later to become apparent was that it followed that it had *always* been the case—ever since the Statute came into force—that measures indicated under Article 41 were binding. The implication was spelled out in the 2007 Judgment in the *Application of the Genocide Convention* case between Bosnia and Serbia, where the Court declared that provisional measures that had been indicated in the case, before the *LaGrand* decision, were just as binding as subsequent ones, because in *LaGrand* 'the Court did no more than give the provisions of the Statute the meaning and scope they possessed from the outset';[6] and that therefore Serbia was in breach of a legal obligation of compliance.[7] There is nevertheless some truth—more truth?—in the view that the binding quality of provisional measures was an idea whose time had come; but it would not have been easy to justify an argument that the interpretation of Article 41 had evolved.[8]

The breach of an international legal obligation gives rise to a duty of reparation. When the obligation is that of compliance with an order for provisional measures, that obligation is independent of the rights and duties of the parties in respect of the original dispute, so long as that dispute has not been settled. In some cases, if the eventual judgment is in favour of the claims of the applicant, or to be more precise in favour of the claims of the party in whose favour the order for measures has been made, the obligation may merge in the obligation to comply with the judgment itself; and this may be so even if there have been acts contrary to the relevant obligation *after* the measures were indicated.[9]

In the recent two combined cases between Costa Rica and Nicaragua, the Court indicated measures to be observed by Nicaragua, and in its judgment on the merits noted that there had been breach of these. It found that Nicaragua had committed breaches in two respects: the first action taken was a breach of a specific directive in the provisional measures order, while the other was objectionable as a violation of Costa Rica's sovereignty.[10] As regards consequent non-material damage, the Court observed that its finding of a breach of territorial sovereignty 'provides adequate satisfaction',[11] but that Nicaragua was under an obligation to compensate Costa Rica 'for material damages caused by Nicaragua's unlawful activities on Costa Rican territory'.[12] It did not apparently find it necessary to distinguish between damage

6 [2007-I] ICJ Rep 43, 230 para. 453. This throws an interesting light on the incident in the *Military and Paramilitary Activities* case ([1986] ICJ Rep 14, 144 para. 287), where the Court failed to respond to a complaint of non-compliance with what we now know to have been a binding order indicating measures.

7 However, in *LaGrand*, the Court indicated that, had Germany made a claim for indemnification (rather than simply for a finding of breach of the order), one of the factors it would have taken into account was the fact that 'when the United States authorities took their decision [not to comply] the question of the binding character of orders indicating provisional measures had been extensively discussed in the literature, but had not been settled by [the Court's] jurisprudence': [2001] ICJ Rep 466, 508 para. 116.

8 Such a process is not impossible: cf. the Court's finding of evolution of the interpretation of Art. 12 of the Charter in the *Construction of a Wall* case: [2004-I] ICJ Rep 136, 149 para. 27; but there would have to be relevant practice to support it, and practice, in the case of Art. 41, pointed, if at all, the other way.

9 See *Application of the Genocide Convention (Bosnia* v *Serbia)* [2007-I] ICJ Rep 43, 235 paras. 467–9.

10 Judgment of 16 December 2015, para. 129.

11 Ibid. para. 139.

12 Ibid. para. 142.

resulting from the breach of sovereignty, a matter of substantive law, and a breach of a binding order of the Court, a matter of procedural or judicial law.

If the claim of the applicant is ultimately held to be unfounded, and *a fortiori* if the Court finds that it has no jurisdiction in the case, the obligation presumably—at the least—ceases to operate for the future. Even when the the applicant's claim on the merits is upheld, it seems that the obligation to comply with the provisional measures ceases, though it may be replaced by the obligation to comply with the decision on the merits. In one of the cases where measures were indicated in an endeavour to suspend execution of the death penalty in the United States, the *Avena* case, Mexico resorted to the expedient of bringing a request for interpretation of the judgment that had confirmed the direction made as a provisional measure, for a stay of the execution proceedings; and in that context was able to ask for and obtain a fresh indication of measures;[13] if the obligation to comply with the earlier measures still subsisted, the new measures would be unnecessary.

However, the Court subsequently decided that 'the matters claimed by [Mexico] to be in issue between the Parties, requiring an interpretation under Article 60 of the Statute, are not matters which have been decided by the Court in its Judgment' in the original case, and therefore dismissed the request for interpretation, thus bringing the proceedings, and the second set of measures, to an end. Nevertheless, the Court considered itself empowered to decide that the US had breached those measures on the basis that

> [t]here is no reason for the Court to seek any further basis of jurisdiction than Article 60 of the Statute [the interpretation article] to deal with this alleged breach of its Order indicating provisional measures issued in the same proceedings. The Court's competence under Article 60 necessarily entails its incidental jurisdiction to make findings about alleged breaches of the Order indicating provisional measures. That is still so even when the Court decides, upon examination of the Request for interpretation, as it has done in the present case, not to exercise its jurisdiction to proceed under Article 60.[14]

If a breach of provisional measures is asserted while the main proceedings, or proceedings specifically on the question of jurisdiction, are in progress, Article 41 of the Statute can be invoked as authorizing action by the Court, on the same basis (existence of prima facie jurisdiction) as supported the making of the original order. This route was, however, presumably not open to the Court in the *Avena (Interpretation)* case, at a moment when the question of merits jurisdiction had been terminated by a negative finding, even one in the guarded terms quoted. The Court's decision 'not to exercise its jurisdiction' in the interpretation proceedings did not vitiate the

[13] Order of 16 July 2008, [2008] ICJ Rep 311. This decision is examined further in the section on Interpretation of Judgments (Ch. 16 sect. A).

[14] [2009] ICJ Rep 3, 19 para. 51. The careful wording of the last phrase will be noted: if the Court had decided specifically that it *had no* jurisdiction under Art. 60, it would be difficult to argue that, having made that finding, it nevertheless could rely on Art. 60 to justify dealing with a breach of the provisional measures order. Note also that the Court did not consider that Art. 60 gave it jurisdiction to examine an allegation of breach of the judgement being interpreted, as distinct from breach of the provisional measures Order made in the interpretation proceedings: [2009] ICJ Rep 3, 20 para. 56.

measures for the past; but presumably they could have no further effect after the finding of invalidity. The Court thus also 'reaffirm[ed] the binding character of the obligations of the United States',[15] not under the provisional measures order, but under the original 2004 judgment.

Non-compliance with a binding order for provisional measures entails responsibility independently of the existence or otherwise of the right protected by the measures.[16] Where non-compliance involves the other party in trouble and expense, it has been argued that the non-complying party could properly be ordered to pay the costs, but the Court has not yet done so.[17]

B. The initiative

Article 41 of the Statute simply confers on the Court the power to indicate measures;[18] the procedure is regulated by the Rules of Court. The starting point is normally a written request by the party that considers that measures are necessary for the protection of its rights (Art. 73 of the Rules). When measures are requested, the President of the Court is empowered to 'call upon the parties to act in such a way as will enable any order the Court may make in the request for provisional measures to have its appropriate effects' (Rules, Art. 74 para. 4); such a request does not appear to be imperative, but failure to observe it might be taken into account by the Court at a later stage.

However, Article 75, paragraph 1, states that '[t]he Court may at any time decide to examine *proprio motu* whether the circumstances of the case require the indication of provisional measures...' The Court has never yet found it necessary to make use of this power;[19] even in a case in which one party was urging it to do so. This occurred at the very outset of the *Construction of a Road in Costa Rica* case, in Nicaragua's Application; and when the Court did not act, it returned to the matter in its Memorial.[20] The reason given for this unusual course was, in effect, that the request was so simple and straightforward that it could and

[15] [2009] ICJ Rep 3, 20 para. 60.

[16] A question that remains somewhat obscure is whether the binding obligation created by provisional measures is an obligation owed by the State concerned to the Court as well as to the other party: if a party chose not to complain of a breach of a measure, could the Court nevertheless sanction it as a defiance of the Court? Such obligations have also been termed 'objective obligations', but the meaning of this is not clear: *Questions Relating to the Obligation to Prosecute or Extradite*, separate opinion of Judge Cançado Trindade, [2012] ICJ Rep 517 para. 79.

[17] See the Joint Declaration of Judges Tomka, Greenwood, Sebutinde, and Judge ad hoc Dugard attached to the Judgment of 16 December 2015 in *Certain Activities by Nicaragua in the Disputed Area*: [2015] ICJ Rep para. 9.

[18] Which of course implies the power to modify or cancel them (see e.g. *Seizure and Detention of Certain Documents and Data, Order of 22 April 2015*, [2015] ICJ Rep).

[19] The need for such an initiative may be expected to be infrequent, since the absence of a request for measures may generally be taken to imply that the situation does not cause concern in the eyes of the party potentially affected.

[20] Memorial of Nicaragua, para. 6.6. Curiously, here and in the Application, the obsolete term 'interim measures of protection' is used. Finally, Nicaragua included the request for the Environmental Impact Assessment in a formal request for provisional measures. In an Order of 13 December 2013,

should be done 'without going through a formal request for [provisional] measures and into the costly and lengthy exercise of public hearings'.[21] But the text of the Article does not say that the Court may indicate measures *proprio motu*, but merely that may decide *proprio motu* to examine the possibility; and it does not seem to follow that if the Court were so to decide, it would also decide to indicate measures without a hearing.[22] The Court has stated that when measures have been requested it 'may, in cases of extreme urgency, proceed without holding oral hearings';[23] the principle *audi alteram partem*, however, surely still applies when the Court decides of its own motion that there may be a need for measures. The only pre-preliminary step, both *proprio motu* and *ex parte*, contemplated by the Rules is a possible appeal by the President of the Court under Article 74 paragraph 3.

C. Required conditions

Whether to order provisional measures is a matter for the discretion of the Court: Article 41 confers a power on the Court, to be exercised 'if it considers that the circumstances so require', so that a party cannot assert a *right* to the indication of measures, however strong its case. The Court has established a number of conditions, outlined below, and if one of these is not met, then measures will be refused, presumably on the basis that the circumstances cannot, in view of this default, be said to 'require' them. If, however, all the recognized conditions are met, is the Court obliged to indicate measures, or does it retain some discretion?[24] Presumably it could be influenced by some other 'circumstance', and would so indicate in its decision; but it could not, it is suggested, recognize compliance with the recognized conditions only to refuse measures.[25]

(1) The jurisdictional question

The distinction should perhaps be emphasized between jurisdiction over the merits of the case in which measures are being requested, and jurisdiction to indicate

however, the Court rejected this particular request on the ground that it would prejudge the Court's decision on the merits (see sect. C).

[21] Application paras. 53–4.

[22] The fact that hearings are provided for in Art. 74 (para. 3) does not imply that they are excluded if the Court is acting under Art. 75. In one case, the Permanent Court did *reject* a request for measures without inviting comment from the respondent, but on the basis that the request was misconceived, as 'not covered by the provisions of the Statute and Rules cited therein': *Factory at Chorzów (Indemnities), PCIJ Series A, No. 12*, 10.

[23] *LaGrand, Order of 3 March 1999*, [1999] ICJ Rep 9, 14 para. 21. The anatomically curious expression 'oral hearings' (rather than 'oral proceedings' or 'hearings') is unfortunate.

[24] The matter is touched on in the dissenting opinion of Judge ad hoc Callinan, Order of 3 March 2014, *Seizure and Detention of Certain Documents*, [2014] ICJ Rep 217–18, 220, paras. 16, 22.

[25] Cf. the decision not to decide on the merits in the *Northern Cameroons* case, where the Court was careful to explain at length why any decision it gave would be 'without object': [1963] ICJ Rep 15, 38.

the measures. The latter jurisdiction flows directly from the Statute, and is not subject to any conditions. One of the recognized conditions *for its exercise*, however, is that the Court be sufficiently satisfied that it has jurisdiction—usually over the merits,[26] but in the context (e.g.) of a request for the interpretation of a previous judgment, it is the jurisdiction to interpret that matters, not the original jurisdiction in the case.

However, a question that has given rise to some difficulty is that of the precise relationship between provisional measures jurisdiction and the 'principal' jurisdiction in this sense. If an indication of measures is requested in a case in which the respondent State has already made it clear that it denies the existence of the 'principal' jurisdiction, what is the relevance of this circumstance to the exercise of the power to indicate measures? At one extreme, it might be argued that if the Court has no jurisdiction to hear the case at all, then it has no power to indicate measures; at the other extreme, it might be said that, since Article 41 confers an independent power (and contains no reference to the question of merits jurisdiction), the Court could indicate measures, if it saw fit, without even inquiring into the question whether it had any jurisdiction over the merits.

The first view has the obvious defect that it would tend to rob the provisional measures procedure of all meaning: if no measures can be indicated until the disputed question of merits jurisdiction has been thrashed out, then the measures cannot serve to meet the urgent needs that they were designed for—and this is so whether or not they have binding effect.[27] The second view may, however, be seen as a threat to the principle of consensual jurisdiction, or even to the sovereign independence of States, if a State can be subjected to an order indicating measures that it is bound to comply with, in a case in which it asserts (justifiably, as it later turns out) that it has never consented to the Court having any jurisdiction at all.[28] The necessary consent conferring or constituting jurisdiction to indicate measures could be said to be given by a State's becoming party to the Statute, a text which contains Article 41; but this merely pushes the argument back a stage, as it were. The question then becomes whether what was thus consented to was a power to

[26] The distinction is slightly blurred by the wording of the Order indicating measures in the *Avena (Interpretation)* case: having found that the conditions for an interpretation under Art. 60 of the Statute were satisfied, the Court added that 'it follows . . . that the Court may address the present request for the indication of provisional measures'. The Court could in fact 'address' that request simply on the basis of Art. 41 of the Statute, and then find that the condition of prima facie merits jurisdiction was more than fully met by Art. 60.

[27] This view was nevertheless put forward by dissenting judges in the *Nuclear Tests* case in 1973 (see e.g. the dissenting opinion of Judge Gros, [1973] ICJ Rep 115, 122); but has not been heard of since.

[28] The difficulty is exacerbated by the ruling in *LaGrand* that the measures indicated constitute an independent legal obligation, one which exists even in face of a later finding of lack of jurisdiction, at least up to the moment that that finding is made. Provisional measures lapse when judgment on the merits is given, the obligations of the judgment being substituted for those under the measures. In the *Avena* (*Interpretation*) case, provisional measures were indicated forbidding the execution of five named individuals, and in its judgment refusing the Request the Court unanimously found that the execution of one of them had been a breach of the obligations of the USA under the provisional measures Order: [2009] ICJ Rep 21 para 61 (2).

indicate measures wholly independently of the existence *vel non* of merits jurisdiction, and if not, subject to what conditions.

So long as it was at least a tenable view that measures indicated under Article 41 *should* be respected, but do not impose a binding obligation, so that no adverse consequence follows for a State that decides not to do so, the jurisdiction problem was not acute. Since *LaGrand*, however, the Court, it seems, must at the very least reach a fairly solid conclusion in favour of the prima facie existence of jurisdiction over the merits before exercising its powers, under Article 41, to impose a non-consensual obligation on a State that, for the time being and provisionally, is before it.

While the possibility or probability of establishing jurisdiction over the merits is one of the factors to be weighed by the Court when considering whether to indicate measures, it is not always necessary for the Court to determine the jurisdictional question; if for other reasons it considers that no measures should be indicated, it could, it seems, deal directly with those reasons. Even if the jurisdictional issue is thus avoidable, the Court, however, seems to prefer to deal with it,[29] as though its jurisdiction to consider whether to indicate measures was *dependent* on prima facie merits jurisdiction.

It is at all events clear that, on the one hand, the Court is not debarred from indicating measures by the mere existence of an objection to jurisdiction; and on the other, that it is open to the Court to decline to indicate measures because there is a 'manifest lack of jurisdiction', or even a serious doubt as to the existence of merits jurisdiction. In some of the cases brought by Yugoslavia against members of NATO, the Court found, when examining the request for provisional measures, that it 'manifestly lack[ed] jurisdiction' to entertain the application instituting proceedings; it was so convinced that jurisdiction could not possibly be shown that it not only rejected the request for measures, but decided to remove these cases from the list at that stage.[30]

The key formula regularly adopted (with verbal variations) in a number of cases, is that

> when dealing with a request for the indication of provisional measures, there is no need for the Court, before deciding whether or not to indicate such measures, to satisfy itself in a definitive manner that it has jurisdiction as regards the merits of the case; but ... it may only indicate those measures if the provisions relied on by the Applicant appear, prima facie, to afford a basis on which its jurisdiction could be founded.[31]

[29] See e.g. the Order of 2 March 1990 in the case of the *Arbitral Award of 31 July 1989*, [1990] ICJ Rep 64, 68–9 paras. 19–22.

[30] See e.g. *Legality of Use of Force (Yugoslavia* v *USA) Order of 2 June 1999*, [1999-II] ICJ Rep 916 para. 29. Removal of a case from the list, without any decision even on jurisdiction, is an exceptional step, only taken in particular circumstances: see e.g. *Legality of the Use of Force (Serbia and Montenegro* v *Belgium)*, [2004] ICJ Rep 279 para. 33.

[31] *Obligation to Prosecute or Extradite*, [2009] ICJ Rep 147 para. 40; see also, e.g., *Certain Activities Carried Out by Nicaragua in the Border Area (Costa Rica* v *Nicaragua)*, [2011-I] ICJ Rep 3,17 para. 49.

Even where the respondent State has not contested jurisdiction at the stage of the request for the indication of measures, the Court maintains this cautious approach;[32] unless the respondent State has expressly reserved the matter, this failure to contest jurisdiction would, however, be likely to constitute *forum prorogatum* (see Ch. 5 sect. A(3)).

(2) Threat of irreparable harm

The purpose of the indication of provisional measures is, as stated in Article 41, to preserve the parties' rights, and this means the avoidance of 'irreparable harm' to those rights. As long ago as the *Eastern Greenland* case, the point arose that, while rights can be infringed, and damage—even irremediable damage—may result, the rights themselves can hardly be said to be 'damaged' or 'harmed'.[33] Similarly the Court has observed that 'no action taken *pendente lite* by a State engaged in a dispute before the Court with another State "can have any effect whatever as regards the legal situation which the Court is called upon to define" '.[34] The intention is, however, clear, and the expression 'irreparable harm to the rights claimed' is convenient and well understood.

Article 41 refers to the protection of 'the rights of *either* party' (emphasis added); it is not merely the applicant State that may ask for measures to protect its rights. Whether a respondent State can ask for measures will depend on the nature of the proceedings, on whether its 'rights' go beyond the mere right to have the application dismissed as unsubstantiated in law or fact. The clearest case would be where a counterclaim had been admitted—or possibly merely presented, since this should suffice for the purposes of an interlocutory application. In the case of *Pulp Mills on the River Uruguay*, brought by Argentina against Uruguay, and relating to the erection of a pulp mill ('the Botnia plant') on the river, Argentinian citizens tried to bring pressure to bear on Uruguay by blockading a bridge over the river. Uruguay presented a request for the indication of provisional measures requiring Argentina 'to take all reasonable and appropriate steps at its disposal to prevent or end the interruption of transit' over the bridge.[35] The Court noted the terms of Article 41, and added that 'the rights of the respondent are not dependent solely upon the way in which the applicant formulates its application'. It continued:

> any right Uruguay may have to continue the construction and to begin the commissioning of the Botnia plant ... pending a final decision by the Court, effectively constitutes a claimed right in the present case, which may in principle be protected by the indication of

[32] *Certain Activities Carried Out by Nicaragua in the Border Area (Costa Rica* v *Nicaragua)*, [2011-I] ICJ Rep 3, 18 para. 50.

[33] *Legal Status of the South-East Territory of Greenland, PCIJ Series A/B, No. 48*, 288: 'even "measures calculated to change the legal status of the territory" could not ... affect the value of such alleged rights'.

[34] *Passage Through the Great Belt*, Order of 29 July 1991 [1991] ICJ Rep 12, 19 para. 32, citing the *Legal Status* decision (see previous note).

[35] Order of 23 January 2007 [2007] ICJ Rep 3, 7 para. 14.

provisional measures; and . . . Uruguay's claimed right to have the merits of the present case resolved by the Court . . . also has a connection with the subject of the proceedings on the merits initiated by Argentina and may in principle be protected by the indication of provisional measures.[36]

The indication of measures is an interlocutory measure justified by urgency: there must be a threat to the rights of a party that is immediate in the sense that the final decision in the case may come too late to preserve those rights. If, therefore, it is to be expected that the case will have been decided before irreparable injury is caused, no measures will be indicated. When Finland complained that the construction by Denmark of a bridge over a particular seaway would block the passage of Finnish drilling rigs, already assembled to be ferried to their position, and thus prevent Finland from exercising its rights to pass through the seaway, the Court declined to indicate measures because the timetable for the bridge works was such that there would be no interference with passage within the time likely to be required for the Court to decide the case.[37] The Court, however, included in its order a warning to the parties (and to Denmark in particular) that a party may not better its legal position by modifications it has made to the status quo, and that consequently the Court might, if it upheld Finland's claim, order Denmark to demolish works already completed that infringed Finland's rights.

The indication of measures presupposes that the eventual victory of the applicant State on the merits, and (where appropriate) the award and payment of compensation, will not be sufficient to restore the status quo.[38] In the *Aegean Sea* case, the Court found that the alleged breach of Greece's rights by Turkey, 'if it were established, is one that might be capable of reparation by appropriate means', and deduced that there was no risk of irreparable prejudice';[39] this, or 'irreparable damage', is the phrase commonly employed in this context. Examples would be the loss of a human life, as in the 'death penalty cases' (*Breard, LaGrand, Avena*[40]), or the destruction of a specific artefact. Territory taken can always be restored, but can be irreparably damaged in the meantime, for example by the cutting down of mature trees.

[36] Ibid. 10–11 paras. 28–9.

[37] *Passage through the Great Belt, Provisional Measures, Order of 29 July 1991*, [1991] ICJ Rep 12. Cf. also the case of the *Electricity Company of Sofia and Bulgaria*, where a request by Belgium for provisional measures was withdrawn in response to assurances that the measures of execution threatened against the Belgian Company would not take place before the Court had given its decision, but had to be reinstated when the measures became imminent: *PCIJ Series A/B, No. 79*, 194, 196.

[38] This is the theoretical impact of 'irreparability', but, as explained above, the case-law has been less rigorous in interpretation of that concept. Cf. the work of arbitral tribunals, operating on the basis of Art. 290 of the Law of the Sea Convention, on applications for release of arrested ships; the harm suffered from retention of the vessel will almost never be 'irreparable': see the dissenting opinion of Judge Kulyk in the *Icelandic Sunrise* case, ITLOS Case No. 22.

[39] [1976] ICJ Rep 3,11 para. 33.

[40] *Vienna Convention on Consular Relations (Paraguay* v *US)*, [1998] ICJ Rep 248; *LaGrand (Germany* v *US)*, [1999-I] ICJ Rep 3; *Avena and Other Mexican Nationals (Mexico* v *US)*, [2003] ICJ Rep 77.

(3) Link with the rights claimed on the merits

Whether it is the applicant or the respondent State that seeks the indication of measures, the same requirement applies: it is often expressed as a condition that there be a 'link' between the measures requested and the rights claimed;[41] thus there will be no reason for the respondent to seek measures unless it has advanced, if not a formal counterclaim, at least something more than a mere denial of the applicant's contentions.

In the *Pulp Mills* case, mentioned above, the Court was not convinced that the blockade of the bridge was interfering with the construction of the disputed Botnia plant, and thus dismissed the argument that the blockade was interfering with the rights claimed by Uruguay to construct it; it therefore refused a measure directing Argentina to keep the bridge open.[42] While the available measures for protection are thus limited by the nature of the rights claimed, that does not mean that the Court similarly can only choose among the specific measures requested by the party for the protection of those rights. It is well established that it may indicate whatever measures it thinks most appropriate for the protection of those rights.[43]

The reasoning behind the requirement of a 'link' is that the purpose of provisional measures is to protect the rights of the State requesting them, but not just any rights that that State may possess—only those asserted or claimed in the application instituting proceedings before the Court, and thus capable of being protected by the eventual judgment. The classic example of a lack of correlation between measures and rights claimed was the request in the case of the *Arbitral Award of 31 July 1989*: Guinea-Bissau and Senegal had submitted a maritime delimitation dispute to arbitration, and an award had been made, but for various reasons Guinea-Bissau considered that the award was null and void, and brought proceedings asking the Court to find that this was so. In that context, it asked for provisional measures whereby both parties should refrain from any action in the disputed area, in order not to prejudice the settlement of the underlying dispute. The Court declined to indicate measures, because it had been asked 'to pass upon the existence and validity of the Award but not . . . upon the respective rights of the Parties in the area in question', so that those rights were 'not the subject of the proceedings before the Court, and 'any such measures could not be subsumed by the Court's judgment on the merits'.[44]

There must thus be a link between the rights claimed and the measures requested; but it has subsequently been ruled, in effect, that this link must not be so close as

[41] See e.g. *Seizure and Detention of Certain Documents*, Order of 3 March 2014, [2014-I] ICJ Rep 147, 152 paras. 22–3.

[42] Order of 23 January 2007, [2007] ICJ Rep 3, 13–14 paras. 40–3. Nor did it accept that a measure was necessary requiring abstention by Argentina from any measures that might aggravate the dispute: ibid. 16 paras. 49–51.

[43] See e.g. *Seizure and Detention of Certain Documents, Order of 3 March 2014*, para. 49, quoting *Request for Interpretation (Temple of Preah Vihear)* [2011-I] ICJ Rep 551 para. 58.

[44] [1990] ICJ Rep 64, 70 para. 26. See also *Questions relating to the Obligation to Prosecute or Extradite (Belgium* v *Senegal)*, Order of 28 May 2009, [2009] ICJ Rep 151 para. 56.

to be equivalent to identity.[45] In the case, for example, of *Construction of a Road in Costa Rica along the River San Juan*, when considering the request by Nicaragua for provisional measures, the Court stated as an issue to be examined 'whether the provisional measures requested are linked to the rights claimed', but added 'and do not prejudge the merits of the case'.[46] The first provisional measure requested was that Costa Rica supply an Environment Impact Statement; as the Court noted, 'this request is exactly the same as one of Nicaragua's claims on the merits contained at the end of its Application and Memorial in the present case'. There was thus an evident 'link'; but the Court considered that a decision to provide the material 'at this stage of the proceedings would . . . amount to prejudging the Court's decision on the merits of the case'.[47]

In the *Guinea-Bissau/Senegal* case just mentioned, the problem was that the requested measures 'could not be subsumed by the Court's judgment on the merits'; in the *Construction of a Road* case, the problem was that they could and would be so subsumed!

Another way of looking at the matter is perhaps by considering whether a proposed provisional measure is reversible. By definition, measures are based on a provisional view of the case, and this view may turn out to be erroneous or unjustified, or the Court may find that it has no jurisdiction over the merits. If that is the situation, it would clearly be unjust for the State that had asked for measures to be able to retain permanently the benefit of a measure—to retain, in the fairly trivial example in point, the Environmental Impact Assessment which, as it turns out, it was never entitled to have.[48] It is not so much that a requested measure may 'amount to prejudging the Court's judgment on the merits' (since the decision to grant it will be surrounded by qualifications as to its provisional nature); it is rather that to grant the measure means that a later negative (in a broad sense) decision on the merits will fail to leave the parties in the same legal position as before the case, as justice would demand.

This view of the matter is also confirmed by the recent case of *Questions Relating to the Seizure and Detention of Certain Documents*. The traditional rule of non-identity would imply that the provisional measures indicated should never be sufficient in themselves to satisfy the claim. However, in that case, the Court indicated a number of provisional measures on the request of Timor-Leste,[49] and Australia complied with them. That State then indicated that the compliance by Australia

[45] Cf. the PCIJ case of *Factory at Chorzów (Indemnities)*, where the Court found that the request for measures 'cannot be regarded as relating to the indication of measures of interim protection, but as designed to obtain an interim judgment in favour of part of the claim': *PCIJ Series A, No. 12*, 10.

[46] [2013] ICJ Rep 404 para. 20.

[47] [2013] ICJ Rep 404 para. 21.

[48] Or, to be absolutely precise, not entitled to obtain on the grounds asserted in the case before the Court. In its judgment on the merits, the Court found that the parties were in agreement as to the existence in general international law of an obligation to conduct an Environmental Impact Assessment where appropriate; it did not rule specifically on whether Costa Rica was under an obligation to supply a copy to Nicaragua, but this may be regarded as entailed in the concept of such an assessment: see Judgment of 16 December 2015, para. 101.

[49] Order of 3 March 2014, [2014-I] ICJ Rep 147. In its judgment on the merits, the Court found that the parties were in agreement as to the existence in general international law of an obligation to conduct an Environmental Impact Assessment where appropriate; it did not rule specifically on

with those measures meant that it had 'successfully achieved the purpose of its Application to the Court', and therefore discontinued the proceedings (to which step Australia made no objection).[50]

However, it is suggested that the fact that what is requested as a provisional measure would be subsumed in the eventual judgment (if the applicant is successful) should be not necessarily be a bar to indication of the measure. This is shown by the non-pecuniary examples of the measures indicated in, for example, *Military and Paramilitary Activities, Nuclear Tests* and *Application of the Genocide Convention*. In a similar context, Germany in the *Chorzów* case made a gallant attempt to suggest urgency ('the prejudice caused by a further delay would be irreparable'[51]), but that element was not present, any more than was demonstrated in respect of the Environmental Impact Assessment in the *Construction of a Road* case.

(4) Plausibility of the rights asserted

Another consequence of the interlocutory nature of proceedings on a request for provisional measures is that, just as the Court cannot, and is not required to, establish firmly its jurisdiction over the case, so also it does not have to be convinced, in face of a denial by the respondent State, that the claimed rights really exist. But obviously, it cannot act to impose a binding obligation on the other party simply on the basis of unproved assertions by the requesting State. Some middle way has to be found; and a stock phrase is now regularly used to express it. This seems first to have appeared in the case of the *Obligation to Prosecute or Extradite*: 'the power of the Court to indicate provisional measures should be exercised only if the Court is satisfied that the rights asserted by a party are at least plausible'.[52] This is the adjective regularly used; perhaps not ideal in view of its overtones of '*apparently* convincing'.[53] However, it is clear that the Court meant to convey that the rights do not, or perhaps the existence of the rights does not, have to be shown by the same substantial evidence or elements as would be required for a decision upholding them definitively; yet at the same time there must appear to be a reasonable chance that the State claiming the rights will be able to bring forward such evidence or elements in due course.

whether Costa Rica was under an obligation to supply a copy to Nicaragua, but this may be regarded as entailed in the concept of such an assessment: see Judgment of 16 December 2015, para. 101.

[50] Order of 11 June 2015, [2015] ICJ Rep. [51] *PCIJ Series A, No. 12*, 6.

[52] [2009] ICJ Rep 149, 151 para. 57; see also *Certain Activities Carried out by Nicaragua in the Border Region* [2011-I] ICJ Rep 6, 19 para. 55; *Seizure and Detention of Certain Documents, Order of 3 March 2014*, [2014] ICJ Rep 147, 152 paras. 22–3. It may not be coincidental that the test appears to have developed (at least in this form) since the *LaGrand* decision that provisional measures are binding; under the law as it was previously thought to exist, a State against which measures were ordered protecting 'rights' that the State considered (and could later prove) not to exist could safely be ignored by that State.

[53] The *OED* indicates that it is 'frequently' used in this sense. The French homonym does not seem to have this flavour, thus the English term may perhaps have first been used to translate it.

(5) Assurances by the other party

In some cases, the respondent State has offered assurances as to its conduct *pendente lite* such as to render, in its contention, the measures requested unnecessary. This is again a question that appears under a different light since the decision in *LaGrand* that provisional measures impose a binding obligation. Previously, the assurance offered, assuming it to be binding,[54] on a basis of treaty-law, would probably offer more security than an order indicating measures that might or might not be complied with, and in respect of which there existed no remedy for non-compliance. Once established that the measures indicated impose or constitute a binding restriction on, or direction as to, the conduct of the respondent State, this will usually be more satisfactory than an assurance that will probably be hedged round with limitations and reservations.[55] To what extent will the offer of such assurances weigh with the Court in deciding whether or not to indicate measures?

In the case concerning *Questions Relating to the Obligation to Prosecute or Extradite* the measures requested were directed to ensuring that M. Habré, the person whose prosecution or extradition was in question, should not leave the territory of the respondent State (Senegal) while the Court proceedings were in progress. Assurances to that effect were given by Senegal. The Court decided not to indicate measures on the basis that there was, in the circumstances, no 'urgency' to justify them.[56] Senegal later announced that it was about to send him back to Chad, his national State, which would have been a clear breach of the assurances given, but backed down as a result of international protests.[57] Assurances were also offered by Nicaragua in the case of *Certain Activities Carried Out by Nicaragua in the Border Area* between itself and Costa Rica, that it 'consider[ed] itself bound not to undertake [certain] activities . . . and to prevent any person or group of persons from doing so'; but the Court was not impressed, pointing out that 'persons under [Nicaragua's] jurisdiction' had already carried out activities contrary to an earlier Order.[58]

In the *Seizure and Detention of Certain Documents* case, confidential documents belonging to the Government of Timor-Leste in a lawyer's office had been seized by the Australian security services, and Timor-Leste was concerned to ensure that they should not be seen by anybody pending the ICJ proceedings instituted to get them returned. Australia, through its Attorney-General and Solicitor-General, gave very carefully worded assurances as to the custody of the documents; the Court was not

[54] It might be so as a unilateral declaration, on the pattern of the *Nuclear Tests* decision; but the Court would probably expect the applicant to say whether or not it accepted it, and if it did, the obligation would be synallagmatic—in effect, based on agreement.

[55] For an example of an undertaking before the Court being treated as binding on the State giving it, see *Maritime Dispute (Peru* v *Chile)*, [2014-I] ICJ Rep 3, 178 para. 65.

[56] Order of 28 May 2009 [2009] ICJ Rep 155, paras. 72–3. The line of thought is a little unclear, as the Court also invoked the idea that 'the risk of irreparable prejudice' was not 'apparent'.

[57] See the account of the incident in the (highly critical) opinion of Judge Cançado Trindade, [2012] ICJ Rep 515–16 para. 24.

[58] Order of 22 November 2013, [2013] ICJ Rep 354, 366–7 para. 50.

satisfied,[59] and indicated provisional measures. However, the measures indicated were not those requested, possibly inasmuch as they were regarded as supplemental to the assurances given[60] (though the Order does not expressly state that the Court regarded those assurances as independently binding). The consideration it gave to the assurances shows that there was no problem of principle in accepting them as grounds for refusing, or indeed limiting, an order.

D. Other questions

(1) Non-aggravation of the dispute

Most indications of provisional measures set out what it is that the party addressed is required to do, or to refrain from doing, as the case may be; these indications require little, if any, commentary. However, one clause that has become fairly standard in Orders for provisional measures does not fit easily into the framework of protection of rights: the 'non-aggravation' clause. Its form is fairly consistent: '[The two Parties] should each of them ensure that no action of any kind is taken which might aggravate or extend the dispute . . . or prejudice the right of the other Party to compliance with whatever judgment the [Court] may render in the case.'[61] Does Article 41, referring to preservation of rights, afford a basis for such an indication? And can it be imposed, as a provisional measure, in isolation, or only as an adjunct to more specific obligations?

When this latter point was raised in the *Aegean Sea* case, the Court found that in the circumstances of the case it was not necessary to decide it, as the parties were already under a parallel obligation by virtue of a decision of the Security Council.[62]

The parties to an international dispute that has been submitted to judicial settlement are, according to the PCIJ, already under a duty to 'abstain from any measure capable of exercising a prejudicial effect with regard to the execution of the decision to be given'.[63] On that basis, it would not seem that a direction to that effect by the Court would add anything; yet in the case in which this observation was made, the PCIJ did in fact indicate measures to the same effect, apparently on the grounds of the dilatory tactics of the respondent State.

[59] Order of 3 March 2014, [2014] ICJ Rep 147. It was influenced in part by the fact that the assurances given were only for the period of the provisional measures proceedings, and in part by the fact that *some* officials might well see the material, and this meant that it 'could reach third parties' (para. 46 of the Order).

[60] This was the view of Judge Cançado Trindade: separate opinion, [2014] ICJ Rep 167, 173 para. 17.

[61] Quoted from *Frontier Dispute (Burkina Faso/Mali), Order of 10 January 1986*, [1986] ICJ Rep 11–12, an Order made by the Chamber of the Court seised of the case. See also *United Diplomatic and Consular Staff in Tehran*, [1979] ICJ Rep 21 para. 47 (B); *Application of the Genocide Convention (Bosnia* v *Yugoslavia)*, [1993] ICJ Rep 24 para. 52 (B); *Land and Maritime Boundary between Cameroon and Nigeria*, [1996-I] ICJ Rep 24 para. 49 (1); *Armed Activities on the Territory of the Congo*, [2000] ICJ Rep 129 para. 47 (1). Kolb (616–20) regards this purpose as, if anything, more important than protecting rights.

[62] [1976] ICJ Rep 3, 13 para. 42.

[63] *Electricity Company of Sofia and Bulgaria, PCIJ Series A/B, No. 79*, 194, 199.

There seems to be no decision upholding an allegation of breach of such an order,[64] so that there is little guidance on this or on what would be regarded as an action tending to aggravate or extend the dispute; it is difficult to see how an act of either type could prejudice the rights claimed in the proceedings, so as to fall within the strict terms of Article 41: as already observed, no amount of infringement of a right can cause that right to cease to exist (except of course in the case of tolerated infringement amounting ultimately to waiver). On this basis, it would not seem that this kind of direction operates to protect the rights claimed in the proceedings. A differing view was expressed by Judge Greenwood in *Seizure and Detention of Certain Documents*, however; he considered it sufficient that 'the link to the merits is still present, since the dispute which the parties are required not to aggravate or extend is the dispute on which the Court is being asked to rule at the merits phase'.[65]

(2) The problem of indemnification

The establishment by the Court that provisional measures are legally binding renders more acute a difficulty already adverted to in the past, in particular in the case of *Passage through the Great Belt*. Compliance with an order for measures may involve more than merely refraining from certain action for a certain time, until the Court has ruled on the merits.[66] It may involve taking positive action, involving expense; and even refraining from action may involve considerable cost. In the case mentioned, Finland was asking that Denmark's project for the construction of a bridge over the Great Belt waterway be suspended until the Court had ruled whether or not its completion as planned would infringe Finland's right of passage. Denmark contended that no right of Finland would be affected by the bridge; but on the question of provisional measures, it also pointed out that to stop work on the project would involve Denmark in expense, the main element of which was estimated at US$500 million.[67] There was some discussion at the hearings of the question whether, if the bridge-works were suspended but Finland's claim was rejected on the merits, Denmark could claim compensation;[68] but since the Court did not order measures, it did not comment on the point. As this example shows, it is one that might acquire considerable financial significance.

[64] In the recent combined *Costa Rica/Nicaragua* cases there was a claim of Costa Rica to this effect, but the Court found that Nicaragua's actions were a breach of more specific measures: Judgment of 16 December 2015, [2015] ICJ Rep para.128.

[65] *Seizure and Detention of Certain Documents*, Order of 3 March 2014 [2014] ICJ Rep 196, Dissenting opinion, footnote to para. 6.

[66] Moreover, in the present state of the Court's calendar, that time may be quite substantial.

[67] *Passage through the Great Belt, Pleadings, Oral Arguments, Documents*, 136–7 (Magid).

[68] A suggestion made at the time by the present writer was that it would be open to the Court to indicate measures subject to the condition that the applicant party, if it was to claim the benefit of these, should give the respondent an undertaking to indemnify it against the consequent expense if the Court found that the claim was unfounded, or that it had no jurisdiction: see Thirlway, 'The Indication of Provisional Measures by the International Court of Justice', in R. Bernhardt (ed.), *Interim Measures Indicated by International Courts*, Max-Planck-Institut (Berlin: Springer, 1994), 33.

The possible need for indemnification was taken up by Judge Greenwood in his dissenting opinion in the case of *Seizure and Detention of Certain Documents*: he regarded it as an aspect of the principle that the measures indicated 'should not go beyond what is considered necessary' to prevent the occurrence of the harm contemplated, and added that this 'is particularly important where those measures may restrict— possibly for some years— the exercise by the party to whom they are directed of rights which that party may subsequently be found to possess'.[69]

[69] [2014] ICJ Rep 196, para.5, and ibid 196–7, para. 7, for the question of indemnity.

14
Preliminary Objections

Reference has already been made, in connection with the Court's jurisdiction, to preliminary objections as a procedural means of challenging the existence of such jurisdiction in a particular case. Jurisdictional issues are, however, not the only matters that may be the subject of such objections: two other categories are generally recognized: objections to admissibility, and a catch-all category of 'objections of a preliminary character'.

The submission of a preliminary objection involves the opening of a new 'phase' of the case,[1] normally to be concluded by a decision ruling on the objection; it is, however, also possible for the Court to open such a distinct phase *proprio motu*. This has been done in particular in cases where the respondent was known to contest the jurisdiction of the Court in the case, but was choosing not to appear in the proceedings, and therefore not submitting any formal objection. In the first such cases, the two *Fisheries Jurisdiction* cases, the Court noted Iceland's allegation (in a letter to the Court) that there was no jurisdiction, and Iceland's refusal to appear or participate; it concluded that 'in these circumstances, it is necessary first of all to resolve the question of the Court's jurisdiction'.[2] The similar procedure adopted in the two *Nuclear Tests* case may have facilitated the Court's unexpected decision to declare the case moot (on the basis of public statements by France) without consulting the applicants for their views.[3]

A. Procedural definition

A preliminary objection is a formal step by which a respondent raises a question that it contends should be dealt with separately, before any other issue in the proceedings is examined. This is usually, perhaps indeed necessarily, on the basis that that question is preliminary in nature; and that as a result, its resolution (in the

[1] See Ch. 7 sect. B(2).

[2] *Fisheries Jurisdiction (UK* v *Iceland), Order of 18 August 1972,* [1972] ICJ Rep 181, 182, and the Order in the *FRG* v *Iceland* case of the same date. Judges Bengzon and Jiménez de Aréchaga dissented, arguing that the Court should have treated Iceland as having raised a preliminary objection, and that the Court needed full details of the case before ruling on jurisdiction: ibid. 184–6. The word 'necessary' certainly seems an overstatement.

[3] [1974] ICJ Rep 253 (Australia) and 457 (New Zealand).

sense contended for by the party raising it) will make examination of the rest of the case unnecessary and inappropriate. The commonest example is therefore a jurisdictional question; if it is asserted that the Court has no jurisdiction to decide a disputed issue, it is evidently its duty to determine that point before examining any other. There is no specific provision in this respect in the Statute of the Court, which simply indicates (Art. 36 para. 6) that '[i]n the event of a dispute as to whether the Court has jurisdiction, the matter shall be settled by the decision of the Court.'[4] The main purpose of this text is, however, to state the principle of the *compétence de la compétence*, and it does not prescribe at what stage the decision on jurisdiction is to be taken, nor does it apply in terms to non-jurisdictional matters raised as preliminary objections. The subject is covered in Article 79 of the Rules of Court.

The definition of a preliminary objection in paragraph 1 of that Article is wide: '[a]ny objection by the respondent to the jurisdiction of the Court or to the admissibility of the application, or other objection the decision upon which is requested before any further proceeding on the merits.' The words 'the decision upon which *is requested*' should be noted; it would not be possible to define the objection as one the decision on which is, for example, *necessary* before any further proceeding, as until the Court has ruled on the objection there will be no way to establish whether it is necessary so to decide it or not. It remains of course possible that the Court may consider that a preliminary decision, as requested, is not necessary, in which case the objection will be rejected or, in case of doubt, reserved by the process formerly called 'joinder to the merits', as will be explained. The paragraph also contemplates the making of an objection 'by a party other than the respondent', that is to say, the applicant,[5] or conceivably a State admitted to intervene as a party. The applicant may wish to raise a preliminary objection to a counterclaim; the hypothesis of an intervening State raising one has never yet been fulfilled. Indeed, the circumstances in which an intervening State might wish to do so are difficult to foresee, given that the participation of such a State in the proceedings in such a manner as to be bound by the decision, or indeed at all, is a consequence of its own direct and specific choice.[6]

It is thus in effect the State making the objection that characterizes the objection as 'preliminary';[7] the Court may find that it is not such, and reject it as an objection, or join it to the merits (to use a convenient, if outdated, term). The wording in Article 79 para. 1 of the Rules quoted above dates from 1978; the 1946 Rules (Art. 62) simply took it for granted that something called a 'preliminary objection'

[4] In the index to the the Statute and Rules (*ICJ Acts and Documents concerning the Organization of the Court*, No. 6), Art. 36 para. 6, is listed under 'Preliminary Objections'.

[5] The hypothesis may seem bizarre: why commence proceedings only to torpedo them oneself? This, however, was done by Italy (raising a 'Preliminary Question') in the case of *Monetary Gold Removed from Rome in 1942*: in the circumstances, too complex to explain here, Italy's action made perfect sense. See [1954] ICJ Rep 19, 25ff.

[6] See the discussion of intervention in Ch. 15.

[7] In this sense, the judgment on preliminary objections in *Barcelona Traction, Light Power Co*, [1964] ICJ Rep 6, 43.

existed, and indicated when it must be filed, the procedure to be followed, etc. The concept had developed before the Permanent Court in relation to matters of jurisdiction and of admissibility; the first occasion on which the Court recognized an objection as a preliminary one though it was not of jurisdiction or of admissibility was in the *Lockerbie* cases (see sect. B(3)). There is some suggestion in these cases that, in addition to being presented as preliminary, a true preliminary objection must have as its purpose 'to prevent, *in limine*, any consideration of the merits';[8] but it is not clear that this really adds anything.[9]

In 2001, Article 79 of the Rules was amended, by the insertion of new paragraphs 2 and 3, to cover the situation in which the initiative for dealing with preliminary issues separately might also be taken by the Court at an early stage: 'the Court may decide that any questions of jurisdiction and admissibility shall be determined separately'; the decision is, however, only to be taken 'after the President has met and consulted with the parties'.[10] Also amended was the time-limit for the filing of a preliminary objection, this in the general interest of avoiding unnecessary delay in the proceedings.

B. Categories

As noted above, the Rules of Court (Art. 79 para. 1) recognize three kinds of preliminary objection: objections to the jurisdiction of the Court, to the admissibility of the application, and any 'other objection the decision upon which is requested before any further proceedings on the merits'. Both jurisdictional defects and inadmissibility may be raised as arguments within the general framework of the merits: the reason why they are singled out from other arguments that may be advanced as grounds for the rejection of the claim is procedural rather than conceptual.[11] The remaining category, that of any 'other objection the decision upon which is requested before any further proceeding on the merits' is useful as providing flexibility, by making it clear that an objection may not be excluded from the 'preliminary' category merely because it is not framed as an objection to jurisdiction or admissibility.[12] It is not uncommon for respondent States to file a whole set of

[8] *Lockerbie (Libya* v *UK)* [1998] ICJ Rep 9, 267 para. 47; (*Libya* v *US*) 115, 131–2 para. 43.

[9] See Thirlway, *Law and Procedure*, i. 973–4.

[10] The Court had already taken action of this kind in the *Aerial Incident (Pakistan* v *India)* case: [2000] ICJ Rep 15–16 paras. 3–4, with the agreement of the parties. Such a procedure was requested by the respondents in the *Legality of the Use of Force* cases, but objected to by the applicant; the adjustment of the Rules may have been suggested by these cases.

[11] On jurisdiction and admissibility generally, and the relationship between them, see Y. Shany, *Questions of Jurisdiction and Admissibility before International Courts* (Cambridge: Cambridge University Press, 2016.

[12] It has been suggested (S. Talmon in Zimmermann et al., *Commentary*, 1160, Art. 43 para. 176) that some paragraphs of Art. 79 of the Rules of Court which specifically mention jurisdiction and admissibility are therefore not applicable to objections of the third category, but this seems to be reading too much into a minor discrepancy of drafting.

preliminary objections, covering all three categories, each of which has to be examined by the Court and disposed of separately.[13]

Whether or not to raise a preliminary objection, and on what points, is a matter for the sole decision of the respondent:[14] the procedural effect of choosing not to raise the objection will depend on its nature, and in particular whether the objection would be to jurisdiction or to admissibility.

(1) Objections to jurisdiction

The nature and the limits of the jurisdiction of the Court have been examined in Chapter 3 above; an objection to jurisdiction will therefore amount to denying that the conditions for the existence of jurisdiction, as there discussed, are not, or not fully, satisfied. A respondent State will generally choose to advance its objections to the Court's jurisdiction as preliminary objections: if it is alleged that the Court has no jurisdiction to go into the matters raised in the application, then not only will it be wasteful of time and effort for those matters to be argued unnecessarily, but the respondent State may prefer that they should not be opened in the public forum of the Court. As indicated in Chapter 4, jurisdiction is essentially based on consent, so a preliminary objection to jurisdiction seeks to show that the consent asserted by the applicant State is non-existent, or does not extend to the matters raised in the application. For the same reason, if the respondent State fails to raise a jurisdictional objection that it could have raised (or if it chooses not to do so), then generally speaking it will be taken to have tacitly consented to the determination of the dispute by the Court.[15]

(2) Objections to admissibility

The same is largely true of objections to admissibility; the Court has observed that these 'normally take the form of an assertion that, even if the Court has jurisdiction and the facts stated by the applicant State are assumed to be correct, nonetheless there are reasons why the Court should not proceed to examination of the merits'.[16] Although an objection of this kind is generally not an assertion of lack of consent, failure to advance it at an early stage may be read as a waiver.

The breadth of the definition by the Court, just quoted, and the inclusion of the word 'normally', indicate that no helpful overall definition is possible, inasmuch as,

[13] In *Land and Maritime Boundary between Cameroon and Nigeria,* e.g., Nigeria, filed eight distinct objections.

[14] In the *Military and Paramilitary Activities* case, for example, the United States did not rely on the 'Connally reservation' in its acceptance of jurisdiction under the optional clause; when dealing with the objections that the US did raise, the Court made no allusion to the point.

[15] This is, of course, provided the matter is one of the consent of the individual State, not if it concerns the extent of the jurisdiction conferred on the Court by the Charter and Statute: for example, if proceedings were brought by a non-State, e.g. an individual, no consent by the respondent State would prevent it being a nullity.

[16] *Oil Platforms*, [2003] ICJ Rep 161, 177 para. 29

like jurisdiction, admissibility is essentially a procedural concept. Some examples of objections of this kind that have been advanced before the Court are the following.[17] (Not all of these have been upheld as objections on the facts, but they have been recognized as falling within the category of matters of admissibility.)

- Objections that the parties have agreed some other method of dispute settlement which takes priority over recourse to the Court;[18]
- where the claim is one of diplomatic protection, objections that the link of nationality is absent,[19] or that local remedies have not been exhausted;[20]
- objections that the claim has been brought with inadmissible delay;[21]
- objections alleging lack of *locus standi* (or 'standing'). This kind of objection amounts to asserting that the applicant is not the party injured by the wrongful act alleged, and may, for example, involve the interpretation of a multilateral convention to determine whether the obligation asserted is one owed *erga omnes partes*.[22]
- Objections that the claim no longer has any object or is 'moot';[23]
- objections related to the applicant's conduct in relation to the subject of the dispute (the concept of 'clean hands');[24]
- objections that the Court cannot consider a question of maritime delimitation until another international body has 'made a determination' in that respect.[25]

(3) Other preliminary objections

The clearest example of a preliminary objection that is not one either of jurisdiction or admissibility is that raised in the two *Lockerbie* cases in 1998.[26] The

[17] This list is based on the enumeration by C. Tomuschat, 'Article 36', in Zimmermann et al., *Commentary*, 700–5 paras. 123–33.

[18] This can also be viewed as a jurisdictional point, the consent relied on by the applicant being limited by, or having been overtaken by, the special consent to the alternative settlement mechanism.

[19] *Barcelona Traction Light & Power Co.*, [1970] ICJ Rep 3.

[20] Numerous cases, including *Ahmadou Siado Diallo*, [2007-II] ICJ Rep 582, 599 para. 40.

[21] '[D]elay on the part of a claimant State may render an application inadmissible . . . [I]nternational law does not lay down any specific time-limit. . . . It is therefore for the Court to determine in the light of the cisrcumstances of each case whether the passage of time renders an application inadmissible': *Certain Phosphate Lands in Nauru*, [1992] ICJ Rep 240, 253–4 para. 32.

[22] Contrast the decisions in *South West Africa*, [1966] ICJ Rep 6, 51 para. 99, and in *Obligation to Prosecute or Extradite*, [2012] ICJ Rep 450 para. 70.

[23] As in the two *Lockerbie* cases; and cf. the *Northern Cameroons* case, though the 'objection' was rather one taken by the Court itself.

[24] As argued by the US in *Oil Platforms*: the Court found that in the circumstances of that case the objection had not been presented as a preliminary one, but impliedly recognizes that it could be so categorized: [2003] ICJ Rep 161, 176–8 paras. 27–30.

[25] *Delimitation of the Continental Shelf between Nicaragua and Colombia beyond 200 nautical miles*: the 'determination' referred to was to be made by the Commission on the Limit of the Continental Shelf. See ICJ CR 2015/27, p. 58.

[26] See n. 8.

objection in those cases was that the Libyan claim had been rendered 'moot' by a decision of the Security Council adopted after the filing of the Libyan applications: the Court found the objection to be 'not of an exclusively preliminary character' (see Rules, Art. 79 para. 9, and sect. C below), and it was never resolved. A decision, on a similar ground, to end a case before the merits had been dealt with, as though a preliminary objection had been upheld, was taken by the Court of its own motion in the *Northern Cameroons* case, in 1963. This involved questions of compliance by the trustee State with an international trusteeship under Article XII of the Charter; but between the institution of the proceedings and the Court's consideration of the matter, the trusteeship had been terminated and the territory had acceded to independence. The respondent (the United Kingdom) raised a preliminary objection to the effect that the Court was without jurisdiction inasmuch as there had never been a dispute as asserted, or that if there had been, it did not fall within the Trusteeship Agreement, or that there was no longer any dispute.[27] The Court did not uphold the objection as such: it specifically left open the question whether there was jurisdiction at the outset, and continued 'circumstances that have since arisen render any adjudication devoid of purpose'—which again seems to leave the jurisdictional issue open. It found that 'the proper limits of the judicial function do not permit to entertain the claims submitted to it . . .'; '[a]ny judgment which the Court might pronounce would be without object'.[28]

C. Procedure on submission, and for disposal, of an objection

Formerly the filing of a preliminary objection was treated as the opening of a new case, separate from the proceedings being objected to, which, however, were suspended until the objection was resolved; since 1952, the objection is treated simply as opening a separate phase in the original proceedings.[29] The Rules contemplate three possible fates for a preliminary objection: the Court, after hearing the parties, 'shall give its decision in the form of a judgment, by which it shall either uphold the objection, reject it, or declare that the objection does not possess, in the circumstances of the case, an exclusively preliminary character' (Art. 79 para. 9).[30] This text dates from the 1972 revision of the Rules: formerly the third option open to the Court was defined as 'joining the objection to the merits';[31] but in the *Barcelona Traction* case the Court already included as an example of this process a decision that 'the objection does not in fact have a preliminary character'.[32] The new definition is

[27] See the UK final submissions at [1963] ICJ Rep 15, 20.

[28] [1963] ICJ Rep 15, 38.

[29] For the consequent modifications in the procedure, see Talmon in Zimmermann et al., *Commentary*, 1163, Art. 43 para. 185. For the concept of a 'phase' of the proceedings, see Ch. 7 sect. B(2).

[30] Restated by the Court in the *Territorial Dispute (Nicaragua/Colombia)* case: [2007-II] ICJ Rep 832, 852 para. 48.

[31] PCIJ Rules (1936), Art. 62 (5) and later texts.

[32] [1964] ICJ Rep 6, 43.

apparently more restrictive, *inter alia* as a result of the addition of the word 'exclusively' before 'preliminary'.

A fourth possibility is that the Court does not need to take any decision on the objection because it is withdrawn by the State submitting it, in which case the discontinuance is recorded of the phase of the proceedings devoted to the objection.[33]

If an objection is upheld, the result—in view of the nature of the objection—is that the case comes to an end, for lack of jurisdiction or because the claim is inadmissible or 'without object'. If the objection is rejected, then the case continues on the merits, new time-limits being set for further pleadings; and if the objection was to jurisdiction, the Court makes a specific finding that it does possess jurisdiction.[34] A finding that the objection 'does not possess . . . an exclusively preliminary character' has substantively the same effect as 'joinder to the merits' under the old Rules: the case continues on the merits, but the fate of the objection is reserved. In effect, by so finding, the Court is saying that it cannot decide the objection until the case has been fully argued on the merits. The eventual judgment will deal first with the objection, and if it is then rejected, will go on to decide the merits.

The change of wording mentioned above was made at a time when the Court's handling of preliminary objections had been exposed to criticism, particularly following two high-profile cases: the *South West Africa* case and, in particular, the *Barcelona Traction, Light & Power Co.* cases. In the first, the Court had dismissed a number of preliminary objections, and proceeded with the merits (including hearing evidence); but when the judgment was given, it proved to be a dismissal of the claims on a fine point of law which was seen by many observers as essentially the same as one of the objections that had been dismissed earlier. In the second case, two preliminary objections were joined to the merits, and after extensive hearing of the merits[35] the case was dismissed essentially on the narrow legal point raised in one of those two objections, all the evidence and argument as to the facts proving superfluous.[36]

A difference between the old and new wording of the Rules is that 'joinder to the merits' describes simply the procedural process, leaving open the reasons that may cause the Court to take it, whereas the new wording requires a specific finding, that the objection does not have an 'exclusively preliminary character'. Under the old Rule, it was sufficient to find, as the Permanent Court had found in *Pajzs,*

[33] See e.g. *Rights of US Nationals in Morocco*, Order of 31 October 1951, [1951] ICJ Rep 109; the case itself was later withdrawn.

[34] For a recent example, see *Obligation to Negotiate Access to the Pacific Ocean (Bolivia* v *Chile)*, [2015] ICJ Rep para. 56(2).

[35] The Court referred in its judgment to 'the unusual length of the present proceedings', for which it blamed the parties, who had asked for long time-limits for their pleadings, and went on to emphasize that 'it is in the interest of the authority and proper functioning of international justice for cases to be decided without unwarranted delay': [1970] ICJ Rep 3, 30–1 para. 27.

[36] Writing in the *American Journal*, President Jiménez de Aréchaga expressly linked the revision of the Rule to the *Barcelona Traction* case: 67 *AJIL* (1973), 13–14: and see the declaration of Judge Bennouna, *Obligation to Negotiate Access to the Pacific Ocean*, [2015] ICJ Rep, 612–14.

Csák, Esterházy, that the 'proceedings on the merits ... will place the Court in a better position to adjudicate with a full knowledge of the facts, and that the preliminary issues and those arising on the merits 'are too intimately related and too closely interconnected for the Court to be able to adjudicate on the former without prejudging the latter'.[37]

It may not always be easy to determine whether an objection is of 'an exclusively preliminary character'; it may be regarded as preliminary, but not exclusively so; and the test probably leaves the Court a considerable measure of discretion. A complex example was the *Territorial and Maritime Dispute* between Nicaragua and Colombia. Whether the Court had jurisdiction under the Pact of Bogotá over a given question in dispute between the parties depended on whether, at the time of the Pact, that question had already been 'settled' between the parties (Art. VI of the Pact): if it had, then the Pact did not confer jurisdiction. Colombia claimed in a preliminary objection that the question in dispute had been 'settled' by a 1928 Treaty, so that there was no jurisdiction under the Pact; Nicaragua contended that the 1928 Treaty was, for various reasons, invalid, so that there was such jurisdiction. Colombia was also relying on the 1928 Treaty to support its claim on the merits of the matter. In view of this intermingling of substantive and jurisdictional questions, Nicaragua argued that the objection was 'not exclusively preliminary', and should be reserved for treatment with the merits. The Court, however, examined the scope of the 1928 Treaty, and also the question whether it was in force in 1928. It thus rejected Nicaragua's argument as to reservation of the matter for the merits,[38] apparently on the basis of considerations of 'the good administration of justice';[39] but it stated that it 'ha[d] already found that the question of whether the 1928 Treaty and the 1930 Protocol settled the matters in dispute does not constitute the subject-matter of the dispute on the merits. It is rather a preliminary question to be decided in order to ascertain whether the Court has jurisdiction.'[40] Whatever the description of the process—joinder to the merits or a finding of 'lack of preliminary character'– the effect, in either case, is that the objection is not resolved, but the Court proceeds to hear the merits, while reserving the possibility to decide, in the light of the presentation of the merits, that the objection should be upheld. There was always a danger of joinder to the merits being used as a device to postpone a problem on which the Court was having difficulty in reaching agreement either way; and if the Court seems narrowly divided on the point at the objection stage, it may be argued that to reserve it might make it possible to determine it, one way or the other, with a more substantial majority at the later stage, particularly if a triennial renewal of the Court will intervene. (There is of course always the risk that the Court in its later composition may be still more divided.) Certainly the new

[37] *PCIJ Series A/B, No. 66*, 9, quoted in *Barcelona Traction, Light Power Co.*, [1964] ICJ Rep 45–6. The whole subject is discussed at length in the separate opinion of Sir Gerald Fitzmaurice at the later stage of that case, [1970] ICJ Rep 64, 110–13, 'The Philosophy of Joinder to the Merits'.

[38] The controversy is stated in [2007-II] ICJ Rep 853, para. 58, and is followed by a cryptic paragraph (59) to the effect the Court 'must apply Article 1 of its Statute'.

[39] [2007-II] ICJ Rep 832, 851 para. 50.

[40] Ibid. 852 para. 51.

formula is not, any more than the expression 'joinder to the merits', one that can be easily and uncontroversially applied.[41]

The Court has declared that '[a] Respondent's right to raise preliminary objections, that is to say, objections which the Court is required to rule on before the debate on the merits begins . . . is a fundamental procedural right.' The context was the raising of a new claim in the Reply, with the consequence that 'the Respondent was no longer able to assert preliminary objections to it, since such objections have to be submitted, under . . . the Rules of Court . . . within the time-limit fixed for the delivery of the Counter-Memorial'.[42]

It is, however, not merely the right to raise objections to jurisdiction and admissibility that is fundamental, but the right to raise such matters as *preliminary* objections, that is to say, 'objections which the Court is required to rule on before the debate on the merits begins'. If a party raises, at any time, an objection to jurisdiction or admissibility, the Court must respond to it, unless of course the circumstances are such that the party concerned can be taken, through inaction or delay, to have waived the objection. Furthermore, because of the preliminary nature of such issues, the Court must dispose of the objections before turning to its decision on the merits, as otherwise it would risk deciding without jurisdiction, or dealing with an inadmissible claim.[43] The principle stated by the Court is that 'A party raising preliminary objections is entitled to have those objections answered at the preliminary stage of the proceedings unless the Court does not have before it all facts necessary to decide the question raised, or if answering the preliminary objection would determine the dispute, or some elements thereof, on the merits.'[44] In the *Diallo* case, the Court ruled, rather curiously, that the right of a respondent to raise preliminary objections is 'infringed' if a new claim is raised late in the proceedings;[45] yet the objection still has to be disposed of in priority, and if the Rules were differently worded, so as to refer to an objection to a belated new claim as a 'preliminary' objection, the problem would apparently disappear. Similarly, when the procedure in a case had been adopted by an Order of the Court, with the parties' agreement, and the respondent sought later to submit a preliminary objection, the Court did not permit this, but did permit the objection to be presented as part of the respondent's first pleading.[46]

[41] For a recent example see *Application of the Genocide Convention (Croatia* v *Serbia)* [2008] ICJ Rep 466 para. 146 (4), the criticism of Judge Tomka, ibid. 525 ff., the subsequent judgment on the merits, 3 February 2015, and the comments of President Tomka in his separate opinion, particularly para. 4.

[42] *Ahmadou Siado Diallo*, [2010-II] ICJ Rep 639, 658 para. 44.

[43] But note the curiously constructed decision in the *Oil Platforms* case, whereby the Court contrived to make a finding against the United States before deciding, in effect, that it had no jurisdiction to do so: [2003] ICJ Rep 161; D. H. Small, 'The *Oil Platforms* Case: Jurisdiction through the (Closed) Eye of the Needle', 3 *LPICT* (2004) 113; F. Berman, 'Treaty "Interpretation" in a Judicial Context', 29 *Yale Journal of International Law* (2004), 319–20.

[44] *Territorial and Maritime Dispute (Nicaragua* v *Colombia)*, [2007-II] ICJ Rep 832, 852 para. 51. The second hypothesis is somewhat obscure; it seems to relate to cases of 'joinder to the merits', but these concerned the possibility of resolving the objection independently of the merits, rather than the impact on the merits of a decision on the objection.

[45] *Ahmadou Siado Diallo*, [2010-II] ICJ Rep 639, 658 para. 44.

[46] *Arrest Warrant of 11 April 2000*, Order of 27 June 2001, [2001] ICJ Rep 559, 562–3.

If a preliminary objection is raised, 'the proceedings on the merits shall be suspended' (Rules, Art. 79 para. 5), and a separate set of proceedings devoted solely to the objection is opened:[47] the applicant responds to the objection in written 'observations and submissions', and hearings are held, leading to the delivery of a judgment of the Court on the objection. In one case already mentioned, the Court deduced from the suspension of the merits proceedings that a claim advanced later in those proceedings had to be treated as a 'new claim' for procedural purposes even if, as the applicant asserted, it had been raised in some form in the course of the proceedings devoted to the objections.[48]

[47] Unless the respondent has indicated that it does not press for the objection and the merits to be handled separately to this extent, e.g. by filing objections and pleading on the merits simultaneously, as did the United Kingdom in *Northern Cameroons*: see [1963] ICJ Rep 15, 27.

[48] *Ahmadou Siado Diallo*, [2010-II] ICJ Rep 639, 654 para. 31: 'As those were incidental proceedings opened by virtue of the DRC's preliminary objections, Guinea could not present any submission other than those concerning the merit of the objections and how the Court should deal with them'.

15

Intervention

A. Introduction

A dispute by definition requires the presence of at least two contesting parties, but may of course involve more than two. The normal number of parties to a case before the Court is thus two, the applicant and the respondent, although either the 'applicant' or the 'respondent' (or each of them) may be constituted by two or more States jointly. There may, however, be more States involved in the underlying dispute than are initially made parties to the proceedings; this is particularly likely in view of the wide variation in the extent to which States have accepted the Court's jurisdiction. A State that observes the introduction of proceedings by other States in a dispute in which it is also involved, and that wishes the Court to hear its side of the question, is of course free to institute a separate case of its own, provided it can find a basis of jurisdiction entitling it to proceed against one or both of the parties to the existing case. While it may be possible for the cases thereafter to be joined,[1] it is desirable that in some circumstances a third State be given the possibility of being involved, in some way, in a case already begun.

This situation is foreseen in the Statute of the Court, which provides for a process called intervention, whereby a third State becomes involved in the procedure, and is entitled to present its arguments and evidence to the Court. There are two possibilities. Under Article 63 of the Statute,

1. Whenever the construction [i.e., interpretation] of a convention to which States other than those concerned in the case are parties is in question, the Registrar shall notify all such States forthwith.
2. Every State so notified has the right to intervene in the proceedings, but if it uses this right, the construction given in the judgment will be equally binding upon it.

Article 62 is more general in scope:

1. Should a State consider that it has an interest of a legal nature which may be affected by the decision in the case, it may submit a request to be allowed to intervene.
2. It shall be for the Court to decide upon this request.

[1] Ch. 7 sect. B(2)b.

B. Intervention under Article 63 of the Statute

Article 63 is based upon a simple concept: that for the judicial interpretation of a multilateral convention, it is desirable to have the views of as many as possible of the parties to the convention. No distinction is made between the original parties, who were presumably involved in drawing up the treaty (and will thus have views—not necessarily the same views—as to what its text was meant to mean), and States who have become parties subsequently. As a result of the ubiquity of multilateral treaty law at the present day, many—perhaps the majority—of the cases brought before the Court now involve the application of Article 63, and the Registrar's duty of notification under that text is quite substantial.

While actual interventions under Article 63 have been few, the question of the notifications has caused difficulties in a number of cases. For example, when the Court receives a request for provisional measures simultaneously with the commencement of proceedings on a matter involving the interpretation of a multilateral convention, how are the parties to the convention to be given an opportunity of considering intervention, consistently with the urgency of the measures that may be called for?[2] Intervention, if it occurs, is in the case as a whole,[3] but if the third State's interest may be affected even by the indication (or non-indication) of provisional measures, that State may seek to intervene at that stage.

The Statute of the Court is itself a multilateral treaty, or part of one,[4] and a case may involve its interpretation, but a specific notification under Article 63 is otiose, in view of the fact that all parties to the Statute are notified of the institution of proceedings.[5] Despite the use, in paragraph 2, of Article 63, of the phrase '[e]very State so notified . . .', Article 82, paragraph 3, of the Rules enables a State that has not been notified, but 'considers itself a party to' the relevant convention, to file a declaration of intervention.

The rarity of interventions under Article 63 may result from States being deterred by the consequence of intervention stated in paragraph 2. It is possible that States tend to consider it better to keep their options open: if they do not intervene, they are free to contend that the Court's interpretation of the convention is not correct, and that interpretation will of course not be binding on them, in view of Article 59 of the Statute. The PCIJ saw only one case of Article 63 intervention;[6] and in only four cases before the present Court have there been interventions of this type.

In the first, *Haya de la Torre*, the intervention of Cuba concerned the interpretation of the Havana Convention, involved in the proceedings, but was devoted

[2] In practice, the request for measures simply has to take its course, with the notification being sent out when possible, sometimes the day before the hearings! See Zimmermann et al., *Commentary, sub* Art. 63 para. 33 (p. 1587).

[3] Though if the proceedings are not devoted solely to the issue of interpretation of the convention, a State intervening under Art. 63 will not be permitted to address the other issues: see the *Haya de la Torre* case, mentioned below.

[4] According to Art. 92 of the Charter, the Statute is an 'integral part' of the Charter.

[5] Statute, Art. 40 (3).

[6] *S.S. Wimbledon, PCIJ Series A, No. 1*, 1, 11, 13.

largely to irrelevant issues;[7] the Court admitted a 'reduced' version of the intervention, limited to the points of interpretation that the Court did then have to decide.[8] The Court indicated in its judgment that it had 'defined in accordance with the Havana Convention the legal relations between the Parties with regard to the matters referred to it'; it did not state specifically that the judgment was binding on Cuba, but Cuba was named as 'intervening Party', and received a copy of the judgment.[9] The second, the intervention of El Salvador in *Military and Paramilitary Activities in and against Nicaragua,* was prompted by the United States; it related to the jurisdiction of the Court, challenged by the US; the Court declined to admit the intervention at any stage of the proceedings. The third case was the anomalous case of the *Request for an Examination of the Situation* submitted by New Zealand in 1995, examined in Chapter 8 section A; a number of Pacific island States sought to intervene under Article 63 (and Article 62) in support of New Zealand;[10] the dismissal of New Zealand's request meant that these attempted interventions were also dismissed, as 'proceedings incidental to' New Zealand's requests.[11]

In the case of *Whaling in the Antarctic* brought by Australia against Japan, New Zealand filed a declaration of intervention under Article 63, with reference to the 'construction' of the International Convention for the Regulation of Whaling, which Australia contended Japan had not been complying with. In its Order admitting the intervention,[12] the Court analysed this form of intervention at some length, by reference to the Statute and Article 82 of the Rules. It carefully distinguished it from intervention under Article 62: there is, for example, no need to show the existence of a 'legal interest that may be affected' by the decision in the case (see sect. C). The third State has, subject to verification of the conditions of the Statute and Rules, a 'right' to be admitted to the proceedings;[13] this must imply that it can be so admitted in the teeth of opposition by both parties. The Court nevertheless sought their observations, presumably so that they could point to any respect in which New Zealand's declaration did not meet the required conditions. Australia, unsurprisingly, supported the intervention; Japan expressed some doubts in relation to procedural equality, in relation to the possible appointment of a judge ad hoc, a matter discussed in Chapter 3 section 2. The intervention was admitted, the Court being unanimous.[14] New Zealand having had the opportunity of expressing its views on the interpretation of the Convention, the role of Article 63 was completed, and the Judgment makes no further reference to New Zealand's interest.

[7] It was addressed to matters already dealt with in the earlier *Asylum* case.

[8] [1951] ICJ Rep 77.

[9] [1951] ICJ Rep 72, 84.

[10] Order of 22 September 1995, [1995] ICJ Rep 288, 292 para. 11.

[11] Ibid. 306–7 para. 67.

[12] [2013] ICJ Rep 3.

[13] Ibid. 4–5 para. 8. This in contradistinction to intervention under Art. 62; yet that form of intervention seems also to be a right, provided the conditions laid down are complied with. Or is intervention under Art. 62 merely by permission, 'at the discretion of the Court, according to what it considers, on a case-by-case basis, to be in the interest of the sound administration of justice'? See the Opinion of Judge Abraham quoted at n. 15.

[14] Ibid. 10 para. 23. It was subsequently unanimous also in its decision on the merits, substantially upholding the claims of Australia: [2014] ICJ Rep 226, 298–9 para. 247.

C. Intervention under Article 62 of the Statute

Since, according to Article 59 of the Statute, the decision in a case has no binding force beyond the parties to it, the rights of third States remain untouched; hence, a right of intervention could not be based upon a threat, real or perceived, to third States' rights. Article 62 therefore contemplates that it is sufficient that a third State perceive that it has an 'interest of a legal nature' that may be 'affected' by the decision.[15] Intervention is intended for the benefit (at least primarily) of the intervening State. In some cases, it might well be useful *for the Court*, before deciding a case, to hear the views of a third State which is somehow involved in the matter, but this is not the criterion. It is only in advisory cases that a State may be treated as 'likely to be able to furnish information', and on that basis give its views on the legal issues involved.[16] Yet in the context of maritime boundary delimitation, where a full picture of claims in the relevant area is essential, even when an intervention is rejected, the Court may 'take note of' the information supplied by the unsuccessful intervenor,[17] with the implication that this information might affect its judgment. On the other hand, a successful intervention apparently may not necessarily carry the consequence that the legal interest will not be affected: the Court has also defined the purpose of intervention as being 'in order to ensure that no legal interest may be "affected" *without the intervener being heard*'.[18]

Before examining the question of the definition of an 'interest of a legal nature', and that of the meaning of 'affected', there is a matter that is left open by the text of the Article: the question of jurisdiction. As between the principal parties, the applicant and the respondent, the existence of a link of jurisdiction is vital; if none is shown, the case may be dismissed on the preliminary point, and the merits never examined. If then a third State wishes to acquire the status of a party, must it also show a jurisdictional link, and if so, with both parties, or merely with one of them?

[15] For the drafting history of the text in the PCIJ Statute and subsequently, see *Continental Shelf (Libya/Tunisia), Application of Malta to Intervene*, [1981] ICJ Rep 3, 13–15,paras. 22–5. A recent decision caused one judge to feel it necessary to reassert that intervention is a right, not merely 'an option whose exercise is subject to permission to be granted or withheld at the discretion of the Court, according to what it considers, on a case-by-case basis, to be in the interest of the sound administration of justice': dissenting opinion of Judge Abraham in the *Territorial and Maritime Dispute* case, [2011] ICJ Rep 384 para. 4.

[16] See Statute, Art. 66 para. 2; 'information' has never been interpreted as limited to *factual* information, but includes information as to the State's view of the applicable law. It has been suggested that, alongside intervention under Art. 63, there should be a similar provision for interested third States to submit observations on legal rules other than those contained in a convention (see G. Gaja, 'A New Way for Submitting Observations on the Construction of Multilateral Treaties to the International Court of Justice', in U. Fastenrath et al. (eds.), *From Bilateralism to Community Interest: Essays in Honour of Judge Bruno Simma* (Oxford: Oxford University Press, 2011), 665.).

[17] *Territorial and Maritime Dispute (Nicaragua* v *Colombia), Application of Costa Rica for Permission to Intervene)*, [2011] ICJ Rep 363 para. 51. Although the Court does not say so, presumably it would also take note of any information supplied by the parties in response to the attempted intervention.

[18] *Land, Island and Maritime Frontier Dispute* [1990] ICJ Rep 130 para. 90 (italics added), quoted in *Territorial and Maritime Dispute*, [2011] ICJ Rep 360 para. 34.

In other words, must the third State be in a position such that it could, in lieu of intervening, have brought separate proceedings for the protection of its 'interest of a legal nature'?[19] If so, it might be thought that Article 62 does not in fact add anything to the procedural rights of parties to the Statute; if not, this may be seen as a derogation from the overriding requirement of consent as the basis of international judicial action.

The problem was illustrated by the attempted intervention of Fiji in the *Nuclear Tests* cases brought by Australia and New Zealand against France. Fiji sought to join in the proceedings, in effect as co-plaintiff, but could not point to any jurisdictional title available to it as against France. Accordingly, Fiji could not validly have brought a separate case against France; could it therefore be allowed to jump on the bandwagon, as it were, to reach the same result by taking advantage of the fact that Australia and New Zealand had brought proceedings? The cases came to a premature end before the Court was called upon to decide the point, but some of the judges felt strongly enough to indicate, in declarations attached to an Order of the Court,[20] that they would have dismissed the intervention for lack of jurisdiction.

The new Rules of Court adopted in 1978 required a State seeking to intervene to indicate in its application (*inter alia*) 'any basis of jurisdiction which is claimed to exist as between the State applying to intervene and the parties to the case' (Art. 81(2)(c)), a wording that seems designed to leave the question open.[21] Around this time, one specific type of dispute made intervention under this Article seem particularly attractive to third States. In a number of cases the Court was asked to rule on the delimitation of seabed areas in a dispute between two States, but in a geographical situation in which the possible rights or interests of other States might be prejudged or infringed in some way—even if in strict law the decision of the Court would be *res inter alios acta* for those States.

It was in this context that the opportunity to settle the point seemed to have come in 1981: Tunisia and Libya had brought a case to determine the limits of their respective continental shelves, and Malta applied for permission to intervene. This was refused (see above), but not on the jurisdictional point, which was expressly reserved.[22] When Italy sought to intervene in the similar case between Libya and Malta, the Court seems to have been united in rejecting this as a possibility, but divided as to the reasons. Unusually, the judgment states successively two alternative arguments, each of which leads to rejection of the intervention.[23] The conclusion that 'the intervention falls into a category which . . . cannot be accepted', the

[19] When Art. 62 of the PCIJ Statute was drafted, it was contemplated that the Court would have universal jurisdiction, so this problem could not, on that basis, have arisen; when the draft was modified to abandon this system in favour of the 'optional clause', no change was made to Art. 62.

[20] See the declarations of Judges Gros, Onyeama, Dillard, and Waldock (jointly), Jiménez de Aréchaga, and Judge ad hoc Barwick, [1974] ICJ Rep 531–3 and 536–8.

[21] See the 1999 decision in the *Land, Island and Maritime Frontier* case, [1999] ICJ Rep 92, 111 para. 44.

[22] *Continental Shelf (Tunisia/Libya), Application by Malta to Intervene*, [1981] ICJ Rep 3, 20 para. 36.

[23] Cf. *Land, Island and Maritime Frontier Dispute (El Salvador/Honduras), Application to Intervene*, [1990] ICJ Rep 92, 132 para. 94.

Court stated, 'follows from either of the two approaches outlined above, and the Court accordingly does not have to choose between them'.[24]

It was eventually a chamber of the Court that cut the Gordian knot. It was the acquisition of the status of party to the case by a State without a link of jurisdiction that appeared objectionable to many judges (and commentators); the Chamber saw that intervention need not necessarily involve acquiring that status. It ruled, in the case of the *Land, Island and Maritime Boundary Dispute* between El Salvador and Honduras, on the application to intervene of Nicaragua, that no jurisdictional link was required for an intervention that did not confer the status of party; and in that context any objection of the original parties to the intervention was to be taken into account, but was not decisive.[25] It resolved the difficulty over lack of consent by observing that the Court's competence in the matter of intervention derives, 'not from the consent of the parties to the case, but from the consent given by them, in becoming parties to the Court's Statute, to the Court's exercise of its powers conferred by the Statute'.[26] These findings were approved by the full Court in the subsequent cases of *Land and Maritime Boundary between Cameroon and Nigeria*,[27] and *Sovereignty over Pulau Ligitan and Pulau Sipadan*.[28] The lack of party status carries with it one important consequence: if the intervener is not a party, the chamber in the *El Salvador/Honduras* case held, then it is not bound by the judgment, and similarly cannot invoke it against the original parties.[29]

It remains the case that intervention as a party is also possible under Article 62, but this apparently requires either the consent of the original parties,[30] or the existence of a jurisdictional title such that the intending intervener could have brought independent proceedings against each of them, or at least against the respondent. No such application to intervene has, however, yet been successfully made.

The cases mentioned have also enabled the Court to consider the conditions for intervention: the nature of a 'legal interest', and how it may be 'affected' for the

[24] *Continental Shelf (Malta/Libya), Application by Italy to Intervene*, [1984] ICJ Rep 24 para. 38.

[25] *Land, Island and Maritime Frontier Dispute (El Salvador/Honduras), Application to Intervene*, [1990] ICJ Rep 92, 132 para. 92; a point already made in *Continental Shelf (Libya/Malta), Application of Italy to Intervene* [1984] ICJ Rep 3, 28 para. 46. See, however, *Land and Maritime Boundary between Cameroon and Nigeria*, [1999] ICJ Rep 1029, 1034 para. 12, where the Court states as a separate paragraph in the *considérants* of its Order the fact that neither party objected to the intervention of Equatorial Guinea.

[26] *Land, Island and Maritime Frontier Dispute (El Salvador/Honduras), Application to Intervene*, [1990] ICJ Rep 133 para. 96.

[27] *Land and Maritime Boundary between Cameroon and Nigeria, Application to Intervene*, [1999] ICJ Rep 1029.

[28] *Sovereignty over Palau Ligitan and Pulau Sipidan (Indonesia/Malaysia), Application to Intervene*, [2001] ICJ Rep 575, 588–9 paras. 35–6.

[29] *Land, Island and Maritime Frontier Dispute (El Salvador/Honduras), Application to Intervene*, [1990] ICJ Rep 92, 610 para. 424. The intending intervener (Nicaragua) had in fact announced in advance that it would accept the judgment as binding, but the Chamber did not find this acceptance legally effective.

[30] In the judgment in the *Land and Maritime Boundary between Cameroon and Nigeria* [2002] ICJ Rep 303 para 12, the Court took note of the fact that the parties had no objection to the intervention of Equatorial Guinea, but that State was not seeking to intervene as a party.

purposes of Article 62.[31] The Court has declared, as a preliminary point, that the decision whether to admit an intervention is not a matter of the Court's discretion; the specific provisions of the Statute have to be applied.[32] An interest of, as it were, an academic nature in the legal rules or principles that the Court would be likely to apply also would not suffice;[33] but if the interest asserted by a would-be intervenor were too specific, so as to amount to a claim parallel to those made in the case, the jurisdictional difficulty, already discussed, would be the more acute. Broadly speaking, the intervention of Malta in *Libya/Tunisia* failed for lack of specificity of the interest asserted, and the intervention of Italy in *Libya/Malta* failed for excessive specificity, in that what was asserted amounted in effect to a claim that could have been made the basis of a separate case. Italy suggested that admission of its intervention would be necessary, or at least desirable, to enable the Court properly to decide on the claims of Libya and Malta; the Court observed that this was not relevant to the issue whether or not Italy had an interest that should not be 'affected' but it also pointed out that, intervention being purely facultative, the Court can never count on such assistance being offered by a third State, and that therefore 'it must be open to the Court, and indeed its duty, to give the fullest decision it may in the circumstances of each case'.[34]

In the *Cameroon/Nigeria* case, the Court went further still; finding at a preliminary stage that its judgment on the maritime delimitation requested might affect the rights and interests of third States, specifically Equatorial Guinea, it virtually invited that State to intervene.[35] Equatorial Guinea duly did so, and the Court (noting that neither of the parties objected to the intervention) found that that State had 'sufficiently established that it has an interest of a legal nature which could [not 'may', as in the Statute] be affected by any judgment' that the Court might give.[36]

In the case of *Pulau Ligitan and Pulau Sipadan*, however, a non-party intervention was refused on the ground that the would-be intervenor had 'not discharged its obligation to convince the Court that specified legal interests may be

[31] The French text of the Article requires that the applicant show that 'un intérêt d'ordre juridique est pour lui en cause'; the Chamber in the *Land, Island and Maritime Frontier* case mentioned this as though it saw a divergence of meaning between the two texts ([1990] ICJ Rep 92, 114 para. 52), but did not pursue the point. The term 'interest' also appears in Art. 31 para. 5, referring to 'parties in the same interest' in connection with the appointment of judges ad hoc (see Ch. 2 B(2)), but the word is clearly there used in a more general sense.

[32] *Continental Shelf (Tunisia/Libya), Application of Malta to Intervene*, [1981] ICJ Rep 3, 12 para. 23. Judge Oda however saw a place also for 'considerations of judicial propriety' (Separate opinion, [1981] ICJ Rep 23 para. 1). Yet subsequent references by the Court to the relevance of considerations of 'the sound administration of justice' have led to some doubt on the point: see the opinion of Judge Abraham, mentioned in n. 15.

[33] As the Court noted approvingly, it was not on this basis that Malta sought to intervene in the *Libya/Tunisia* case: [1981] ICJ Rep 3, 17 para. 30; and on the intervention of Nicaragua in the *Land, Island and Maritime Boundary Dispute*, the Chamber rejected the idea that 'an interest of a third State in the general legal rules and principles likely to be applied by the decision can justify an intervention': [1990] ICJ Rep 92, 124 para. 76.

[34] *Continental Shelf (Libya/Malta), Application of Italy to Intervene*, [1984] ICJ Rep 3, 25 para. 40.

[35] *Land and Maritime Boundary between Cameroon and Nigeria*, [1998] ICJ Rep 275, 324 para. 116 in fine.

[36] Ibid. [1999] ICJ Rep 1029, 1034 paras. 12, 13. The uncontroversial character of the decision is emphasized by its being cast in the form of an Order, unanimously adopted.

affected in the particular circumstances of this case'.[37] The would-be intervenor, the Philippines, had argued that since Article 62 refers to the possibility that a State may 'consider' that it has a legal interest that might be affected, to intervene it need only meet a subjective test, of showing that it did so consider; but the Court stated, as it had in an earlier decision, that the State must 'demonstrate convincingly what it asserts' in this respect.[38] The parties to the case were in dispute as to sovereignty over the two islands named in the case-title, and the Philippines asserted no claim in respect of the islands in dispute between the parties, but it feared that the Court, when dealing with the 'treaties, agreements and any other evidence' produced by the parties in support of their respective claims, might make pronouncements with 'a direct or indirect bearing on the legal status of North Borneo', and thus 'affect' the Philippines' claim concerning that territory.[39]

At the stage of the decision to admit or refuse intervention, the eventual content of the decision on the merits can only be guessed at; but the Court can, it seems, be content with the possibility that it 'might find it necessary to consider' the matters raised as affecting the third State's interests.[40]

More recent jurisprudence has brought out a difficulty—at least theoretical—in reconciling intervention under Article 62 with the general principle of the relativity of the effect of judicial decisions, expressed in Article 59 of the Statute. If, as that Article indicates, a judgment of the Court cannot affect the rights (or interests) of States not parties to the proceedings, then logically it should be impossible to show that such an interest 'may be affected' by a future judgment, and no non-party intervention could ever be justified. In the *Territorial and Maritime Dispute* between Nicaragua and Colombia, Costa Rica, seeking to intervene, was unable to show 'that its interest of a legal nature in the maritime area bordering the area in dispute between Nicaragua and Colombia needs a protection that is not provided by the relative effect of decisions of the Court under Article 59 of the Statute'.[41]

It has been suggested that intervention under Article 62 is valuable in the general interest of affording the Court wider opportunities to develop the law, with the participation of more States; and that therefore the conditions for such intervention should be made less restrictive.[42] This may, however, be a

[37] *Sovereignty over Palau Ligitan and Pulau Sipidan (Indonesia/Malaysia), Application to Intervene*, [2001] ICJ Rep 575, 600 para. 67, and 607 para. 93.

[38] Ibid. 590 para. 40 and 598 para. 58, citing the *Land, Island and Maritime Frontier Dispute* [1990] ICJ Rep 92, 117–18 para. 61.

[39] Ibid. 589 para. 36. When formulating its application to intervene, the Philippines was also hampered by the Court's refusal to give it sight of the pleadings, under Art. 53 para. 1 of the Rules, so that it did not know exactly what was being argued and what evidence was being offered.

[40] *Jurisdictional Immunities of the State, Intervention of the Hellenic Republic*, [2011-II] ICJ 494, Rep 500–1 para. 25.

[41] [2011] ICJ Rep 372 para. 87; the decision was adopted by 9 votes to 7.

[42] A. Cassese, 'The International Court of Justice: It is High Time to Restyle the Respected Old Lady', in A. Cassese (ed.), *Realizing Utopia: The Future of International Law* (2012), 239, 242–3.

unrealistic view of the likely attitude of States; as has been pointed out, parties to ICJ proceedings are anxious to retain control of their dispute, and a greater likelihood of third States intervening 'might further discourage states from litigating because of the uncertainty [the proposal] could introduce into the proceedings'.[43]

[43] I. Scobbie, '"All right, Mr. DeMille, I'm ready for my close-up": Some Critical Reflections on Professor Cassese's "The International Court of Justice: It is High Time to Restyle the Respected Old Lady"', 23 *EJIL* (2012), 1071, 1078.

VII

THE POST-ADJUDICATIVE STAGE

16

Interpretation and Revision of Judgments

A. Interpretation of judgments

The text of Article 60 provides for the Court to 'construe' (French '*interpréter*') a judgment; the English term is rather old-fashioned, but the meaning seems to be exactly the same as the French. The Permanent Court, when first asked to interpret a judgment, was 'of the opinion that the expression "to construe" must be understood as meaning to give a precise definition of the meaning and scope which the Court intended to give the judgment in question'.[1] Only judgments are subject to interpretation: this follows from (or is at least implied by) the mention of interpretation in the Statute (Art. 60) immediately after the mention of the binding force of a judgment (Art. 59). This means that a problem now arises in respect of Orders indicating provisional measures: whether these are binding was for long controverted, with the more accepted view being perhaps that they were not. Since the *LaGrand* decision, examined in Chapter 13 section A, it is established that such Orders have binding force; are they then subject to interpretation? Article 76 paragraph 1 of the Rules expressly provides for revocation or modification of provisional measures 'at the request of a party',[2] but does not contemplate a request for interpretation. Since a party is bound at its peril to observe the measures directed, it would, however, seem simple justice that it may ask for clarification if they are not clear.

On the other hand, if the judgment the interpretation of which is being requested was not on the merits of the case, but on preliminary objections, this does not exclude the possibility of interpretation.[3] It seems theoretically possible to request the interpretation of a judgment given on a request for interpretation (presumably a case of *obscurum per obscurius*!) or on a request for revision, since Article 100 paragraph 2 of the Rules provides that decisions of this kind are to be 'given in the form of a judgment'. The power to interpret a judgment being a statutory one, it is

[1] *Interpretation of Judgments Nos. 7 and 8 (Factory at Chorzów), PCIJ Series A, No. 13*, 10.

[2] And see the implementation of this text in the case of *Certain Activities carried out by Nicaragua in the Border Area (Costa Rica* v *Nicaragua)* [2013] ICJ Rep 230.

[3] *Request for Interpretation of the Judgment of 11 June 1998 in the Case concerning the Land and Maritime Boundary between Cameroon and Nigeria (Cameroon v Nigeria), Preliminary Objections* [1999-I] ICJ Rep 31,3 5 para. 10. In the *South West Africa* case, the Court left open the question whether a preliminary objections judgment is *res judicata*, or a 'final' decision: [1966] ICJ Rep 36–7 para. 59.

not open to the parties to exclude it or fetter its exercise, by (e.g.) provision in the special agreement.[4]

The precondition for a request for interpretation is that there be a 'dispute as to the meaning or scope of a judgment': that is, such a request cannot be made simply by one party that does not understand (or does not like!) a particular provision.[5] If the parties agree on a meaning of an ambiguous phrase, no interpretation is needed; this may be regarded as a corollary of the principle of consent underlying all judicial jurisdiction. The term used in the French text of Article 60 of the Statute to correspond to 'dispute' is not *différend*, as in Article 38, but *contestation*. The Court has noted in this connection that

> although in their ordinary meaning, both terms in a general sense denote opposing views, the term 'contestation' is wider in scope than the term 'différend' and does not require the same degree of opposition . . . compared to the term 'différend', the concept underlying the term 'contestation' is more flexible in its application to a particular situation . . . a dispute ('contestation' in the French text) under Article 60 of the Statute, understood as a difference of opinion between the parties as to the meaning and scope of a judgment rendered by the Court, therefore does not need to satisfy the same criteria as would a dispute ('différend' in the French text) as referred to in Article 36, paragraph 2, of the Statute . . .

It concluded that

> in the present circumstances, a meaning shall be given that best reconciles the French and English texts of Article 60 of its Statute, bearing in mind its object[,] . . . notwithstanding that the English texts of Article 36, paragraph 2, and Articles 38 and 60 of the Statute all employ the same word, 'dispute' . . . the term 'dispute' in English also may have a more flexible meaning than that generally accorded to it in Article 36, paragraph 2, of the Statute . . .[6]

The existence of the dispute thus does not have to be established with formality: it is 'sufficient if the two Governments have in fact shown themselves as holding opposite views as to the meaning or scope of a judgment of the Court'.[7]

The limitation, implied in the Statute, of interpretation to decisions having binding force also implies a limitation on the category of points on which the interpretation of a given judgment may be asked for. The Permanent Court had stated that the point in dispute must be one that was decided with binding force;[8] in the *Land and Maritime Boundary* case the Court therefore considered that the request had to 'relate to the operative part of the judgment and cannot concern

[4] *Application for Revision and Interpretation of the Judgment of 24 February 1982 in the Case concerning the Continental Shelf (Tunisia/Libyan Arab Jamahiriya)*, [1985] ICJ Rep 192, 216 para. 43: Judge Ruda dissenting, ibid. 234–5 paras. 13–14.

[5] See *Request for Interpretation of the Judgment of 20 November 1950 in the Asylum Case* [1950] ICJ Rep 403.

[6] *Request for Interpretation of the Judgment of 31 March 2004 in the Case concerning Avena and Other Mexican Nationals (Mexico* v *USA)* Order of 16 July 2008 [2008] ICJ Rep 311, 325 para. 53.

[7] *Interpretation of Judgments Nos. 7 and 8 (Factory at Chorzow), PCIJ Series A, No. 13*, 10–11, quoted in the 1985 decision (see n. 8).

[8] *Application for Revision and Interpretation of the Judgment of 24 February 1982 in the Case concerning the Continental Shelf (Tunisia/Libyan Arab Jamahiriya) (Tunisia* v *Libyan Arab Jamahiriya)*, [1985] ICJ Rep 192.

the reasons for the judgment except in so far as these are inseparable from the operative part'.[9] In the *Tunisia/Libya* case the matter was complicated by the fact that the Court had been asked, not to establish a delimitation of the shelf, but to indicate the international legal principles and rules applicable; but the Court nevertheless regarded the points in its earlier decision that it was asked to interpret as *res judicata* for this purpose.

The *Avena* case brought by Mexico against the United States involved an unusual employment of the right to seek interpretation of a judgment. Mexico had obtained an Order for provisional measures requiring the US not to execute a number of named Mexican nationals pending the final judgment in the case;[10] and in the subsequent 2004 judgment on the merits a similar obligation was found to rest on the US not to execute these persons until their cases had received 'review and reconsideration'.[11] Mexico then brought a request for interpretation of the 2004 judgment, asking the Court to say whether the US obligation stated in the judgment was an 'obligation of result'. In that context, it also asked for provisional measures; and by an Order of 16 July 2008 the Court indicated measures requiring that the Mexican nationals referred to should not be executed 'pending judgment on the Request for interpretation submitted by the United Mexican States, unless and until these five Mexican nationals receive review and reconsideration' on the lines already laid down.[12] One of the named Mexican nationals was nevertheless executed. As to the claim for interpretation itself, the US conceded that the obligation under the 2004 judgment was such an obligation, and contended that there was therefore no 'dispute' for the purposes of Article 60 of the Statute. The Court however based its decision, refusing the interpretation, on the ground that the matters that Mexico alleged to be 'in issue' between the parties, and was thus seeking to have resolved, were not matters that the 2004 judgment had decided, so that they could not give rise to an interpretation under Article 60.[13] Mexico had, however, also asked that the Court declare that the US was in breach of the 2008 Order indicating provisional measures (in the context of the request for interpretation) inasmuch as one Mexican national had been executed, and the Court acceded to this request.

The jurisdiction of the Court under Article 60 of the Statute was therefore found to be wide enough to encompass the indication of provisional measures, and where appropriate a finding of non-compliance with such measures.[14]

[9] *Request for Interpretation of the Judgment of 11 June 1998 in the Case concerning the* Land and Maritime Boundary between Cameroon and Nigeria, [1999-I] ICJ Rep. 31, 35 para. 10. See further below (following pages).

[10] Order of 5 February 1003, [2003] ICJ Rep 3.

[11] [2004-I] ICJ Rep 12, 72 para. 153 (9). The reason why Mexico was able to require this of the US as an international obligation was through the operation of the Vienna Convention on Consular Relations.

[12] [2008] ICJ Rep 311. It is not unreasonable to suppose that the request for provisional measures was the essential purpose of the request for interpretation.

[13] *Request for Interpretation of the Judgment of 31 March 2004 in the Case concerning Avena and Other Mexican Nationals (Mexico* v *USA)*, [2009] ICJ Rep 3, 20–1 para. 61 (1).

[14] See *Request for Interpretation of the Judgment in the Avena case*, [2009] ICJ Rep 3, 19 para. 51, and Ch. 13 sect. A.

This case also brought out the fact that the purpose of interpretation is to clarify the earlier judgment, not to supplement it, even if it is suggested that it failed fully to decide the matter submitted to it. The Court has ruled that

> [t]he real purpose of the request must be to obtain an interpretation of the judgment. This signifies that its object must be solely to obtain clarification of the meaning and the scope of what the Court has decided with binding force, and not to obtain an answer to questions not so decided. Any other construction of Article 60 of the Statute would nullify the provision of the article that the judgment is final and without appeal.[15]

The argument is apparently that to add anything to the earlier judgment would, by the same token, alter what had there been decided. This suggests that the parties could not, even by agreement, obtain from the Court 'an answer to questions not . . . decided'. They could not attain this end by a request for revision either, since, as explained below, revision must be based on something that has happened since the judgment was given; and everything in this chronological category must remain outside the Court's purview on a request for interpretation.[16] The conclusion must apparently be that if the Court were to leave undecided a point that was in dispute, and one which the parties had wanted to see decided, nothing but the bringing of a new case would suffice.[17]

A related limitation on the scope of interpretation of a judgment is that 'a dispute within the meaning of Article 60 of the Statute must relate to the operative clause of the judgment in question and cannot concern the reasons for the judgment except in so far as these are inseparable from the operative clause . . . or, in the words of the Permanent Court, constitute "a condition essential to the Court's decision"'.[18] In the case in question, the Court had no difficulty in finding that there was a dispute between the parties relating to various provisions of the operative clause, so there is little guidance on what would, and what would not, be regarded as a reason 'inseparable from the operative clause'.

The limitation, according to the Permanent Court, derives from Article 60 itself: that article begins by stating the principle that the judgment is final and without appeal, and then provides for disputes 'as to its meaning or scope'. From

[15] *Request for Interpretation in the Asylum Case*, [1950] ICJ Rep 395, 402; see also *Request for Interpretation in the case of the Land and Maritime Boundary between Cameroon and Nigeria*, [1999-I] ICJ Rep 31, 36–7 para. 12. The PCIJ had already ruled that an interpretation 'adds nothing to the decision': *Factory at Chórzow, PCIJ Series A, No. 13*, 21, cited in *Application for Revision and Interpretation, Continental Shelf (Tunisia/Libya)*, [1985] ICJ Rep 192, 228 para. 65.

[16] '[T]he Court when giving an interpretation, refrains from any examination of facts other than those which it has considered in the judgment under interpretation, and consequently all facts subsequent to that judgment': *Interpretation of Judgments Nos. 7 and 8 (Factory at Chorzów), PCIJ Series A, No. 13*, 21, quoted in *Temple of Preah Vihear (Interpretation)*, [2013] ICJ Rep 281, 308 para. 75.

[17] Similarly, it appears that neither interpretation nor revision will serve if the complaint is simply that the other party has failed to comply with the judgment given: cf. the recent case between Nicaragua and Colombia, *Delimitation of the Continental Shelf between Nicaragua and Colombia beyond 200 nautical miles*, Judgment of 17 March 2016, [2016] ICJ Rep paras. 14, 62ff.

[18] *Temple of Preah Vihear (Interpretation)*, [2013] ICJ Rep 281, 296 para. 34, citing the Order indicating provisional measures in the same case, [2011-II] ICJ Rep 542 para. 23, and *Interpretation of Judgments Nos. 7 and 8 (Factory at Chorzów), PCIJ, Series A, No.13*, 20.

this the Permanent Court deduced that the second sentence 'was inserted in order, if necessary, to enable the Court to make quite clear the points which had been settled with binding force', and from this that 'a request which has not that object does not come within the terms of the provision'.[19] The logic is perhaps not inexorable, as may be recognized by the qualifications as to 'inseparable' or 'essential' reasons being equally subject to interpretation.

Some assistance as to the scope of these terms is provided by a joint declaration of three judges attached to the judgment in the *Temple Interpretation* case: in their view, '[r]easons are "inseparable" when the operative part of the Judgment is not self-standing and contains an express or implicit reference to these reasons.'[20] They insisted that 'inseparable' reasons are not the same as 'essential' reasons—a criterion used by the Permanent Court in this context: in their view, '"[e]ssential" reasons are those on which the dispositive [operative clause] is based. They may sustain the operative part of the judgment even if this is self-standing.' The importance of the distinction, in their thinking, was that to extend interpretation to part of a judgment that is not part of the operative clause, even if 'essential' to it, would be in effect to decide something that the parties had not submitted to the Court's jurisdiction.[21] It was suggested by Judge ad hoc Guillaume that the 'inseparable' or 'essential' reasoning 'constituted . . . the *ratio decidendi*', not having 'the executory force attaching to the operative parts of judgments', but having 'the authority of *res judicata*, that is to say, binding force'.[22] Possibly the criterion in view is that if a difference of view as to the *reason* for an operative finding does not make it impossible, or difficult, to comply with that provision, then interpretation is unnecessary.

But does a judgment always decide something with binding force? One would suppose so; but there have been a number of cases, particularly in the field of maritime delimitation, in which the parties have not asked for a judgment *directing* one or both of them to act in a certain way, or declaring the existence of a specific international obligation, but have come near to asking the Court for an advisory opinion. The first of these was *North Sea Continental Shelf*, in which the parties simply asked the Court to say '[w]hat principles and rules of international law are applicable to' the delimitation of areas of continental shelf.[23] Could the general rules and principles so declared amount to a binding decision? In the context of interpretation, the problem arose when Tunisia asked for (*inter alia*) an interpretation of the 1982 judgment on the delimitation of marine areas between Tunisia and

[19] *Interpretation of Judgments Nos. 7 and 8 (Factory at Chorzów), PCIJ, Series A, No.13*, 11; see also *Request for Interpretation, Land and Maritime Boundary between Cameroon and Nigeria*, [1999] ICJ Rep 31, 35 para. 10.

[20] *Declaration of Judges Owada, Bennouna and Gaja*, [2013] ICJ Rep 320 para. 1, citing as example the judgment on preliminary objections in *Land and Maritime Boundary between Cameroon and Nigeria* [1998] ICJ 275, as read in the judgment on the interpretation of that judgment, [1999-I] 31, 36 para. 11.

[21] The problem was the status of a map (the 'Annex I map') that had not, in the original judgment, been declared, in the operative clause, to be defining of a relevant boundary, though the operative part of the judgment was, in effect, only referable to that map.

[22] Declaration of Judge Guillaume, [2013] ICJ Rep 346, 348.

[23] [1969] ICJ Rep 3, 6.

Libya.[24] In this context, the Court considered it useful 'to make certain observations as to the meaning of "binding force" and the significance of the principle of *res judicata* in the circumstances of the present case'.[25] The Special Agreement under which the Court was seised used a similar formula to that in the *North Sea* case, though it was also asked to specify how the principles and rules should be applied. The Court noted that it would be a treaty, as provided for in the Special Agreement, that would contain the final delimitation.

> The treaty will however be the implementation of an obligation already entered into, in Article 2 of the Special Agreement; and that provision is not a bare *pactum de contrahendo*. The Parties have undertaken not merely to conclude a treaty, but in doing so to apply the principles and rules indicated by the Court in its 1982 Judgment.

The parties might agree to a delimitation not corresponding to the judgment; but

> failing such mutual agreement, the terms of the Court's Judgment are definitive and binding. In any event, moreover, they stand, not as something proposed to the Parties by the Court, but as something established by the Court.[26]

In this sense, then, the Court's indications would be matters of binding force, so as to be subject to a request for interpretation.

Still less, one would have thought, would the Court be entitled, on the basis of a request for interpretation of a judgment to comment on one party's compliance or non-compliance with it. It was for this reason that Judge Abraham recorded his disagreement with part of the operative clause of the decision in the *Avena (Interpretation)* case, and it is respectfully suggested that he was right.[27]

B. Revision of judgments

Article 61 of the Statute qualifies the finality of a judgment referred to in Article 60, by providing for revision, but in carefully restricted terms:

> An application for revision of a judgment may be made only when it is based upon the discovery of some fact of such a nature as to be a decisive factor, which fact was, when the judgment was given, unknown to the Court and to the party claiming revision, always provided that such ignorance was not due to negligence.[28]

Revision is therefore not a procedure for correction of a mistake allegedly made by the Court on the basis of the material that was before it when it gave the judgment, but a process whereby the Court can be made aware of a relevant fact that was not

[24] *Continental Shelf (Tunisia/Libya)*, [1982] ICJ Rep 18.

[25] *Application for Revision and Interpretation of the 1982 Judgment in the Continental Shelf (Tunisia/Libya) case*, [1985] ICJ Rep 192, 218 para. 47.

[26] *Application for Revision and Interpretation of the 1982 Judgment in the Continental Shelf (Tunisia/Libya) case*, [1985] ICJ Rep 192, 219 para. 48.

[27] [2009] ICJ Rep 27ff.; the argument is too complex to be examined in a footnote, but the essential point is as stated above.

[28] The last qualifying clause was presumably only intended to refer to the *party*'s ignorance!

then known to it, and can, if necessary, modify its decision accordingly. In one case it was sought to have the Court correct an 'error' in its judgment; the Court found that there had been no error, and reserved the question whether such a correction procedure existed.[29] In another case, there was no application for revision, but a mistake in a judgment was identified by the Court itself in a later judgment in the same case; the mistake did not affect the decision, but had led to some argument that was probably unnecessary.[30]

The fact discovered and advanced as grounds for revision is referred to in Article 61 paragraph 2 as 'the new fact'; this expression has been a source of confusion, as it is clear from the text of the paragraph that the fact must be an old fact (prior to the judgment to be revised) newly discovered (after that judgment). In the case between Bosnia and Yugoslavia, the Court observed (at first sight paradoxically) that 'a fact which occurs . . . after a judgment has been given is not a "new" fact within the meaning of Article 61'.[31] It distinguished between an Article 61 fact and 'the legal consequences' as to a pre-existing state of affairs drawn from 'facts subsequent to the Judgment';[32] but the distinction is not entirely convincing.

An unusual feature of the procedure is that it is divided by the Statute into two stages: Article 61 paragraph 2 provides that '[t]he proceedings for revision shall be opened by a judgment of the Court expressly recording the existence of the new fact, recognizing that it has such a character as to lay the case open to revision, and declaring the application admissible on this ground.' In the context of general proceedings on the merits of a case, the case may be divided into 'phases':[33] for example, the respondent may raise a preliminary objection on grounds of inadmissibility, or the Court may decide of its own motion to examine admissibility in a separate preliminary phase; but revision is the only context in which the Court is *directed* by the Statute to divide the procedure relating to a suggestion of inadmissibility in this way.[34] When an application was made requesting both revision and interpretation, the Court sensibly dealt with the question of interpretation simultaneously with the admissibility of the revision.[35] At the present time, no application for revision

[29] *Application for Revision and Interpretation of the Judgment of 24 February 1982 in the Case concerning the Continental Shelf (Tunisia/Libyan Arab Jamahiriya)*, [1985] ICJ Rep 192, 221 para. 52. The Court made clear that it has in any event power to correct an *érreur matérielle* in the text of a judgment: ibid. 198 para. 10. This term is not defined, but would seem to mean the sort of error that is obvious when pointed out (e.g. a mistake in a date or spelling), and over which there would be no disagreement.

[30] *Ahamadou Sadio Diallo*, [2010-II] ICJ Rep 639, 655 paras. 33–4, referring to [2007-II] ICJ Rep 600 para.45.

[31] *Application for Revision of the Judgment of 11 July 1996 in the case concerning Application of the Genocide Convention (Bosnia* v *Yugoslavia)*, [2003] ICJ Rep 7, 30, para. 67.

[32] Ibid. para. 69. [33] See the terminology guide in Ch. 7 sect. B(2).

[34] The logic of the division seems to be that at the first stage the Court satisfies itself that there may be grounds for revision, and then in the second stage decides what revision, if any, is necessary. Since already at the first stage it will, as a condition of admissibility, have found that the 'new fact' is 'of such a nature as to be a decisive factor', most of the heavy lifting would seem to have been done before the second stage is reached.

[35] *Application for Revision and Interpretation of the Judgment of 24 February 1982 in the Case concerning the Continental Shelf (Tunisia/Libyan Arab Jamahiriya)*, [1985] ICJ Rep 192, 197–8 para. 10.

has been found admissible, so that how Article 60 would operate in the second stage of the proceedings is a matter of speculation.

The decisions in the following cases have been the subject of subsequent applications for revision: *Continental Shelf (Tunisia/Libya)*; *Application of the Genocide Convention (Bosnia* v *Yugoslavia)*; and *Land, Island and Maritime Frontier Dispute*. This last case was heard by a chamber specially formed for the purpose; Article 100 provides that in such case the application for revision 'shall be dealt with by that chamber'. The difficulties encountered in applying the text when the chamber no longer exists are discussed in Chapter 2 section C.

The provisions of Article 60 of the Statute are supplemented by Articles 99 and 100 of the Rules of Court, which provide for the party to the original case other than the one seeking revision to submit 'observations', and the Court 'may' afford the parties 'a further opportunity of presenting their views' (Art. 99 para. 3). This leaves open the question of whether oral proceedings will be held; in all three of the cases listed above, there were such proceedings, and it seems likely that the parties will always ask for them unless the revision sought is comparatively simple and trivial.

VIII

THE COURT AND THE FUTURE

17

The Court at 70: Concluding Reflections

On 4 December 2006, in commemoration of the Court's sixtieth anniversary, the UN General Assembly adopted resolution 61/37, by which it 'solemnly commend[ed] the International Court of Justice for the important role that it has played as the principal judicial organ of the United Nations over the past sixty years in adjudicating disputes among States, and recognize[d] the value of its work'. This commendation, it is suggested, confirms the conclusion to which the preceding chapters point, namely that the Court is making an important and valuable contribution to the settlement of present international disputes, through its decisions when they are submitted to it, and to the settlement of future disputes through the establishment and clarification of international law.[1] Of course, not every individual litigant State may have been happy with the decision in a particular case—submission of a dispute for settlement entails that there is going to be a loser as well as a winner, if only as a matter of degree![2]—but only in comparatively few cases have there been refusal to appear, or refusals to accept the Court's verdict.[3]

Each decision has added also to the general corpus of international law. The Court's judgments and advisory opinions are treated, not only in academic discussion but, it is understood, in relations between States, as defining or reflecting the state of international law, despite the insistence of Article 59 of the Statute on their non-binding nature for third parties. From this standpoint, the wider the use of the Court, the better; and this also was recognized in the 2006 General Assembly resolution.[4]

Nor has the picture changed during the intervening years: this was the tenor of a paper submitted by the writer to the 2010 Annual Conference of the European Society of International Law,[5] and of an article shortly to appear in the *Leiden Journal*.[6] It is also the picture delineated in a Seminar held by the ICJ in April

[1] See e.g. C. J. Tams and J. Sloane (eds.), *The Development of International Law by the International Court of Justice* (Oxford: Oxford University Press, 2013), *passim*.

[2] Or, of course, one of those 'verdicts . . . | Which send away both parties to a suit | Nor puffed up nor cast down—for each a crumb | Of right, for neither of them the whole loaf': Robert Browning, *The Ring and the Book*, ii. 749–52.

[3] See Ch. 7 sect. B(3)c; Ch. 10 sect. B.

[4] Para. 4, which 'encourages' States to use the Court, and in general to accept its jurisdiction.

[5] *The ICJ 1989–2009: At the Heart of the System*, 57 *NILR* (2010) 347–96.

[6] 'The International Court of Justice: Cruising Ahead at 70', 29 *LJIL* 4 (June 2016).

2016.[7] The problem discreetly referred to in another paragraph of resolution 61/37, one in which the Assembly 'expresse[d] its appreciation of the measures adopted to operate an increased workload with maximum efficiency', with the implication that more might be achieved in this respect, is very much less acute, even though the number of cases submitted to the Court each year has been generally higher than in the early years,[8] and the time required by even the most devoted and efficient judge to study their often complex facts is necessarily also greater.

There has, of course, been a general development since 1922 of recourse to international judicial settlement, with far more international courts and tribunals now operating.[9] Of these, however, only the WTO dispute settlement system and the dispute mechanism established by UNCLOS, including the International Tribunal for the Law of the Sea, share some of the workload that might otherwise be the Court's;[10] and it is difficult to see any other field of inter-State dispute settlement in which a new separate tribunal, on the model of ITLOS, would be appropriate.

Is all well, then?[11] As recently as 2012, a distinguished internationalist argued that reform of the Court is urgently needed if it is to keep its place in the world.[12] This elicited a response from another well-known scholar;[13] without suggesting that perfection had been achieved in the establishment and operation of the Court, he disagreed with the conception advanced of the judicial role of the Court. He suggested that the criticisms expressed were more idealistic than practical; though their author claimed rather the status of 'judicious reformer'.[14]

More radical is the approach taken in a study published with the bold title 'The Failings of the International Court of Justice'.[15] This appeared just before the

[7] 'The International Court of Justice at 70: in Retrospect and in Prospect'. See the records of the Seminar, to appear shortly in *JIDS*.

[8] See in particular the paper by Dapo Akande at the ICJ Seminar, 'Selection of the ICJ as a Forum for Contentious and Advisory Proceedings (Including Jurisdiction)', to appear shortly in *JIDS*. Since the Seminar was held, no less than three new cases have been brought before the Court: see ICJ Press Releases 2016/16, 2016/18, and 2016/19.

[9] See e.g. Y. Shany, *The Competing Jurisdictions of International Courts and Tribunals* (Oxford: Oxford University Press, 2003).

[10] Arbitral tribunals under Annex VII of ITLOS, though not permanent bodies, are also competitors. Already the phenomenon of 'forum-shopping' has made its appearance: see the '*Swordfish*' dispute between Chile and the EC, and generally L. E. Salles, *Forum Shopping in International Adjudication: The Role of Preliminary Objections* (Cambridge: Cambridge University Press, 2014).

[11] Mention has already been made of the work of A. von Bogdandy and I. Venzke, *In Whose Name? A Public Law Theory of International Adjudication* (Oxford: Oxford University Press, 2014), which offers a conception of an international court extremely different from the present institution. This, however, forms part of a rethinking of the whole of international society, and therefore does not call for discussion here.

[12] A. Cassese, 'The International Court of Justice: It is High Time to Restyle the Respected Old Lady', ch. 19 of A. Cassese (ed.), *Realizing Utopia: The Future of International Law* (Oxford: Oxford University Press, 2012).

[13] I. Scobbie, '"All Right, Mr. de Mille, I'm ready for my close-up": Some Critical Reflections on Professor Cassese's "The International Court of Justice: It Is High Time to Restyle the Respected Old Lady"', 23 *EJIL* (2012), 1071–88.

[14] Introduction, Cassese, *Realizing Utopia*, p. xvii.

[15] A. M. Weisburd, *Failings of the International Court of Justice* (Oxford: Oxford University Press, 2016). The book is written from an evident US perspective; by way of contrast, another US scholar has recently argued forcibly that it is in the US national interest to accept fully the jurisdiction of the ICJ:

present work went to press; it thus cannot receive as full an attention as it may perhaps deserve, but some basic points will be considered here. The author offers 'an evaluation of the Court, and thus must focus principally on how well the Court has carried out [its] obligation', namely 'to resolve such cases as came before it by applying international law to the issues the parties presented'.[16] Much of the book is thus taken up with what are seen as errors, both procedural and substantive, committed by the Court in its judicial decisions. Even if these are correctly so designated, prima facie, they are not here our concern, which is whether it can be shown that the Court has succeeded or failed *as an institution*, or whether it is to be regarded as a body successfully filling the role it was designed for, but liable, like all human enterprises, to make mistakes.[17]

But any such errors would presumably affect the Court's contribution to the development of the law. It is of course the case, as the author states, that 'the Court lacks the *formal* authority to determine the content of international law', that is to say, by defining it for others than the parties to the decision—this is the effect of Article 59 of the Statute. He concedes, however, that the Court might possess 'very significant de facto authority over international law whatever the limits on its de jure authority'. Most scholars would say that this indeed is what it does possess; but the author considers that 'the Court has not performed well enough to have earned that type of authority'.[18] Thus the contention is that the cumulative, but—as it were—incidental, errors add up to an *institutional* failure; and this is demonstrated, or buttressed, by the suggestion that in fact States 'have not relied on the Court to a very great degree either to settle particular disputes or to establish rules of law governing subjects seen by states as involving significant political stakes'.[19] The suggestion is, in effect, that the Court is not equipped, on its present constitutional basis, to fulfil the role in the world it was destined for, or, perhaps, the role that has now become required of an international tribunal.[20]

It is probably correct that, where they can, States prefer to keep out of the hands of the Court issues seen as 'involving significant political stakes'; but it was always contemplated that this would be possible, at least on an individual basis by limitations imposed on any acceptance of jurisdiction.[21] What is arguably the case is that the range of disputes that States might prefer not to see submitted to judicial settlement is now wider than what was contemplated in 1920, or even in 1945. These

J. D. Ohlin, *The Assault on International Law* (Oxford: Oxford University Press, 2013), particularly 217–22.

[16] Weisburd, *Failings of the ICJ*, 21.

[17] The present writer would, however, agree with Professor Weisburd on the existence of at least of some of the mistakes he identifies, though perhaps not on their seriousness.

[18] Weisburd, *Failings of the ICJ*, 4, (both quotations), italics added. [19] Ibid.

[20] The generally favourable conclusion of Yuval Shany as to the effectiveness of the ICJ in meeting the goal for which it was established was qualified with the reflection that '[t]he propriety and sufficiency of this goal, however, remains an open question': *Assessing the Effectiveness of International Courts* (Oxford: Oxford University Press, 2014), 188.

[21] Professor Weisburd considers that the term 'legal disputes' in the PCIJ Statute was intended to exclude disputes 'involving conflicts of interest, a political question, or inalienable rights of states', unless specifically requested by the parties: *Failings of the ICJ*, 353–4.

may include cases where 'the political consequences of a legally correct decision could well be negative' or cases where 'a merits judgment would require the Court to make a policy decision'[22]—cases which, the author apparently contends, the Court ought to refuse to decide at all.[23]

Is the Court then not doing what States in general want it to do, or doing what States in general do not want it to do?[24] On a general level, General Assembly resolution 61/37 may serve, if not as a rebuttal, at least as an indication that the Court has not failed, or was not, ten years ago, failing the expectations of the generality of States, either as regards the actual settlement of disputes or as to contributing to development of the law.[25] In this latter connection, it is universally accepted, if not self-evident, that every decision the Court hands down will have an influence (to put it no higher) on how the law in the relevant field will thereafter be understood; and the Court itself sometimes in effect treats its own earlier decisions as precedents to be followed, and not merely in matters of its own procedures.[26]

May then States expect the Court, as also part of its function, to exercise that influence consciously, to seek to steer the development of international law? Or is this at least permitted to the Court? This is a question on which much has been written, by authors and by individual judges in opinions.[27] As observed by Hernández, the very fact that the Court's decisions are, and are expected to be, reasoned, implies that the Court 'claims authority based on the soundness of its decisions and not through any compulsive power it might have'; and he draws attention to what has been judicially referred to as 'the tradition of using advisory opinions as an opportunity to elaborate and develop international law'.[28]

The widening of the class of disputes that may be brought to the Court, mentioned above, is relevant to another question raised from time to time,[29] namely whether the Court should have wider, or general, compulsory jurisdiction. The 'optional clause' of the Statute went as far in the direction of universal jurisdiction for the Court as in 1920 the States were able to accept, but its proponents probably

[22] Ibid. 363.

[23] Professor Weisburd also deplores 'the absence of any legal mechanism for addressing legal errors that the Court may make'; 'there is no way to compel the Court to comply with its Statute': ibid. 357. He does not, however, argue that there should be such an appeal mechanism (and indeed this would merely push the problem back a stage); the suggestion is apparently that the Court should be aware of this finality, and therefore be more careful what it does decide.

[24] It is also argued—apparently as a criticism—that 'the Court will have reason to avoid rendering judgments that will anger significant groups of States' (ibid. 363), but the author cites numerous decisions that seem to have done just that.

[25] However, there seems also to be an unavowed implication in Weisburd's thesis that what matters is the body of expectations of one or more of the 'great powers' (see e.g. ibid. 355–6) and much is made of decisions against the interests of the United States, particularly the *Armed Activities* case.

[26] See e.g. the cases discussed in Thirlway, *Law and Procedure*, ii. 1207–8.

[27] For a useful and balanced survey, see Gleider Hernández, *The International Court of Justice and the Judicial Function* (Oxford: Oxford University Press, 2013), ch. III-D, 'The Court and the Development of International Law'.

[28] Hernández, ibid., citing Judge Higgins, Separate Opinion in the Palestine *Wall* case, [2004-I] ICJ Rep 207, 212–13.

[29] e.g. by Cassese, 'The International Court of Justice: It is High Time to Restyle the Respected Old Lady'.

hoped that this was only a stage in the development of the international judiciary. This position did not change in 1945; and there seems at present to be no realistic prospect of moving further toward universality, in the sense that all parties to the Statute would *ipso facto* accept ICJ jurisdiction over all disputes with other parties.

It has from time to time been suggested that the principle, that the Court only has jurisdiction over a State, or over a particular activity of a State if, and to the extent that, the consent of that State can be demonstrated, might be, or needs to be, tempered in certain circumstances: in particular if the matter is one relating to the application or observance of a peremptory norm. Where a reservation to a treaty excludes the Court's jurisdiction in a matter of this kind, should it—could it—be declared invalid? A number of judges have raised this question, specifically with regard to the validity of reservations to Article IX (the jurisdictional clause) of the Genocide Convention;[30] and apparently felt that international law should develop, or have developed, in the direction of invalidating such reservations.[31] One argument is that if a peremptory norm declares certain conduct unlawful, there must exist an equally peremptory norm barring the exclusion of the Court from examining conduct alleged to be of this nature,[32] but this is highly questionable, in view of the origins and present status of the concept of *jus cogens*.[33] Nor is it easy to see how such a development could come about since it goes to State consent at a universal level; and even the existence of peremptory norms is not universally and unambiguously accepted.

A separate question is whether more States should accept the Court's jurisdiction, and in wider terms, than is at present the case. That is certainly to be recommended,[34] but outside the Court's control; nor is it easy to see what the Court could do to encourage it, except possibly by offering more immediate and speedy resolution of cases. This depends on, inter alia, the Court's workload and its working methods.

The encouragement of States to use the Court, contained in resolution A/RES/61/37, in a sense runs counter to the rest of the text: could the Court cope with more cases than it already has? In this respect, the most valuable reform—if reform were needed—might be the enlargement of the achievable output of the Court. Both in terms of the number of cases dealt with each year, and the number of unresolved cases on the list, the general pattern seems fairly stable;[35] but if account is taken also of the complexity of the issues raised, it has been such as to suggest that

[30] *Armed Activities on the Territory of the Congo (DRC* v *Rwanda)*, dissenting opinion of Judges Higgins, Kooijmans, Elaraby, Owada, and Simma, [2006] ICJ Rep 71 para. 29.

[31] Ibid. para. 25.

[32] See in particular *Fisheries Jurisdiction (Spain* v *Canada)*, dissenting opinion of Judge Bedjaoui, [1998] ICJ Rep 534 para. 44.

[33] See the First Report of the ILC on the subject, mentioned in Ch. 3 sect. D.

[34] An excellent UN publication, due to an initiative originally taken by Switzerland, is the *Handbook on accepting the jurisdiction of the International Court of Justice: model clauses and templates* (A/68/963); this goes further in recommendations than the ICJ itself, or the Registry, would probably feel able to undertake.

[35] The average number of cases brought, and the number of cases resolved, in a single (calendar) year seems to be around three in both respects. The number of cases pending at any one time has been around twelve to thirteen; at the time of writing there are fourteen, but three (the Marshall Islands

the structure devised in 1920 may not be adapted to current demands. The nature of the cases that the Court is called upon to decide differs markedly from what was probably contemplated by the original draftsmen of the PCIJ Statute. Furthermore, few international legal disputes turn solely on whether one view or another of the applicable legal rule is found to be correct; thus the resolution of such a dispute will often also involve deciding a disputed question of fact, even if it is not one crucial to the correct application of the law. Yet the sort of factual disputes foreseen in 1920 would probably not have included assessments of the environmental impact of chemical processes (as in the *Pulp Mills* case),[36] or even analysis of the obscurities of the accounts or evidence of events in a situation of hostilities, as in the two cases involving Serbia, or the case concerning the *Racial Discrimination Convention*.[37]

While many courts, both national and international, get through considerable work by allocating cases to separate chambers, the full court sitting only (if at all) for cases requiring special treatment for one reason or another, this is not possible under the terms of the ICJ Statute. Nor would States as litigants necessarily be content with the attention of a limited group of judges rather than of the whole bench; and the principle of 'the representation of the main forms of civilization and the principal legal systems of the world'[38] would have to be compromised or tempered.[39]

Might a solution be to enlarge the membership of the Court? The experience of ITLOS, with its twenty-one members, shows that there is nothing magical about the figure fifteen for efficient working; but nor does it show any gain in efficiency. A larger Court sitting *en banc* is not to be recommended:[40] such a Court might perhaps be planned to operate in two separate chambers, each as widely representational as possible, with cases allocated to the one or the other by the Court, not (or not necessarily) according to the parties' choice, to ensure division of the total workload.[41] However, there must be much doubt whether States would accept such a system.

cases) are really one case, and two cases are in fact resolved for all practical purposes (*Armed Activities on the Territory of the Congo*, and *Gabčíkovo-Nagymaros Project*).

36 Though the complaints that eventually led to the pioneering 1936 *Trail Smelter* decision were already the subject of a domestic arbitration as early as 1924. It has been suggested that the Court has not shown itself competent enough in handling complex technical material, in particular relating to environmental protection, and that States may be reluctant in the future to entrust to it disputes of this kind: T. Meshel, 'The Permanent Court of Arbitration and the Peaceful Resolution of Transboundary Freshwater Disputes', *ESIL Reflection* 5:1 (2016).

37 *Application of the Genocide Convention (Bosnia* v *Serbia)* and (*Croatia* v *Serbia)*; *Application of the International Convention on the Elimination of All Forms of Racial Discriminaion (Georgia* v *Russian Federation).*

38 Art. 9 of the Statute; the exact meaning of the expression seems never to have been clear: see O. Spiermann, *International Legal Argument in the Permanent Court of International Justice: The Rise of the International Judiciary* (Cambridge: Cambridge University Press, 2005), 68.

39 Cf. E. McWhinney, 'Law, Politics and "Regionalism" in the Nomination and Election of World Court Judges', 13 *Syracuse Journal of International Law* (1986), 1–28.

40 See Ch. 2 sect. C.

41 Allocation would not necessarily be by alternation, but would take account of the 'size' of the case in terms of expected workload.

The time-lag at present between institution of proceedings and the final decision on the merits is usually a matter of years; this, though regrettable, is probably inevitable with a single court with a heavy workload. Moreover, the proceedings are often prolonged as a result of the filing of preliminary objections, which are dealt with in an independent phase of the proceedings; if the objections are rejected, it is only thereafter that proceedings on the merits can be resumed. It is important to preserve the right of the respondent to have jurisdiction (at least) established, before being called upon to plead to the merits;[42] and the fact that such objections are from time to time upheld shows that not all applications have a sound jurisdictional basis. However, the resulting delay, and the established practice as to composition of the court where there are successive phases, means that the composition of the Court for the eventual merits may be substantially different from its composition when it dismissed preliminary objections—and if provisional measures were requested at an early stage, probably even more different from its composition then. The principle is clear: judges sitting in the merits phase may not reopen matters decisively settled at the preliminary objection stage, even if they think that the decision at that stage was unfounded. But the examples of the *South West Africa* and *Barcelona Traction* cases suggest that a change of the balance of thinking within the Court may nevertheless have its effects.

Whether the long-established system of ICJ deliberation[43] is or is not ideal cannot really be judged by those outside the Court:[44] it may seem to outsiders to take a long time, but who can say whether this is more than necessary?[45] A feature of judicial organization that has been suggested is that of a *juge rapporteur*, analogous to the *conseiller rapporteur* of the French *Conseil d'État*; this is already the mechanism adopted by the European Court of Justice and the European Court of Human Rights. Under the Court's Resolution on Internal Judicial Practice, every judge takes an equal part in the deliberation up to the moment when the Drafting Committee is elected, and the members of that Committee are concerned only with how best to express what remains, to the fullest extent, a collective decision. A *juge rapporteur* for each case would, however, be the only judge to study the whole case, and he would present a full report on it, with his own proposals as to how it should be decided. Whether this would in fact save time in a Court with a tradition of full participation by every Member must remain uncertain.

[42] Though this right is not always available in certain forms of arbitration: see e.g. the Procedural Order of 15 January 2013 of the PCA Arbitral Tribunal under UNCLOS Annex VIII in the case between Mauritius and the UK, rejecting a request for 'bifurcation of the proceedings'.

[43] Governed by the Resolution on the Internal Judicial Practice of the Court of 12 April 1976, which, however, in broad lines followed the previous resolution, and that employed by the PCIJ: and see Ch. 10 sect. D.

[44] There have been some intermittent liftings of the veil: see e.g. M. Bedjaoui, 'La "fabrication" des arrêts de la Cour internationale de justice', *Le Droit international au service de la paix, de la justice et du développement (Mélanges Viraly)* (Paris: UNESCO, 1991), 87; Thirlway, 'The Drafting of ICJ Decisions: Some Personal Recollections and Observations', 5 *CJIL* (2006), 15.

[45] What is clearly unnecessary is the kind of judge's opinion (separate or dissenting) that bears only a tenuous relationship with the case, being essentially an article or lecture published at UN expense: see Ch. 12, in particular text and n. 9.

Finally, a more delicate question is the quality of the membership of the Court. In terms of impartiality, the Court ranks high. Judges—both judges ad hoc and elected Members—may occasionally appear to give more weight to the arguments or interests of their national States, but not to such a degree as to suggest unjudicial bias; and there is no example known to the writer in which there has been even a suspicion of a corrupt motive that could be attributed to a judge. As to competence and effectiveness, all that can be said is that there have in the past undoubtedly been Members of the Court whose contribution to its work, or even whose intellectual fitness for the office, have given rise to doubts, among their colleagues[46] or elsewhere.[47] There have in the past been unsuccessful candidates for election to the Court who might have made a greater contribution than some, at least, of the successful ones. But there is no human institution in which election, as a process of representational selection intended to meet the requirements of democracy, is also one in which the ideal result is also always achieved.

The Court itself is not perfect, either in conception or in operation, but it achieves a great deal in the maintenance of legal stability and international peace, and in the development of international law, and fully deserves the respect it has gained. If the vision of the founders of the PCIJ, from the shadow of the 1914–18 conflict, of a world governed by law, laid down and administered by a judicial body with universal jurisdiction, has not become reality, it is because that is not—or not yet?—a vision universally shared. Justice by consent is no contradiction; how well an international system on that basis has served, will, it is hoped, have been shown by the account given in this book.

[46] In relation to the PCIJ, some revealing observations in private papers of its Members are mentioned by Spiermann, *International Legal Argument*. The propriety of citing any corresponding indiscretions relating to the Members of the post-war Court (if such exist) must be doubtful.

[47] It is striking to compare the intellectual level and knowledge of international law displayed in present day judges' separate and dissenting opinions with that offered in those of *some* of their predecessors.

Select Bibliography

Note: The International Court of Justice itself regularly issues a bibliography compiled by the staff of the Library (with the assistance of the Library of the Peace Palace); this is probably by far the most complete available, and is conveniently divided into sections devoted to various aspects of the Court and its work. Unfortunately, at the time of writing the most recent edition was No. 57, issued in 2007. The following bibliography therefore lists books and articles which have appeared since 2007, together with some earlier ones already mentioned in the ICJ Bibliographies but of continuing interest.

A. INTERNATIONAL JUDICIAL SETTLEMENT IN GENERAL

Ascensio, Hervé, 'L'Amicus Curiae devant les juridictions internationales', *RGDIP* (2001), 897.

Bennouna, Mohamed, 'How to Cope with the Proliferation of International Courts and Coordinate Their Action', in A. Cassese (ed.), *Realizing Utopia: The Future of International Law* (Oxford: Oxford University Press, 2012), 287–94.

von Bogdandy, Armin, and Venzke, Ingo, *In Whose Name? A Public Law Theory of International Adjudication* (Oxford: Oxford University Press, 2014).

Boisson de Chazournes, L., Kohen, M. G., and Viñuales, J. E., *Diplomatic and Judicial Means of Dispute Settlement* (Leiden: Nijhoff, 2013).

Brant, L. N. C., *L'Autorité de la chose jugée en droit international public* (Paris: LGJD, 2003).

Brown, Chester, *A Common Law of International Adjudication* (Oxford: Oxford University Press, 2007).

Collier, J., and Lowe, Vaughan, *The Settlement of Disputes in International Law* (Oxford: Oxford University Press, 2000).

Distefano, G., and Buzzini, G., *Bréviaire de jurisprudence international: Les Fondamentaux du droit international public* (Brussels: Émile Bruyant, 2010).

Doehring, Karl, 'Zur Befangenheit internationaler Richter', in Ando, N., et al. (eds.), *Liber amicorum Judge Shigeru Oda* (The Hague: Kluwer, 2002), i. 23–9.

Dupuy, Pierre-Marie, 'Competition among International Tribunals and the Authority of the International Court of Justice', in U. Fastenrath et al. (eds.), *From Bilateralism to Community Interest: Essays in Honour of Judge Bruno Simma* (Oxford: Oxford University Press, 2011), 862.

French, D., Saul, M., and White, N. D., *International Law and Dispute Settlement: New Problems and Techniques* (Oxford: Hart, 2010).

Guillaume, Gilbert, 'Le Précédent dans la justice et l'arbitrage international', *Clunet* 3 (2010).

Guillaume, Gilbert, 'The Use of Precedent by International Judges and Arbitrators', 2 *JIDS* (2011) 5.

Kingsbury, Benedict, 'International Courts: Uneven Judicialisation in Global Order', in J. Crawford and M. Koskenniemi (eds.), *The Cambridge Companion to International Law* (Cambridge: Cambridge University Press, 2012), 203–27.

Leandro, A., *La Validità Della Sentenza Internazionale Nelle Controversie fra Stati* (Padova: CEDAM, 2012).

Lowe, Vaughan, 'The Function of Litigation in International Society', 61 *ICLQ* (2012), 209–22.

Merrills, John, *International Dispute Settlement*, 4th edn. (Cambridge: Cambridge University Press, 2005).

Reismann, W. Michael, and Skinner, Christina, *Fraudulent Evidence before Public International Tribunals: The Dirty Stories of International Law* (Cambridge: Cambridge University Press, 2015).

Romano, Cesare, Alter, Karen, and Shany, Yuval, *The Oxford Handbook of International Adjudication* (Oxford: Oxford University Press, 2014).

Schill, Stephan W., 'The Overlooked Role of Arbitration in International Adjudicatory Theory', *ESIL Reflections* 4:2 (2015).

Shany, Yuval, 'No Longer a Weak Department of Power? Reflections on the Emergence of a New International Judiciary', 20 *EJIL* (2009), 73.

Shany, Yuval, *Assessing the Effectiveness of International Courts* (Oxford Scholarship Online, 2014).

Shany, Yuval, *The Competing Jurisdictions of International Courts and Tribunals* (Oxford: Oxford University Press, 2016).

Thirlway, Hugh, 'The Proliferation of International Judicial Organs and the Formation of International Law', in W. P. Heere (ed.), *International Law and The Hague's 75th Anniversary* (The Hague: Asser, 1999).

Thirlway, Hugh, 'The International Court of Justice and Other International Courts', in N. M. Blokker and H. G. Schermer (eds.), *Proliferation of International Organizations* (The Hague: Kluwer, 2001), 251–78.

Venzke, Ingo, 'The Role of International Courts as Interpreters and Developers of the Law: Working Out the Jurisgenerative Process of Interpretation', 34 *Loyola of Los Angeles Comparative Law Review* (2011), 99–131.

Zoppo, L., 'Considerazioni sul concorso tra le giurisdizioni internazionali: i modelli di conflitto e le modalità di coordinamento', *Rivista di diritto internazionale* (2014), 88.

B. HISTORY: THE PCIJ

The Permanent Court of International Justice (The Hague: ICJ, 2012). [Published to mark the 90th anniversary of the PCIJ.]

Spiermann, Ole, '"Who attempts too much does nothing well": the 1920 Advisory Committee of Jurists and the Statute of the Permanent Court of International Justice', 73 *BYBIL* (2002), 187–260.

Spiermann, Ole, *International Legal Argument in the Permanent Court of International Justice: The Rise of the International Judiciary* (Cambridge: Cambridge University Press, 2005).

C. THE ICJ: GENERAL

Akande, Dapo, 'Selection of the International Court of Justice as a Forum for Contentious and Advisory Proceedings (including Jurisdiction)', *ICJ 70th Anniversary Seminar* (2016), *JIDS*.

Amr, M. S. M., *The Role of the International Court of Justice as the Principal Judicial Organ of the United Nations* (The Hague: Kluwer, 2003).

Apostolidis, C. (ed.), *Les Arrêts de la Cour international de justice* (Dijon: Éditions Universitaires de Dijon, 2005).

Bannelier, K., Christakis, T., and Heathcote, S. (eds.), *The ICJ and the Evolution of International Law: The Enduring Impact of the Corfu Channel Case* (Abingdon: Routledge, 2012).

Bennouna, M., 'La Cour internationale de justice en son environnement politique', in M. Kamba and M. M. Mbengue (eds.), *Liber Amicorum en l'honneur de Raymond Ranjeva* (Paris: Pedone, 2013), 429.

Cassese, A., 'The International Court of Justice: It is High Time to Restyle the Respectable Old Lady', in A. Cassese (ed.), *Realizing Utopia: The Future of International Law* (Oxford: Oxford University Press, 2015), 239–49.

Eisemann, P. M., and Pazartzis, P., *La Jurisprudence de la Cour international de justice* (Paris: Pedone, 2008).

Espaliú Berdud, Carlos, *Desarollos jurisprudenciales y práctica reciente en la jurisdicción contentiosa de la Corte internacional de justicia* (Madrid: Dykinson, 2000).

Fitzmaurice, Malgosia, and Lowe, Vaughan, *Fifty Years of the International Court of Justice: Essays in Honour of Sir Robert Jennings* (Cambridge: Cambridge University Press, 1986).

Forlati, Serena, *The International Court of Justice: An Arbitral Tribunal or a Judicial Body?* (Heidelburg: Springer, 2014).

Gaja, G., and Grote Stoutenberg, J., *Enhancing the Rule of Law through the International Court of Justice* (Leiden: Brill, 2014).

Guillaume, Gilbert, *La Cour international de justice à l'aube du XXIème siècle* (Paris: Pedone, 2003).

Handbook of the International Court of Justice, 6th edn. (The Hague: ICJ, 2014).

Hernández, Gleider, *The International Court of Justice and the Judicial Function* (Oxford: Oxford University Press, 2014).

Kolb, Robert, *The International Court of Justice* (Oxford: Hart, 2013).

Lang, Andrew, 'The Role of the International Court of Justice in a Context of Fragmentation', 62 *ICLQ* (2013), 777–812.

Lucht, Silvia, *Der Internationaler Gerichtshof Zwischen Recht und Politik (Europäisches und Internationales Recht)* (Baden-Baden: Nomos, 2005).

Muller, A. S., Raic, D., and Thuránsky, J. M., *The International Court of Justice: Its Future Role after Fifty Years* (The Hague: Martinus Nijhoff, 1997).

Peck, Connie, and Lee, Roy, *Increasing the Effectiveness of the International Court of Justice*, Proceedings of the ICJ/UNITAR Colloquium to celebrate the 50th Anniversary of the Court (The Hague: Nijhoff, 1997).

Rosenne, Shabtai, *The Law and Practice of the International Court of Justice, 1920–2005*, 3rd edn. (Leiden: Nijhoff, 2005).

Scobbie, Iain, ' "All right, Mr. de Mille, I'm ready for my close-up", Some Critical Reflections on Professor Cassese's "The International Court of Justice: It is High Time to Restyle the Respected Old Lady" ', 23 *EJIL* (2012) 1071–88.

Tams, Christian J., and Sloan, James, *The Development of International Law by the International Court of Justice* (Oxford: Oxford University Press, 2013).

Thirlway, Hugh, 'The International Court of Justice 1989–2009: At the Heart of the Dispute Settlement System', 62 *NILR* (2012) 347.

Thirlway, Hugh, *The Law and Procedure of the International Court of Justice: Fifty Years of Jurisprudence* (Oxford: Oxford University Press, 2013).

Thirlway, Hugh, 'The International Court of Justice', in M. D. Evans, *International Law*, 4th edn. (Oxford: Oxford University Press, 2014), 586–614.

Thirlway, Hugh, 'The International Court of Justice : Cruising Ahead at 70', 29 *LJIL* (2016).

Weisburd, A. Mark, *Failings of the International Court of Justice* (Oxford: Oxford University Press, 2016).

Zimmermann, Andreas et al., *The Statute of the International Court of Justice: A Commentary*, 2nd edn. (Oxford: Oxford University Press, 2012).

D. THE ICJ: PARTICULAR ASPECTS

(1) Jurisdiction

Alexandrov, S. A., *Reservations in Unilateral Declarations Accepting the Compulsory Jurisdiction of the International Court of Justice* (Dordrecht: Brill, 1995).

Crawford, J. R., 'Jurisdiction and Applicable Law', 25 *LJIL* (2012), 471–9.

Eick, Christophe, 'Die Anerkennung der obligatorischen Gerichtsbarkeit des Internationalen Gerichtshofs durch Deutschland, 68 *Zeitschrift für ausländisches öffentliches Recht und Völkerrecht* (2008), 763.

Oellers-Frahm, Karin, 'The Principle of Consent to International Jurisdiction—Is It Still Alive? Observations on the Judgment on Preliminary Objections in the Case Concerning Application of the Convention on the Prevention and Punishment of the Crime of Genocide (Croatia v. Serbia)', 52 *German Yearbook of International Law* (2009), 487–524.

Papdakis, M., 'Compromissory Clauses as the Gatekeepers of the Law to be "Used" in the ICJ and the PCIJ', 5 *JIDS* (2014), 560–604.

Shany, Yuval, Questions of Jurisdiction and Admissibility before International Courts (Cambridge: Cambridge University Press, 2016).

Spatafora, Ersiliagrazia, La reciprocità nella giurisdizione dell Corte internazionale di giustizia (Milan: Guiffrè, 2001).

Szafarz, R., *The Compulsory Jurisdiction of the International Court of Justice* (Dordrecht: Kluwer, 1993).

Thienel, Tobias, 'Third States and the Jurisdiction of the International Court of Justice: The *Monetary Gold* Principle', 57 *German Yearbook of International Law* (2015), 321–54.

Thirlway, Hugh, 'Reciprocity in the Jurisdiction of the International Court', XV *NYBIL* (1984), 97.

(2) Procedure and working methods

Bowett, D. W., Crawford, J., Sinclair, I., and Watts, A. D., *The International Court of Justice: Efficiency of Procedures and Working Methods*, Report of BIICL Study Group, January 1996 (issued as a Supplement to ICLQ).

Fontanelli, F., and Busco, Paolo, 'The Function of Procedural Justice in International Adjudication', 15 *LPICT* (2016), 1–23.

Gardner, J. P., et al., *The International Court of Justice, Process, Practice and Procedure* (London: BIICL, 1997).

Guyomar, G., *Commentaire du Règlement de la Cour international de Justice adapté le 14 avril 1978—Interprétation et pratique* (Paris: Pedone, 1983).

Malintoppi, Loretta, 'Fact-finding and Evidence (Notably in Scientific-Related Disputes)', *ICJ 70th Anniversary Seminar* (2016) *JIDS*.

Peat, Daniel, 'The Use of Court-Appointed Experts by the International Court of Justice', 84 *BYBIL* (2013), 271–303.

Pellet, Alain, 'Remarks on Proceedings Before the International Court of Justice', 5 *LPICT* (2006), 163–82.

Riddell, A., and Plant, B., *Evidence before the International Court of Justice* (London: BIICL, 2009).
Rosenne, S., 'Visit to the Site by the International Court', in E. Yakpo and T. Boumedra, *Liber Amicorum Mohammed Bedjaoui* (The Hague: Kluwer, 1999), 46.
Teitelbaum, Ruth, 'Recent Fact Finding Developments at the International Court of Justice', 6 *LPICT* (2007), 119–58.
Thirlway, Hugh, *Non-Appearance before the International Court of Justice* (Cambridge: Cambridge University Press, 1985).
Zanobetti, Alessandra, *La non comparazione davanti alla Corte internazionale di giustizia* (Bologna: Guiffrè, 1996).

(3) Particular procedures

(a) *Provisional measures*

Iwamoto, Yoshiyuki, 'The Protection of Human Life Through Provisional Measures Indicated by the International Court of Justice', 15 *LJIL* (2002), 345.
Kammerhofer, Jörg: 'The Binding Nature of Provisional Measures of the International Court of Justice: the "Settlement" of the Issue in the *LaGrand* Case', 16 *LJIL* (2003), 16.
Kempen, B., and He, Zan, The Practice of the International Court of Justice on Provisional Measures: The Recent Developments', *Heidelberg Journal of International Law* 69 (2009), 919–29.
Marotti, Loris, '"Plausabilità' dei diritti e autonomia del regime di responsabilità nella recente giurisprudenza della Corte internazionale di giustizia in tema di misure cautelari', 97 *Rivista di diritto internazionale* (2014), 614–66.
Saccucci, Andrea, 'Fond du litige et indication de mesures conservatoires: Réflexions en marge des ordonnances de la CIJ dans l'affaire des usines de pâte à papier', 112 *RGDIP* (2008), 795–832.
Sloane, Robert D., 'Measures Necessary to Ensure: The ICJ's Provisional Measures Order in *Avena and Other Mexican Nationals*, 17 *LJIL* (2004), 673.
Uchkanova, Inna, 'Provisional Measures before the International Court of Justice', 12 *LPICT* (2013), 391–430.

(b) *Intervention*

García Rubio, Mariano, 'Intervention before the International Court of Justice: The Nicaraguan Intervention in *El Salvador/Honduras* Case', 1 *Anuario mexicano de derecho internacional* (2001), 165–95.
Günther, Konstantin, 'Zulässigkeit und Grenzen der Intervention bei Streitigkeiten vor dem IGH', 34 *German Yearbook of International Law* (1991), 254.
Torres Bernárdez, Santiago, 'L'Intervention dans la procedure de la Cour international de justice', 256 *Recueil des cours* (1995), 1996.
Uchkanova, Inna, 'The Minotaur's Labyrinth: Third State Intervention before the International Court of Justice', 13 *LPICT* (2014), 178–98.

(4) Decisions

Bedjaoui, Mohamed, 'Expediency in the Decisions of the International Court of Justice', 71 *BYBIL* (2000), 1–27.

Boisson de Chazournes, L., and Angelini, A., 'After "The Court Rose": The Rise of Diplomatic Means to Implement the Pronouncements of the International Court of Justice', 11 *LPICT* (2012), 1.

Brant, L. N. C., 'L'Autorité de la chose jugée et la revision devant la Cour international de justice à la lumière des derniers arrêts de celle-ci (Yougoslavie *c.* Bosnie et El Salvador Ic. I Honduras)', 49 *Annuiaire français de droit international* (2003), 248–65.

Guillaume, Gilbert, 'Les Déclarations jointes aux décisions de la Cour internationale de Justice', in C. A. Barea (ed.), *Liber amicorum "in memoriam" of Judge José María Ruda* (The Hague: Kluwer, 2000), 421–34.

Kulovesi, Kati, 'Legality or Otherwise? Nuclear Weapons and the Strategy of *Non Liquet*', X *Finnish Yearbook of International Law* (1999), 55–89.

Palchetti, Paolo, 'La Corte internazionale di giustizia alle prese con i propri "errori": il problema dell'estensione della *res judicata* nella sentenza Diallo', *Rivista di diritto internazionale* (2011), 173.

Schulte, C., *Compliance with Decisions of the International Court of Justice* (Oxford: Oxford University Press, 2004).

Scobbie, Iain, '*Res judicata*, Precedent and the International Court', 20 *Australian Yearbook of International Law* (1999), 299.

Thirlway, Hugh, 'The Drafting of ICJ Decisions: Some Personal Recollections and Observations', 5 *ChJIL* (2006), 15.

(5) Various

Álvarez-Jiménez, Alberto, 'Methods for the Identification of Customary International Law in the International Court of Justice's Jurisprudence, 2000–2009', 60 *ICLQ* (2011), 681–712.

Brown, Chester, 'The Inherent Powers of International Courts and Tribunals', 76 *BYBIL* (2006), 199–244.

Chan-Tung, L., 'Les Exceptions préliminaires devant la CIJ: les clairs-obscurs d'une théorie', 40 *Revie belge de droit international* (2007), 437–73.

Chesterman, S., 'The International Court of Justice in Asia: Interpreting the Temple of Preah Vihear Case', 5 *Asian Journal of International Law* (2015), 1–6.

Ciampi, Annalisa, 'The International Court of Justice between "Reason of State" and Demands for Justice by Victims of Serious International Crimes', 96 *Rivista di diritto internazionale* (2013), 374–98.

Elias, O., and Lim, C., 'The *Right of Passage* Doctrine Revisited: An Opportunity Missed', 12 *LJIL* (1999), 231–46.

Forlati, Serena, 'Protection diplomatique, droits de l'homme et réclamations "directes" devant la Cour international de justice', 111 *RGDIP* (2007), 89.

Forlati, Serena, 'La sentenza della Corte internazionale di giustizia in merito alla richiesta di rivizione della pronuncia sulla giurisdizione resa fra Bosnia e Iugoslavia', 86 *Rivista di diritto internazionale* (2003), 426–48.

Fry, James D., 'Non-participation in the International Court Revisited: Change or *Plus Ça Change?*', 49 *Columbia Journal of Transnational Law* (2010), 35–74.

Gattini, Andrea, 'La corte internazionale di giustizia fra *judicial activism* e *judicial self-restraint*: il curioso caso della richiesta di interpretazione della sentenza resa nella affare *Avena*', *Rivista di diritto internazionale* (2009), 476.

Guillaume, Gilbert, 'La "cause commune" devant la Cour international de justice', in E. Yakpo and T. Boumedra, *Liber Amicorum Mohammed Bedjaoui* (The Hague: Kluwer, 1999), 325.

Hamuli Kabumba, Yves, 'Incidence de la jurisprudence de la CIJ sur les règles d'interprétation du Statut de Rome, sur la qualification des faits et sur la preuve devant la CPJI', 114 *RGDIP* (2010), 779–809.

Higgins, R., 'Human Rights in the International Court of Justice', 20 *LJIL* (2007) 745–51.

Jacobs, D., and Yannick, R., 'Waiting for Godot: An Analysis of the Advisory Opinion on Kosovo', 24 *LJIL* (2011), 331–53.

Kawano, Mariko, 'The Administration of Justice by the International Court of Justice and the Parties', in S. Yee and J.-Y. Morin, *Multiculturalism and International Law: Essays in Honour of Edward McWhinney* (Leiden: Nijhoff, 2009), 285.

Keith, Kenneth J., 'The International Court of Justice and Criminal Justice', 59 *ICLQ* (2010), 895–910.

Kerbrat, Yann, and Maljean Dubois, S., 'La Cour international de justice face aux enjeux de la protection de l'environnement: Réflexions critiques sur l'arrêt du 20 avril 2010', *Usines de pâte à papier su la fleuve Uruguay*', 115 *RGIP* (2011), 39–75.

Kooijmans, Pieter H., 'The Legality of the Use of Force in the Recent Case Law of the International Court of Justice', in S. Yee and J.-Y. Morin, *Multiculturalism and International Law: Essays in Honour of Edward McWhinney* (Leiden: Nijhoff, 2009), 455.

Llamson, Aloysius P., 'Jurisdiction and Compliance in Recent Decisions of the International Court of Justice', 18 *EJIL* (2008), 815.

Mendelson, Maurice, 'The Curious Case of *Qatar* v. *Bahrain*', 72 *British Yearbook of International Law* (2001), 183–212.

Mendelson, Maurice, 'The *Cameroon/Nigeria* Case in the International Court of Justice: Some Territorial Sovereignty and Boundary Delimitation Issues', 75 *BYBIL* (2004), 223–48.

Miron, Alina, 'Les Méthodes de travail de la Cour', *ICJ 70th Anniversary Seminar* (2016), *JPICT*.

O'Connell, Mary Ellen, 'The Natural Superiority of Courts', in U. Fastenrath et al. (eds.), *From Bilateralism to Community Interest: Essays in Honour of Judge Bruno Simma* (Oxford: Oxford University Press, 2011), 1040–54.

Rennie, Ian, 'Philosophical Influences at the International Court of Justice as Demonstrated in the *Lockerbie* Case', 32 *Cambrian Law Review* (2001), 65.

Runavot, M.-C., 'L'Oxymore, nouvel exercise de style pour la CIJ: un avis inattendu pour une solution sans surprise', *Clunet* 3 (2012), 859–86.

Scobbie, Iain, '"Une hérésie en matière judiciaire": The Role of the Judge ad hoc in the International Court', 4 *LPICT* (2005), 421.

Tams, Christian J., 'Meta-Custom and the [International] Court: A Study in Judicial Law-Making', 14 *LPICT* (2015), 51–79.

Tams, C. J., and Tzanakopoulos, A., '*Barcelona Traction* at 40: The ICJ as an Agent of Legal Development', 23 *LJIL* (2010), 781–800.

Tancredi, Antonello, 'Il parere della Corte interzionale di giustizia sulla dichiarazione d'indepenza del Kosovo', *Rivista di diritto internazionale* (2010), 994.

Thiele, Carmen, 'Der Schutz der Mensenrechte durch den IGH', 51 *Archiv des Völkerrechts* (2013), 1–14.

Thierry, Hubert, 'Par la voix prépondérante du Président . . .', in E. Yakpo and T. Boumedra, *Liber Amicorum Mohammed Bedjaoui* (The Hague: Kluwer, 1999), 525.

Thirlway, Hugh, 'Dilemma or Chimera?—Admissibility of Illegally Obtained Evidence in International Adjudication, 78 *AJIL* (1984), 623.

Thirlway, Hugh, '"Normative Surrender" and the "Duty" to Appear before the International Court of Justice: A Reply', 11 *Michigan Journal of International Law* (1990), 912.

Thirlway, Hugh, 'Judicial Activism and the International Court of Justice', in N. Ando et al. (eds.), *Liber Amicorum Judge Shigeru Oda* (Leiden: Kluwer, 1992), 75–106.

Thirlway, Hugh, 'The Contribution of the International Court of Justice to the Development of Law: The *South West Africa* Experience', African Society of International and Comparative Law, *Proceedings of the Seventh Annual Conference* (1995), 103.

Thirlway, Hugh, 'Counterclaims before the International Court of Justice: The *Genocide Convention* and *Oil Platforms* Decisions', 12 *LJIL* (1999), 197.

Thirlway, Hugh, 'Injured and Non-Injured States before the International Court of Justice', in M. Ragazzi (ed.), *International Responsibility Today* (Leiden: Brill, 2005), 311.

Thirlway, Hugh, 'Some Observations on Recent Trends in the Work of the International Court of Justice', 55 *Japanese Yearbook of International Law* (2012), 4.

Thirlway, Hugh, 'Peace, Justice and Provisional Measures', in G. Gaja and J. Grote Stoutenberg (eds.), *Enhancing the Rule of Law through the International Court of Justice* (Leiden: Brill, 2014), 75–86.

Tomka, Peter, 'Custom and the International Court of Justice', *LPICT* (2013), 195.

Vermeer-Künzli, A., '*Diallo* and the Draft Articles: The Application of the Draft Articles on Diplomatic Protection in the *Ahamadou Sadio Diallo* Case', 20 *LJIL* (2007), 941–54.

Vidmar, J., 'The *Kosovo* Advisory Opinion Scrutinised', 24 *LJIL* (2011), 353–83.

Villalpando, Santiago, 'On the International Court of Justice and the Determination of Rules of Law', 26 *LJIL* (2013), 243–51.

Vukas, Budislav, 'Some Provisions of the Statute of the International Court of Justice which Deserve Amendments', in S. Yee and J.-Y. Morin, *Multiculturalism and International Law: Essays in Honour of Edward McWhinney* (Leiden: Nijhoff, 2009), 277.

Weil, Prosper, '"The Court Cannot Conclude Definitively . . .": *Non Liquet* Revisited', 36 *Colombia Journal of International Law* (1997), 109.

De Wet, Erika, 'Judicial Review as an Emerging General Principle of Law and its Implications for the International Court of Justice', *NILR* (2000), 181.

Wilde, Ralph, 'Human Rights Beyond Borders at the World Court: The Significance of the International Court of Justice's Jurisprudence on the Extraterritorial Application of Human Rights Treaties', 12 *ChJIL* (2013), 639–77.

Wyler, Eric, 'Les Rapports entre exceptions préliminaires et fond du litige à la lumière de l'arrêt de la CIJ du 11 juillet 1996 dans l'affaire du Génocide', *RGDIP* (2001), 25.

Wyler, Eric, 'La CIJ lit-elle Shakespeare? Retour sur l'interprétation de l'Avis consultatif du 8 juillet 1996 relatif à la menace et l'emploi de l'arme nucléaire', *Journal du droit international* (2011), 67–89.

Yee, Sienho, '*Forum prorogatum* and the Indication of Provisional Measures in the International Court of Justice', in G. S. Goodwin-Gill and S. Talmon (eds.), *The Reality of International Law: Essays in Honour of Ian Brownlie* (Oxford: Oxford University Press, 1999), 565–84.

Yee, Sienho, '*Forum prorogatum* returns to the International Court of Justice', 16 *LJIL* (2003), 701–33.

Yee, Sienho, 'We Are All "Civilised Nations": Arguments for Cleaning-Up Article 38 (1) *(c)* of the Statute of the International Court of Justice', in S. Yee (ed.), *Towards an International Law of Co-progressiveness, Pt. II* (2014), 21–35.

Yee, Sienho, 'Article 38 of the ICJ Statute and Applicable Law: Selected Issues in Recent Cases', ICJ 70th Anniversary Seminar, *JPICT* (2016).

Yusuf, Judge A. A., 'The Notion of "Armed Attack" in the *Nicaragua* Judgment and Its Influence on Subsequent Case Law', 25 *LJIL* (2012), 461–70.

Index